GROUNDING A WORLD

Essays on the work
of
Kenneth White

The St Andrews Symposium
organised by Gavin Bowd and Charles Forsdick
at the University of St Andrews
10-11 October 2003

Edited by

Gavin Bowd, Charles Forsdick and Norman Bissell

alba editions

First published in 2005 by Alba Editions

Alba Editions is the imprint of the Scottish Centre for Geopoetics
Director: Norman Bissell 340 Lincoln Avenue Glasgow G13 3LP
E-mail norman@rbissell.fsnet.co.uk

Unless for the purpose of a review, applications to publish any part of
this book should be made to the above address.

The Scottish Centre for Geopoetics is affiliated to
the International Institute of Geopoetics
Website: www.geopoetique.net

British Library Cataloguing in Publication Data
A catalogue record is available on request from the British Library.

ISBN 0-9529337-2-1

The publisher gratefully acknowledges subsidy from

the School of Modern Languages
the University of Liverpool
and
the Carnegie Trust for the
Universities of Scotland

towards the publication of this book.

Cover photograph: Norman Bissell
Cover design: John Hudson

Typeset in Sabon by Markings Publications
1 Longacres Road Kirkcudbright DG6 4AT

Printed and bound in Scotland by
Buccleuch Printers Ltd., Galashiels TD1 2UH

living in obscurity
            like Hakuyu
      his name meant
            White Obscurity
      his name meant
            he who lived in the hills
            back of Northern White Water -
or secretly though not unconsciously
      in the cities of Europe
   living my life
            founding and grounding
      a world.

(Kenneth White, *Walking the Coast*)

He is more than a poet in the banal sense of the word, he is a strategian of mutation.

(Osip Mandelstam, *Essay on Dante*)

CONTENTS

INTRODUCTION
Gavin Bowd

> *From Strathclyde to Whiteness lies the way*
> *through all the wild weathers of the world*
> *and through all the dog-days:* si con Escos
> qui porte sa çavate, de palestiaus sa chape ramendée
> deschaus, nus piés, affublez d'une nate
>
> *Kenneth White, 'A Personal Winter', Wild Coal*

In October 2003, in St Andrews, a colloquium was held on 'Forty Years of the White World', organised by the University of St Andrews in collaboration with the University of Liverpool, and with the kind and essential support of the Embassy of France, whose nationality Kenneth White took in 1980. The occasion for this meeting was the fortieth anniversary of the publication, in Paris, of Kenneth White's first collection of poetry, *Wild Coal*. The setting, the Senior Common Room of the Faculty of Theology, under the implacable gaze of John Knox, alluded half-humorously, half-seriously, to a culture and history that Kenneth White could be seen to owe much to while striving to go far beyond. For two days in that room gathered and spoke, among dozens of others, a journalist, an architect, a trade union activist, a Buddhist monk, a cultural attaché, poets, academics, and, in apparent contradiction of Roland Barthes's dictum that 'the author is dead', the 'object of study' himself (although there was, symptomatically, no representative from St Andrews' almighty School of English). The essays in this volume are by participants as well as those who, for some reason or other, were unable to make the physical journey.

In his closing remarks on 'grounding a world', Kenneth White defined a colloquium, in his extravagantly erudite way, as meaning both 'speaking together' and a 'relocation of perspectives'. Both things can be found in the colloquium of these pages. There are timely attempts to bring the work of White into dialogue with that of other figures. Stuart Kelly explores White's relation to the canon of Scottish letters, placing him in an avant-garde tradition that is not properly acknowledged in Sandy Moffat's painting of the *Poets' Pub*. For the first time, Charles Forsdick brings to the attention of the English-speaking reader White's long and rich relationship with the work of Victor Segalen. Pierre Jamet, with suitable iconoclasm, points to the influence on the boy from Fairlie not only of Pelagius and Duns Scotus, but also the Scottish Reformation. Other affinities are indicated: Michael Tucker on the spirit of shamanism, Padmakara on the Buddhist Way, Tony McManus on poetic 'possibilism' and Marco Fazzini on 'ecocriticism'. Michèle Duclos emphasises the ground shared by White and TS Eliot, despite their radically different social origins: both take cognizance of a 'psychical split between thinking and feeling' and search for a 'new aesthetics', although their particular solutions prove to be radically different.

The very public self of the White of the 'White world' is therefore placed among other selves, but, in the process, the self itself is redefined. Anne Bineau, in her close study of White's use of quotation, and his poems focussed on individuals such as Artaud, Hölderlin and Ovid, argues that White denies the myth of original genius and identifies with other selves in a critical fashion with, as ultimate horizon, a 'poetic idea of the earth'. John Hudson takes head-on the thorny issue of White's, irksome for some, use of his surname in mapping a mental geography: punning, asserts Hudson, is part of the poet's armoury, while the embarrassed sniggers at White's positive narcissism are the unfortunate legacy of western cultural attitudes to the self. Not for the first time in this collection, the mystic Meister Eckhart points the way to a recasting of 'self' and 'world'.

With this emphasis on finding 'open spaces', a militant and passionate use of the ideas of Kenneth White makes itself felt. For Anne Scott, Kenneth White maps out a new way of thinking that is 'ex-act', outside the violence and mediocrity of the present. For Khalid Hajji and Omar Bsaïthi, two young scholars from the

University of Oujda in Morocco, the 'white world' offers post-colonial Arab intellectuals with an alternative to ridiculous imitation of the mutilating and uprooting culture dominant, they claim, in the West. For Jean-Paul Loubes, White's essays stimulate the search for a 'situated architecture', beyond the wreckage of the Modern Movement.

This passionate engagement with the world of White inflects the style of many of the contributions. Norman Bissell offers not only an invaluable narrative of Kenneth White's tumultuous passage through the worlds of avant-garde and academe - the Universities of Glasgow, Pau and Paris; groupments and reviews such as Jargon, Feuillage, Raster and Feathered Egg - but also bears witness to the effect on his own life of encountering White's work and personality. Olivier Delbard forgoes certain conventions of the academic essay - the impersonal, or royal?, we, the ternary structure and concluding conceit - for a 'walk' into Kenneth White's 'landscape-mindscape'.

What we have here is a topologically coherent body of texts on an author who is, in the lucid words of Stuart Kelly, 'precariously poised between veneration and suspicion'.

KENNETH WHITE:
A TRANSCENDENTAL SCOT
Tony McManus

Kenneth White occupies a paradoxical situation in Scottish letters. André Breton remarked upon the 'high note of originality' which he brought to writing and thought and Lawrence Durrell praised his 'poetry with marrow and purity',[1] saying that it was bound to be seen as in the forefront of English-language literature. However, the work of Scotland's writer of greatest European and global standing since Hugh MacDiarmid only became available in Scotland in 1989. Translated into many world-languages, he barely features as yet on the syllabuses of the Scottish universities. Founder of the International Institute of Geopoetics with centres in various parts of the globe, his essays have only recently become available in Scotland. While Scottish to the bone, White, then, cannot easily be described in national terms, nor fitted into the established categories: 'I'm what you might call a transcendental Scot', he writes in 'The Ballad of Kali Road.'[2]

White works in three forms of literary expression. His prose narrative 'waybooks' follow a narrative figure out of the contemporary western context through the cultures of the earth and into its empty spaces where he is imbued with a 'sense of world' – a clarification of perception in relation to the earth itself. The essays chart a similar movement in a more analytical form. The poetry is of two kinds. The long poems White refers to as 'peregrinations' in the spaces of the earth and the mind. The short, 'diamond' poems evoke intense moments of perception. The three forms overlap considerably – analytical passages are found in the 'waybooks' which are also scattered with poems; the poems can be long analyses of ideas or significant cultural figures; the essays reach moments of poem-like imagery and focus.

One of the key contributions Kenneth White has made to Scottish cultural discourse is to transcend the identity complex manifested in the constant reference to England as that in opposition to which a distinct Scottish identity is created – Scotland and Scots always trying to define themselves as not-England, non-English. He even comes across this kind of thing in francophone Canada:

> *The motto of Quebec is* Je me souviens *(I remember).*
> *I asked somebody what the remembering was all about.*
> *'The time the English came.'*
> *God almighty! Who cares about the English, whether coming or going?*
> *If I bothered about what the English did, I'd be up there in old Caledonia with a historical chip on my shoulder, scrawling long political poems in Lallans and waving a wee flag.*
> *Shit, you can't be a Scotsman all your life. At least, you can't always be harping on it. You've got to get out there and mix it more.* Make *something of it.*[3]

This is a little image of Kenneth White's itinerary and of the nature of his considerable oeuvre. In its rejection of dominant culture, its imperative to 'get out there and mix it more' and its appeal to '*make* something of it' we can see reflected the three-part movement which grounds and permeates White's work. Firstly, there is a nihilism in the face of a western civilisation at its 'endgame';[4] secondly, 'intellectual nomadism' – a movement out of this in physical and mental exploration of the world;[5] thirdly, the apprehension of a new or re-newed 'sense of world', which requires to be expressed in a new, or renewed, poetics. This is the movement towards 'geopoetics'.[6]

A Supernihilist Itinerary

White starts from the modern condition, the sense that things are lacking coherence. Alienation – from work, from others, from oneself, from the world – is the identifying feature of the modern context. This is not simply an intellectual severance, it is also an existential one – we feel the problem as well as think about it. Here is Barcelona in this perspective:

> *away at the dead end of the Calle San Pablo, where there are no longer any women visible, only men humped in sordid drink-shops with pale blue TV screens flickering in the darkness, yes, this is the end, with a pale-green-painted little hospital-looking shop there advertising* lavajes-siphilis, *the syphilitic end of the overhuman bloody world.*[7]

The scene is full of signs of a civilisation at its end – the 'dead-end' street is that of St. Paul, establisher of Christian orthodoxy, the 'darkness' in which the TV screens flicker is a cultural and intellectual darkness. The human hopelessness of it recalls the extreme negativist E.M. Cioran's dark definition of contemporary man: 'a convalescent aspiring to disease.'[8]

White's 'waybooks' always start in this sense of the 'overhuman bloody world'. *Travels in the Drifting Dawn* searches the ports and landscapes of Europe for signs of 'something else' in the air. *Incandescent Limbo* recounts White's experiences in seven rooms in Paris in the early sixties and reflects an initial interest in surrealism that later moved out, as does the book, towards a radical culture-analysis.[9] Later books such as *The Blue Road* and *Pilgrim of the Void* accentuate the more comic tone also present in the earlier books.[10] A movement is then charted towards a 'clarified space'. In *Letters from Gourgounel*, a thunderstorm, 'a field of energy' in the world, gathers and breaks during the course of the book and parallels the enlightenment which gathers and breaks in the book's narrative figure through intellectual penetration into the philosophies of the east, especially through the translation of Chinese poetry, and through penetration into the landscape.[11]

In his essays,[12] which range with great erudition and acute intelligence over the cultural map, White casts a critical eye upon the two main attempts which have been made to deal with the existential problem outlined here – the political method of Marxism and the psychoanalytical method originating with Freud. Close to European critics such as, among others, Gilles Deleuze[13] and Jean-François Lyotard,[14] he indicates how the function of psychoanalysis is to repatriate the sick spirit back into the alien context which made it sick in the first place, and how political movements have offered no genuine path out of the malaise. What White proposes is a larger field of thought and action.

Along with a negativist awareness of the modern context, there is an awareness of another reality which White discovers, at least in its initial signs, in his childhood territory and which becomes the potential focus for that renewal of culture which he seeks. This is the territory around the west coast village of Fairlie[15] – what he calls 'the white world of arctic gulls, breaking waves and silver birches'.[16] This sense of an 'energy-filled' and spacious reality is also an experience felt in both mind (knowledge of and mental penetration into nature) and body (sensual enjoyment of wind, tree, bird flight, salt of sea, smell of earth). Here he is instinctively aware of the presence of what is missing in contemporary culture – 'a sense of world'. 'Morning Walk' is an early poem of White's which describes that sensation:[17]

MORNING WALK

It was a cold slow-moving mist
clotted round the sun, clinging
to the small white sun, and the earth
was alone and lonely, and a great bird
harshly squawked from the heronry
as the boy walked under the beeches
seeing the broken pale-blue shells
and the moist piles of mouldering leaves.

The key word is 'seeing': this is a poem about perception. One might have expected 'looking' – what 'seeing' does is to heighten and deepen the perceptual experience the boy is having. The word's force is strengthened by its use in participial form just after two active verbs, 'squawked' and 'walked', whose rhyme helps transmit their active nature into the participial form of 'seeing': this 'seeing' is not something that is happening *to* the boy, he is *doing* it. This form also allows the word to act as a noun and a verb at the same time, that is, to make the abstract and the concrete co-exist: *this* boy seeing *those* pale-blue shells, but also the *idea* of 'seeing pale-blue shells'. This, plus the apt expression of colour, 'pale-blue shells' (the repetition of the *l* sound unites the three words into a strongly visual expression) also leads the reader, to 'see' them too. The final line is an image of the necessary focus of perception, the earth in a sensual, erotic expression: 'moist, mouldering leaves'.[18]

The reality being perceived seems to lie outwith the parameters of western culture. This leads White to consider that perhaps it is the obsession with the socio-personal context itself which is wrong. Perhaps we need to look at the whole cultural context, its roots, ideas and expression. This is what White calls the 'supernihilist' movement, the desire to go beyond nihilism's infinite pessimism and, without indulging in facile optimism, to seek possibilities.[19] This is to initiate a move away from the western mainstream, not just, as with so many modern Scottish writers, its anglo-centric manifestation, towards the study of the 'fundamental question' – culture. This requires a radical analysis of the roots of western culture. Using the image of the 'motorway of western civilisation', White traces its humanist and sacred development from Platonic idealism and Aristotelian categorisation, through the Christian paradigm of 'creator' and 'created' and the modern Cartesian dualisms of mind and body, man and nature, to the Romantics' attempt to refocus on the earth.

The real inspirational break, as far as White is concerned, arrives in the shape of two figures who, beginning a movement off this 'motorway', prefigure the geopoetic field: Rimbaud who says, 'if I have any taste it is only for earth and for stones',[20] and Nietzsche who says, 'remain true to the earth'.[21] These figures, the French philosophical poet and the German poetic philosopher, break out of the Hegelian line which led to the twentieth century's dream of the superstate and illusion of the 'supermarket of happiness',[22] and, from their movements, White develops a method, leaving the main road of culture and delving in to the wild terrain. It is a movement he calls 'intellectual nomadism'.[23]

The Intellectual Nomad

If White's sense of alienation is both intellectual and existential, the intellectual nomadism which explores ways beyond the alienation consists of intellectual enquiry – reading and writing, the cultivation of the mind – but also existential experience – errance and residence, the cultivation of the body and the senses. We separate them for the purpose of explaining and interpreting them. However, our idealising and categorising culture has seen that separation become almost permanent. In fact, as Kenneth White proceeds in to his territory, he is aware that these apparent dualisms – mind and body, man and nature – are fundamentally one and this awareness can lead to a genuine perception of the world.

Dissatisfied with the 'mediocratic' cultural context of sixties Britain,[24] White settled in France in 1967. However, in leaving Scotland-Britain, he found himself penetrating into a more authentic Scotland which, chiming with the intuitions he felt as a child on the west coast and evoked in the poem quoted above, seemed connected to that bigger 'sense of world' which he was seeking.

Always beginning with the ground, White's vision of Scotland goes back to its origins in the glacier and its shaping movement out of which:

> *the land emerges*
> *bruised and dazed*
> *in the arctic light*[25]

The humans he sees inhabiting this land develop a highly poetic culture with totemic references to the natural world and cosmological considerations in their engravings.[26] In the Christian era they evolve ways of seeing and expressing which put them at the margins of establishment culture. This pelagian line[27] which, in direct conflict with the establishment,[28] holds that there is no original sin, permeates the teaching and poetry of the early Christian monks who travelled Europe teaching a Christianity which was expressed in terms of the natural world not as metaphor for 'the human condition', but as the locus of reality. In his essays White refers us to Ernest Renan's comment on:

> *the quite particular vivacity with which the Celts informed*
> *their feeling for nature...*[29]

White's departure from anglo-centric mainstream culture and his adoption of alternative routes to the perception of reality is summed up in his statement, 'there is a pelagian line running through the whole of Western culture.'[30] That is, there is an alternative way to perception of reality. This movement is summed up in the poem 'Brandan's Last Voyage'[31] about the saint whose journeys inspired the remarkable medieval poem on his life which gave Europe the original model for the vision of the 'other world' and which furnished Dante with some of the models and images which inform *The Divine Comedy*. At the end of White's poem, Brandan and his followers go off in their little boat:

> *farther and farther they pulled away*
> *into the white unknown.*

White traces a Scottish line of the descendants of these 'studious philologians and rugged philosophers'[32] from Erigena's ninth century philosophy of nature[33] to Duns Scotus[34] who, in opposition to Thomas Aquinas affirms the 'thisness' (*haecceitas*) of the phenomena of the world. George Buchanan,[35] teacher of Montaigne, wrote a long Latin poem on the subject of the cosmos. Patrick Geddes sought a unification of the branches of knowledge through what he began to see as an *aesthetic*.[36] Hugh MacDiarmid's intellectual aim extended to cover world literature and philosophies, science, anthropology and grammar. The tradition of 'extra-vagant' Scots reaching out from Scotland to the world and promulgating an alternative tradition of perception of reality is a long and distinguished one which Kenneth White synthesises and develops.[37]

However, this tradition stands in opposition to Cartesian modernity with its explicit separation of human from nature, mind from body, and the ever more minute separation of the branches of knowledge and the specialising of the sciences to which it led. Paradoxically, as White points out in many essays on the scientific theme, that very specialising finally led to discoveries which have re-opened the cosmological perspective, notably Einstein's *Cosmological Considerations* through which 'the notion of 'cosmos' returns'.[38] Subsequent developments in science have put in question the basic foundations of mainstream western culture. Quantum physicists refer to the impossibility of the subject-object dualism in a manner which reminds us of the perceptual force in the poem 'Morning Walk' quoted above.

In linguistics and literary theory, the American Ernest Fenollosa comes to a parallel conclusion which is also mirrored in that poem:

> *A true noun, an isolated thing, does not exist in nature.*
> *Things are only the terminal points, or rather, the meeting*
> *points of actions...The eye sees noun and verb as one.*[39]

In philosophy, White indicates Edmund Husserl's dismissal of objectivism as 'naivety',[40] which leads him to propose the aim of a subject who, in unencumbered contemplation of the world, can realise its thereness. Here not only is modernity's subject/object dualism being questioned but so is the materialist/idealist dualism. Husserl's pupil Martin Heidegger takes this further still, attempting to re-establish the meaning of the basic concepts of western thinking as they were originally conceived, and positing an idea of 'being' where phenomena 'emerge', 'stand' and 'endure in the light' and are 'apprehended' by humans.[41] These notions, which Heidegger grounds in pre-Socratic thinking, connote movement, event, experience and presence. In post-Socratic times – White's 'motorway of western civilisation' – they become static, formulaic, to do with opinion and interpretation. This, then, is the 'loss of world' which underpins the modern feeling of alienation. It is a cultural problem to do with a weakening in thought or 'apprehension' of the world.

For White, this pelagian movement in western thought dismantles the orthodox western categories and turns the mind, at least in the first instance, towards the East, and demands a re-orientation of thought. This is not, as one critic put it,[42] to embrace 'thin-witted international zennery' (White is as scathing of pseudo-movements as anyone), but to explore a thought and expression unconditioned by western traditions – the experience of the void, the emptiness in which the socio-personal identity is lost and one experiences an 'enlargening of identity'.[43] A major source of inspiration is the Japanese haiku and prose master, Matsuo Bashō,[44] whose advice to the poet sums up the points being made in this brief survey of White's intellectual nomadism:

> *You must leave your preoccupations with yourself. Your*
> *poetry issues of its own accord when you and the thing*
> *have become one... if your feeling is not natural – if the*

thing and yourself are separate – then your poetry is not true poetry but merely a counterfeit.[45]

Geopoetics

This nomadising in the byways of civilisation leads White, like the figures and cultures through which he has 'nomadised', to the conclusion that instead of attempting to understand the human in relation to itself, we must perceive the human in relation to the earth, that is develop that 'sense of world' whose felt loss has been the spur of all his work. This is the 'geo' in 'geopoetics'. The 'poetics' covers the realisation, also derived from that nomadising, that when the human being hits upon genuine perception of reality, the desire to express that perception is part of it.

> *Geopoetics is concerned with 'worlding' (and 'wording' is contained in 'worlding'). In my semantics, 'world' emerges from a contact between the human mind and the things, the lines, the rhythms of the earth. When this contact is sensitive, subtle, intelligent, you have 'a world' (a culture) in the strong, confirming and enlightening sense of the word. When that contact is insensitive, simplistic and stupid, you don't have a world at all, you have a non-world, a pseudo-culture, a dictatorial enclosure or a mass-mess. Geopoetics is concerned with developing sensitive and intelligent contact, and with working out original ways to express that contact.*[46]

For White, then, 'poetics is a fundamental word, underlying science, literature, philosophy, and coordinating elements arising from all these disciplines'.[47] Because the 'normal' condition of man is artificial, so is his language. Therefore, the geopoetical poem seeks a new form of expression. This leads to a radically different approach to the form of poetry than the norm in the English and western canon. For White, the language of poetry must reveal the world. Poetry as we are accustomed to it in the English canon rarely reveals world. We are offered an artefact constructed of metaphors, metrics, word and sound-play, beautifully made often, but only revealing the poet. Poetry which reveals a world will not point back in on itself like this, rather it will be, to use Gaston Bachelard's memorable description, 'the flare-up of being in the imagination'.[48] White's writing is full of such incandescent moments as this from 'In the Sea and Pine Country':[49]

> an occasional cry
> enlarges the silence

This image pares the poet's experience down to the essential sign and simplest language but it has the opposite effect on the reader whose mind is filled, from this starting point, with the 'sense of world' which has inspired the lines. And the lines themselves reflect the poetic practice being pointed to – it's the small 'cry' of the poet which indicates the vast 'sense of world'.

This is not to say that 'form' is irrelevant. It may be correct to a certain extent, as one critic has said,[50] that White reveals a 'distrust of style and technique' (although there is a lot more craftsmanship in White's poetry than is initially apparent), but he is utterly wrong in accusing him of 'lack of form'. On the contrary the 'poetics' in 'geopoetics' refers precisely to the idea of 'composition'. The focus of the poet's attention, though, is, primarily, not on (artificial) form, but on that point at which essential perception of the world, so truly felt as to necessitate its being expressed, meets its form in its emergence into being (its voicing).

'No metaphor-mongering/no myth-malarkey', as 'Ovid' puts it in one of White's longer poems, 'Ovid's Report',[51] which offers a useful example of White's content and method. These long poems trace the development of certain key historical cultural figures from their personal-social contexts to vaster and clearer fields of perception. 'At first I found it hard to swallow,' says Ovid of his exile 'on the Scythian coast'. Then,

> the citizenship of Rome
> dropped off me
> like some old skin

and he begins to delight in this 'land of wind and shadow' which is 'at the world's edge'. Normal perception will see that phrase as meaning 'the world's end'; in the intellectual nomad's perspective, it means 'the world's beginning'. Now, Ovid contemplates the known world and speculates on unknown worlds:

> *between the Scythians and the Hyperboreans*
> *a hundred peoples, a thousand tribes*
> *Rome has never heard of*

and begins to discover the 'strange poetry hidden / in these barbarian lands'. The poem finishes with Ovid, echoing Brandan, seeking to 'get further into this unspoken space' and:

> *find, who knows, the source*
> *of another light.*

The poem starts in apparent prosaic form, its tone bitter and proud – 'just imagine me... all alone among uncouth clods...' – with Ovid still writing his 'finely wrought discourses'. But as the rough, cold, Black Sea landscape begins to penetrate, images of it begin to accumulate in the conversational tone, signs of an enlargening and illuminating perspective growing in the Latin poet. In a river-like movement common to many of these poems, the poem's rhythm, mirroring its content, becomes slower and more open, becoming calmer as it becomes more aware of the expansive void to which the content has directed itself – the geopoetical sea of potentiality opening up at the end which is, in fact, a beginning.

Similarly, in the short poem form, a sense of apparent prosaicness is the initial response to a poem such as this image of Venice:

HOTEL WINDOW, EVENING

> *Night falling*
> *voices fading from the quays*
> *gondoliers covering their barques*
>
> *and suddenly, all along the lagoon*
> *the lighting up of the hidden channels*[52]

The ordinary scene from the window reveals illuminating signs of a hidden reality, the light which the darkness reveals to those who can see it. And the poet must say, as well as see it, in a language apparently as ordinary as the scene but also full of signs brought to the reader's attention by slight rhymes, alliteration and word echoes which, in unifying the poem as a complete image, offers the reader the opportunity to see exactly what the poet has seen, and unifies the reader's mind with the poet's. The effect is, contrary to the poetry described above, to open up the reader's mind to an image of the world and its significance. As White says in 'Broken Ode to White Brittany':

> *May it never, don't forget*
> *smell the poet*[53]

Gerard Manley Hopkins, drawing on Duns Scotus' *haecceitas*, sought to express phenomenal reality and to forge the language which it necessitated. T.S. Eliot exposed the 'waste land' of western culture to the critical analysis of the poetic imagination. Ezra Pound, influenced by Fenollosa, reoriented western poetry towards the 'image', which would, when perfected, become the building block for long, all-embracing poems. Hugh MacDiarmid pointed to the knowledge of all the disciplines of human endeavour and knowledge as the true subject-matter of poetry. Kenneth White has taken up these most significant attempts to return poetry to its central role as clear and perceptive expression of human experience in the world and renewer of culture. But more than that, he has developed them, and evolved a poetic language which is as remarkable for its simplicity, its musicality and its oral tone as it is for its intensity, profundity and formal astuteness. The 'possibilism' which he espouses does not see 'endgame' in the degeneration of western culture, but new beginnings:

> *Today, for the first time in the history of humanity, winds*
> *blow from all regions of the globe at once, and each and*
> *everyone of us has access to all the cultures of the world.*
> *That can give rise to cacophony, to disarray, lassitude in*
> *front of so much accumulated richness, but it can also give*
> *rise, with analytical work and synthesis...to a new way of*
> *thinking, a great world poem, liveable by everyone.*[54]

NOTES

1 Breton in a letter to White in 1965 after reading a draft chapter of *Incandescent Limbo* in *Les Lettres nouvelles* of January 1965 (ed. Maurice Nadeau). Durrell quoted in *Presenting Kenneth White*, a publisher's brochure published by Mainstream Publishing (Edinburgh) in 1989.
2 In *The Bird Path* (Edinburgh: Mainstream Publishing, 1989), p.20.
3 From *The Blue Road* (Edinburgh: Mainstream Publishing, 1990), p.16.
4 Samuel Beckett's expression. White writes of Beckett pushing the boundaries of nihilism further and further out while White seeks to take the step across those boundaries.
5 The expression partly originates with Emerson, but White made it his own with a doctoral thesis on 'intellectual nomadism' presented at the Sorbonne in Paris in 1979.
6 The word first occurred to White in Labrador in 1979 and soon developed into the concept which unifies his life and work and gives them forward impetus especially through the International Institute of Geopoetics.
7 From 'Night in Barcelona', in *Travels in the Drifting Dawn* (Edinburgh: Mainstream Publishing, 1989), p.125.
8 *A Short History of Decomposition* (London: Quartet Encounters, 1990), pp.24-25.
9 Unpublished in English as yet, French version: *Les Limbes incandescents* (Paris: Denoël, 1976).
10 *The Blue Road* recounts a journey up the St. Lawrence River from Quebec City to Ungava Bay in Labrador; *Pilgrim of the Void* (Edinburgh: Mainstream Publishing, 1992) recounts travels in Asia and incorporates two books published separately in France: *Le Visage du vent d'est* (Les Presses d'aujourd'hui, 1980), which brings in Hong Kong, Thailand and Taiwan, and *Les Cygnes sauvages* (Grasset, 1990) which relates a journey from Tokyo to Hokkaido in the footsteps of Matsuo Bashō (1644-94). French translations of White's work are by his wife, Marie-Claude.
11 *Letters from Gourgounel* was published by Jonathan Cape in London in 1962 but is now out of print. The revised edition in translation, *Lettres de Gourgounel*, was published first at the Presses d'Aujourd'hui (Paris, 1979), then in Grasset's Cahiers Rouges series (Paris, 1986). It recounts White's experiences in an old farmhouse in the Ardèche in Southern France, 1961.
12 Four volumes of essays have been published in France: *La Figure du dehors* (1982), *Une Apocalypse tranquille* (1985), *L'Esprit nomade* (1987) and *Le Plateau de l'Albatros* (1994) – all by Grasset in Paris. Individual essays on Victor Segalen, Antonin Artaud and Hokusaï have also been published as well as collections of interviews.
13 Notably Gilles Deleuze and Félix Guattari, *L'Anti-Œdipe* (Paris: Les Editions de Minuit, 1972).
14 Notably J.-F. Lyotard, *Dérive à partir de Marx et Freud* (Paris: Union Générale d'Editions, 1973).

15   Village south of Glasgow on the west coast of Scotland where White was brought up from the age of three, having been born in Glasgow.

16   In 'Following out world lines' an interview with Alistair Paterson in *Coast to Coast*, a volume of interviews edited by Norman Bissell (Glasgow: Open World in association with Mythic Horse Press, 1996), p.78.

17   *Handbook for the Diamond Country* (Edinburgh: Mainstream Publishing, 1990), p.17.

18   White's insistence on bringing together sensual and intellectual experience is expressed in phrases such as 'eros, logos, cosmos' and 'erotic logic'.

19   White refers to the three early books *Travels in the Drifting Dawn*, *Incandescent Limbo* and *Letters from Gourgounel* as 'a supernihilist itinerary'.

20   'Une saison en enfer' in *Œuvres poétiques* (Paris: Garnier Flammarion, 1964), p.133.

21   In *Thus Spoke Zarathustra* (Harmondsworth: Penguin, 1961), p.41.

22   White's expression for the twentieth century terminus of the 'motorway of western civilisation', the degeneration of the nineteenth century's utilitarian goal of 'the greatest happiness of the greatest number' and of Hegelian ideas of inevitable historical 'progress'.

23   See note 6.

24   Mediocracy - one of White's neologisms: a society geared to mediocrity. For White, the most insidious threat to democracy.

25   From 'Scotia Deserta' in *The Bird Path*, p.123.

26   The archaeological, lithographical and mythographical records of Scotland's pre-christian peoples constitute a tantalising field of study to which White refers throughout his work.

27   Pelagius, a fourth century philosopher of British origin, whom White considers among his spiritual ancestors, denied original sin and shifted the theological balance away from divine grace towards individual responsibility for salvation; excommunicated three times by the Vatican. White plays a lot on the word 'pelagian', referring at one and the same time to this current of thought, currents in the sea, and fish.

28   St. Augustine sent St. Jerome, unsuccessfully, to sort out the pelagian Britons. The Synod of Whitby in 663AD referred to the Scots as 'the only people stupid enough to put themselves out of step with the entire world' (a phrase White often quotes, both in texts and lectures).

29   Ernest Renan, 'La Poésie des races celtiques', in 'Essais de morale et de critique', in vol. 2 of *Œuvres complètes*, ed. Henriette Psichari (Paris: Calmann-Lévy, 1948), p.269.

30   Kenneth White 'Ces moines venus de la mer', pamphlet, St. Malo, 1992, p.6.

31   *The Bird Path*, pp.188-193.

32   Renan, 'La Poésie des races celtiques', p.292.

33　John Scot Erigena was invited to the court of Charles le Chauve, King of France, in the ninth century where, protected from the wrath of Rome regarding his pelagian ideas, he translated the Greek philosophers and wrote his great work – *Periphyseon (de Divisione Naturae)*.

34　John Duns Scotus, thirteenth century franciscan philosopher.

35　George Buchanan (1506-1582), renowned teacher in Paris and Bordeaux, termed 'prince of poets' by his contemporaries.

36　Patrick Geddes (1854-1932), biologist, town-planner, teacher, ecologist... He demonstrated 'the paradoxical generalisation that (human) production – though fundamentally for maintenance – is mainly for "art"'.

37　'*Extra vagans*' was an epithet used in the Middle Ages for the wandering Scots.

38　White, in 'Elements of Geopoetics', *The Edinburgh Review*, 88 (1992), p.164.

39　Ernest Fenollosa, 'The Chinese Written Character' (1906).

40　Edmund Husserl, *Phenomenology and the Crisis of Philosophy*, trans. Quentin Lauer (New York: Harper, 1965), p.185.

41　Martin Heidegger, *An Introduction to Metaphysics* (Yale University Press, 1987) – especially chapter 4, 'The Limitation of Being'.

42　Douglas Dunn 'Bird Path of an Exile', review in the *Glasgow Herald*, May 13th 1989.

43　An expression used throughout White's work in various contexts.

44　White's *The Wild Swans* (in *Pilgrim of the Void*) follows Bashō's footsteps in *The Narrow Road to the Deep North*.

45　Quoted widely; see the introduction to *The Narrow Road to the Deep North and other travel sketches* (Harmondsworth: Penguin Classics, 1966), p.33.

46　In 'From the Centred Complex', an interview with Tony McManus, in *The Edinburgh Review*, 92 (1994), p.126.

47　'From the Centred Complex', p.128.

48　Gaston Bachelard, *The Poetics of Space* (Boston: Beacon Press, 1969), p.xiv.

49　*The Bird Path*, p.104.

50　Edwin Morgan, in *Books in Scotland*, 31 (1989).

51　*The Bird Path*, pp.34-40.

52　*Les Rives du silence* (Paris: Mercure de France, 1997), p.196.

53　*The Bird Path*, p.206.

54　Kenneth White, *Sources*, 32 (1991), p.44.

KENNETH WHITE AS EDUCATOR
Norman Bissell

When we're thinking about Kenneth White as educator, we can forget the idea of an academic whose career has moved in a straight line from start to finish. His career has been full of ups and downs, and he's made decisions and followed a path, not on the basis of an academic career, but on something much wider and deeper than that.

In 1963, he accepted an assistant lecturer's post offered him by Alan Boase, Professor of French at the University of Glasgow, and within two years he was promoted to full lecturer. Yet two years later he resigned his post, dropped everything, and moved to France, to Pau in the Pyrenees. There, starting again from scratch, he got himself a job as *lecteur* (a post more lowly and more precarious than that of assistant), which he lost because of his active participation in the cultural and political revolt of 1968. After two years' unemployment, he got himself another *lecteur's* job, this time at the leftist university of Paris VII. He was a *lecteur* there for twelve years – probably the longest period of *lecteur* in the history of French education. After defending his state thesis on "intellectual nomadism" at the end of the 70s, he became a *docteur*, as well as *lecteur*, almost a contradiction in terms. As a Doctor of Letters of the French state, he directed research, but as *lecteur*, he wasn't allowed to sign the papers, one of his colleagues had to do that.

It was the kind of paradox that must have amused White, like those Zen stories where the smartest man in the monastery is not the head-man, but the doorkeeper. Eventually, however, he took steps to normalise his situation by adopting French nationality in 1980 (which gave him dual nationality since he retained his British passport) and in 1983, he was nominated to the Chair of Twentieth Century Poetics at Paris IV, Paris-Sorbonne, where he stayed until he decided to leave in 1996. Since then he's been Visiting Professor here and there and gives lectures in many different institutions and contexts.

So, what has he taught during this time? Well in Scotland, he taught French literature, mainly French poetry from Rimbaud onwards. In France, he taught Anglo-American literature, mainly American, from Whitman on. In the 70s and early 80s, within a department of English and American literature, he gave an East-West seminar, where he was teaching Taoism and Zen Buddhism, illustrating his teaching with examples of Far Eastern influence on European and American writers and thinkers. From the early 80s on, his seminar at the Sorbonne was entitled "World Poetics", and brought in material, not only from literature and poetry, but from philosophy and science – in fact, it was more or less geopoetics without the name.

But one of the things which has distinguished Kenneth White from other educators is that he has always been a creator of groups. In Glasgow, in the early 60s, it was the Jargon Group, devoted to "cultural revolution". In France, in the late 60s and early 70s, it was the Groupe Feuillage, then the group he called The Feathered Egg, to indicate a potential in society that hadn't yet found its full wings. And then in 1989 he started up the biggest group of them all, the International Institute of Geopoetics.

His academic qualifications are outstanding: a first class Honours degree, named first student in the faculty of Arts at Glasgow University, a state doctoral thesis in Paris, which not only received maximum honours, but was recognised as opening a whole new field of research and study, as well as two honorary degrees. But White, let it be repeated, is no 'orthodox academic'. His manner is different, his method is different, and his perspectives are different. For a start he never uses the terms professor or doctor, he sees himself simply as a teacher. He is a teacher and a poet. When White

first read Walt Whitman he saw those two words in juxtaposition:
"Will you be a poet and teacher to these States?" His answer to old
Walt was an unqualified 'Yes!' So perhaps we should think of him,
in the context of education, as a poet-teacher.

1

As an educator, Kenneth White has to be seen in the context of
a long Scottish cultural line, though one that has been largely
neglected, except by him.

There's more than a mere analogy between the movement and
style of Kenneth White and that of the old Scoto-Celtic monks,
especially the travelling ones, and later the wandering Scottish
scholar, the *Scotus vagans*. As he's mentioned more than once in
poem and prose, he first became aware of this line when, around the
age of nine, he attended the Parish Church in the village of Fairlie in
Ayrshire. On a stained glass window, there was, and still is, an
image of Kentigern, (later known as St Mungo) standing on a shore
with a book in his hand, preaching to the gulls. White has said that
this image constituted a root concept in his mind: natural space, a
man speaking out, a book.

Here's an excerpt from the poem *Scotia Deserta*:

Other figures cross the scene
like this one:
Kentigern they cried him

in the church I attended
around the age of nine
was that stained glass window
showing a man
with a book in his hand
standing on a seashore
preaching to the gulls

I'd be gazing at the window
and forgetting the sermon
(all about good and evil
with a lot of mangled metaphor
and heavy comparison)

eager to get back out
on to the naked shore
there to walk for hours on end
with a book sometimes in my hand
but never a thought of preaching in my mind
trying to grasp at something
that wanted no godly name
something that took the form
of blue waves and grey rock
and that tasted of salt

There are at least passing references to this line in practically every book that White has written and on more than one occasion he has gone into the field in detail and in depth. In his poem *Letter from Harris*, referring to the village of Rodel, he says this is "where the 'great cleric' lived, who founded the grammar school in Paris". One of the more complete presentations was the lecture he gave in French, at Fort Lalatte in the North coast of Brittany, in the winter of 1992: "Ces moines venus de la mer – conférence pérégrinante et pélagienne" ("Those monks who came in from the sea – a peregrine and pelagian lecture"), where, leaving aside the faiths and beliefs of these monks, he insists on their travelling and their thought. Again in *Scotia Deserta*, he makes the area of his interest clear:

One left traces of his presence
out there in Bute and the Garvellach Isles
and in Kilbrannan Sound –
the holy voyager, Brandan

Brandan was maybe a believer
but that's neither here nor there
first and foremost
he was a navigator
a figure moving mile by mile
along the headlands
among the islands
tracing a way
between foam and cloud
with an eye to outlines:

Sound of Islay
The Firth of Lorn
Tiree passage
The Sound of Mull
Skerryvore and Barra Head
Loch Alsh, Kyle Rhea
Sound of Raasay

Ah, the clear-sounding words
and a world
opening, opening!

The main current of thought White was interested in was pelagianism, elaborated by the monk Pelagius, who denied the Augustinian theory of Original Sin, saying that (human) nature was a good enough basis, so long as you worked at it and cultivated it. Hence, in these monasteries particular practices, but, mostly *studium*: study. The idea, via Gaelic, Latin, Greek and Hebrew, was to become *nobilissime instructus* (very nobly learned). White brought all this out in his lecture, making reference to figures like the one known as *magnus mundi magister* (the great teacher of the world).

It was especially when they began leaving the Isles of the West and moving as *peregrini* over the continent – like Malo to Brittany, and Malcallan to the Ardennes, founding monasteries, libraries and schools on the way that their peculiarities and capabilities began to be recognised. Ernest Renan in Brittany was to call them bold philosophers and ingenious linguists, teachers in literature, thought and grammar to all the west.

Kenneth White has not only studied all this movement, evoking it in poems and prose, he continues it.

In the later Middle Ages, the figure of the peregrine monk became that of the wandering scholar, the *Scotus vagans*, a well-known figure on the Continent and particularly in France. In a poem *A Personal Winter* in his very first book, *Wild Coal*, White quotes a medieval French poem describing the poor Scottish scholar out on the roads "barefoot, with his shoes slung over his back, wearing a ragged, patched cloak". Another poem, previously uncollected, but probably written about the same time, which appears in his latest book, *Open World*, entitled *The Wandering Scot*, presents the student White moving through France up to Aurillac in Auvergne, carrying in his rucksack a copy of Thomas Carlyle's *Sartor Resartus* and an empty notebook, clearly continuing the tradition.

Further down the centuries, after George Buchanan, scholar, poet, teacher, in Paris and Bordeaux, after David Hume, philosophising in Edinburgh and Paris, after Robert Louis Stevenson, meditating in Fontainebleau and at Hyères, this figure, carrying the energies of poet, scholar, teacher, opens out in White's mind and practice into the figure of the Intellectual Nomad, with a scope that is truly global, as you find in *Open World*.

2

It was as a student that Kenneth White began to think about the university and about education, calling in question a great deal of what was going on.

In his essays on culture and education, White often refers at least in passing to Carlyle, as well as to others such as John Ruskin and John Stuart Mill. In the chapter "Pedagogy" in *Sartor Resartus*, we can see why. Carlyle says of Professor Teufelsdröckh: "He seems himself universally animated on the matter of Education, and not without some touch of what we might presume to be anger", a phrase which White used as epigraph to his first pamphlet on education, *The Phoney University*. We also find there: "Thought kindling itself at the fire of living Thought? – How shall *he* give kindling, in whose own inward man there is no live coal?" There is an obvious reference here not only to White's general stance, but to *Wild Coal*, the point of departure of this conference.

Among other books that fired his own thought with regard to education were Rousseau's *Emile*, Schiller's essays on "The Aesthetic Education of the Human Being" and, especially, Nietzsche's five lectures on "The Future of our Educational Institutions" delivered at Basel in 1872, followed, in 1874, by his book *Schopenhauer as Educator*, from which I borrowed my title for this paper.

When he returned to Glasgow in 1963, after four years in Paris during which he had studied the existence in Europe from the Middle Ages on of anarchic, antinomian groups such as the *Homines Intelligentiae*, he had this idea and project in mind.

I was fortunate to have Kenneth White as my tutor in French in my first year at Glasgow University, and I still remember the exercise he set us of translating into English a poem of Bertholt Brecht which he'd translated from German into French, and how he would encourage us to write from direct experience in our French compositions. To those continuing with French he provided a radical initiation into poetics via Arthur Rimbaud, André Breton, Henri Michaux and others among those that constitute his spiritual family. From the outset I joined the Jargon Group which he set up outwith the formal structures of the university, where he gave talks on themes as varied as Nietzsche, Whitman, Autopsy of the Modern, Taoism, Poetry and Revolution 1917, D.H. Lawrence, The Beat Poets of America, and Henry Thoreau. He opened your mind to so many ideas, poets and thinkers, and made you want to read them for yourself. He was an inspiring teacher, not only in what he introduced you to, but in his ability to communicate the life essence, the essential spark of life, of those of whom he spoke.

This comes across in Jargon Paper 1: *It is the animation to life with which we are concerned, and with those more-than-literary books that pull the doors of the mind off their hinges : releasing the spirit.*

And again: *It is not for nothing (i.e. because they have 'artistic leanings') that the Taoist and Zen masters who have arrived at Nature (Cosmos-Chaos), are also poets. It is because they are men alive, and exalting in their aliveness.*

You can imagine the effect this had on me as a young man. This exaltation in aliveness is what he taught us then and continues to teach us today. Those feelings of what Coleridge called joyance engendered by his talks were continued in discussions late into the night at his and Marie-Claude's flat, and one time walking home along Great Western Road I felt so exhilarated that the leaves on the trees seemed to be dancing above me. Their movement gave me a tremendous feeling of well-being. It is White's ability to touch in some deep way not only minds but hearts, and make the world come alive, which above all distinguishes him from so many other scholars, poets and teachers.

The Jargon Papers, signed K.W., were first distributed in the streets of Glasgow and later relayed worldwide from London by Alex Trocchi's Project Sigma movement. We felt part of a worldwide movement of cultural revolution, but not of the Maoist kind.

Our fortnightly meetings in the city were also continued by what White called field work: excursions into the country and along the shores. These weren't sing-song trips of the 'I love to go a wandering' kind, nor field work in the scientific sense (though that could come into it), they were aimed at keeping contact with the initial world, getting direct experience of the earth, renewing and enlarging sensation, perception, and contemplation carried on into meditation. For White, in poetics and in education, that is a necessary basis. He's a man of ideas, but he's no idealist. For him, there's no Platonic essence behind phenomena, what he's saying is that the real is bigger and has more potential than what we think and make of it.

But the specific text on education which White wrote at this time was the one I mentioned earlier: *The Phoney University*, an indictment of the university as mere "degree factory" and of education as seen and practised in purely utilitarian terms.

> *Goliath, that unfortunate Philistine, is the paragon of socio-cultural excellence when compared with the average Z student after close on twenty years in the educational penitentiary. ...*
> *Being awake to the real and radical problems is something for which you don't get paid in our society. In fact you might even lose your job. ...*
> *In the place of teaching, we find mere instruction and a cultural matter of the most trite and washed-out kind. ...*
> *We need new groupments which can, beyond the deadness, introduce the life-thing. ... It is this kind of movement we must be on the look-out for. And engage in it. Initiate it. This is to go beyond criticism. Into creativity. 'The cleanest expression', writes Whitman 'is that which finds no sphere worthy of itself and makes one.' The University as a sphere is phoney. Let us make another. Others. New spheres of life.*

White has always begun from a fundamental critique of what he's found and this essay was hitting out at absurdities and highlighting problems that would become worse, indeed virulent, over the following decades.

Meanwhile, feeling that the times were not yet ripe in Britain for real change, and that he had momentarily done his bit, White gave up his post in Glasgow and left again for the Continent.

3

In France, White continued the work he had begun in Glasgow, but this time it coincided, at least for a time, with a general movement, the revolt of 1968.

As soon as he arrived in Pau in the Pyrenees, White set up another group, the Groupe Feuillage, with a magazine *Feuillage*, having borrowed the term from Whitman: "Always our old feuillage, always the free range and diversity".

White's teaching was ostensibly in the field of Anglo-American literature, but whatever the material in hand, he always gets down to radical ground, and, even before the revolt in May, his work, while arousing enthusiasm among the students, was disquieting to those in higher office. After May, it was considered not only as disquieting, but as downright subversive.

Kenneth White directed the first three numbers of *Feuillage* – till he was put out of the university in July. In the following year, it was continued by a small group of students, despite its being banned and despite threats of the students' not obtaining a diploma if they dared pursue the publication.

In the first editorial, White talks about "a living earth", "live knowledge" and a "living university". He's continuing his central theme from the Jargon days, and he illustrates it in various ways in the first three numbers. In No. 4, produced after the May Revolt, he goes into it all in more detail, with two long essays, one in French, "Poésie et révolution", and one in English, "The Phenomenon of May", an analysis of the whole unrest and movement of the past few months. This continues in No. 5, in another two essays by White: one in French, "Origines de l'université bourgeoise en France" (Origins of the bourgeois university in France), the other in English: "Towards a Creative University". The first is among other things, a critique of Scottish Common Sense philosophy, introduced by Napoleon into his imperial university as a bulwark against free thought. In the second, White moves from what he calls "the boulevard of culture" that flattens out live reality, into the margins, where he sets out new perspectives and lays out the groundwork of a Creative University. For White this does not mean tacking on creative writing courses to the University as it is. He wants the teaching itself to be creative, based on an active sense of culture amongst teachers and students. *Feuillage* 7, which closes the series is a "Spécial Kenneth White", with the students on the editorial board speaking of the influence White's teaching had on them.

Here are a few highlights from *Towards a Creative University*:

The bourgeois university tends, then, to be a vast accumulation of knowledge without synthesis or movement (all those theses without a thesis ...).

But where is the Creative University, it may be asked, where is it situated? Many of us, at one time or another, have envisaged the creation of new centres, outwith the existing institutions. But this creation of new institutions, however enticing, and however fertile they might be, would still leave the existing institutions, with the weight of existent economy and politics behind them, in the hands of the 'last men'.
The Creative University must situate itself (as a kind of ghost) within the existing institutions, and pursue its work there. Its critical-creative work.

Perhaps again there need be no 'revolutionary moment', and the movement will be a long slow underground process, appearing now and then, here and there, 'on dove's feet' (Nietzsche). This long slow underground process is the concern of teaching. The desires and forces are there - needing a teaching that corresponds to them.

The ethos of the Creative University, far from being an ethos of conformity and production, will be an ethos of self-realisation, based on the notion of auxesis, *the increase of life.*

It's this long process of critical-creative teaching that Kenneth White has been engaged in from the start.

4

By 1971, White was teaching again, this time at the University of Paris VII, living at first in Paris where he completed his Paris book, *Incandescent Limbo*, then commuting once a week between Pau and Paris.

At Paris VII, White started off teaching a course he called "At the Limits of Literature", beginning with Samuel Beckett, and going into the whole field of nihilism. He was working at the concept of supernihilism which runs through *Incandescent Limbo,* and he gave a research seminar he called officially, the "East-West Seminar", but which came to be known more familiarly as the "Old Pond Seminar" (after Bashō) or the "Cold Mountain Seminar" (after Han Shan). Here he was getting at Buddhist negativism and the notion of Emptiness by looking at Eastern figures like Bashō, Han Shan, and Nagarjuna, and Western poets and thinkers involved at one time or another with various aspects of Eastern art and thought, such as Fenollosa, Pound etc. One year he devoted entirely to the haiku, going so far as to present the further reaches of Heidegger's thought in the form of haiku.

By 1972, he had started up another magazine, *The Feathered Egg*.

Its first issue, entitled "Underground, Other Ground", he wrote entirely himself, but under pseudonyms. In the editorial he explained why he was doing this on his own – for speed, and because he says it's creative subjectivity, not committees, that opens up the widest perspectives. Then came a piece "London Underground" (which was to be the first chapter in *Travels in the Drifting Dawn*), signed "Kenzen", then an essay "Essays and Experiments", which laid out his work with the Jargon Group and Feuillage, signed "K le Métèque" (K the Stranger), thereafter an essay "Into the White World", published much later in *On Scottish Ground*, on his conception of poetics, which sets out so much of what was to become geopoetics, signed "Kenjavajra" (a reference to the mahayana school of Buddhism), and finally a poem "Fragments of the Thule Culture", signed Kengaktok (obviously an Eskimo shaman).

By the second number, White had gathered another group together. Under the title *University and Creativity*, there was, for example, an essay by one of his colleagues on "The Crisis in Literary Criticism", with White contributing "A Few Gull Cries in the Void", notes on poetics, "A Note on Methodology" signed Steppenwolf, and reproducing his essay "Towards a Creative University".

This work continued at Paris VII for the next eleven years, and his seminar became well known outside purely university circles. As well as students doing theses with him, there were also a lot of regular listeners-in, and at times people just passing through Paris would also turn up and ask to come in, a request which he very rarely refused, and some 'lifelong students' came back year after year.

Although his *lecteur's* post was from an economic point of view a bad proposition, because about half of his salary went to the French National Railways since he persisted in commuting, preferring to live in the Pyrenees than Paris, it had some advantages in that he had no administrative duties, no examination correction, and none of the soul-destroying chores that more and more kill creative work in the universities.

When he was appointed to a Chair of Twentieth Century Poetics at Paris-Sorbonne, some of his students simply had their dossiers transferred and went along with him. There he gave an amphitheatre lecture once a week on about twelve British and American poets (mostly American) he felt close to. Through them he was in fact putting forward his own conception of poetics, which, using a deliberately non-literary title, he called "Fields of energy". As professor, he made his course optional, rather than compulsory, and reached an even wider audience than before, since it was regularly broadcast over the Paris area from Radio-Sorbonne.

His research seminar was now called Open World Poetics. 'Open world' in at least two senses: one, in that he brought in texts from around the world, and two, in that, he was going into the concepts of "world" and "openness". To do this, he again brought in work other than literary, for example psychological, philosophical and scientific work, and this gradually turned into a seminar on geopoetics.

White has never been much concerned with career as such, his concern has always been, one way or another, to open up a field, and to do this he has constantly made breaks and breakaways, which is why, to everybody's surprise, he resigned his prestigious post at the Sorbonne in 1996.

Sometimes, at the introduction of his East-West Seminar at Paris VII, White would quote an old Chinese description of the real teacher: "Great capacity, deep learning, fullness of expression – and freedom to come and go".

5

Well, since 1996, White has come and gone quite a lot, increasing the scope of his poetic teaching still further. He has been visiting professor in several places, and visiting lecturer in many more.

In particular, here in Scotland, since renewing his contact in 1989, he has given a whole series of lectures which were brought together with other texts in *On Scottish Ground*, such as the "Scotland, Intelligence and Culture" lecture at the Advisory Council for the Arts conference at Edinburgh in 1989; the lecture "A Shaman Dancing on the Glacier", delivered at the Goethe Institut, Glasgow in 1990; "The Scot Abroad", at the Celtic Connections Festival, Glasgow in 1996; "The Franco-Scottish Connection" at the University of Edinburgh in 1996; "Scotland, Europe and the Culture-Question" at the University of St Andrews in 1998; the lectures "The Re-Mapping of Scotland" and "On the High Line", delivered at the Edinburgh International Book Festival respectively in 2001 and 2002. These lectures will be seen more and more as marking a new tide in the affairs of Scotland.

Content apart, White practises the lecture as an art. In his writing there is a strong oral thrust, and it is this he uses to great effect in his lecturing. Tony McManus remarked in an article on the electrifying effect on the audience of White's talk "A Shaman Dancing on the Glacier". When he finished, the audience simply erupted in a flow of discussion. He has developed and deepened his knowledge and skills since the Jargon days, but the Wild Coal and the fire are still there, and one cannot help thinking of that golden period of lecturing in the first half of the 19th century, with figures like Coleridge and Carlyle on the platform.

The historian Michelet speaks in one of his texts of "a great art of education and initiation". White represents that, and generations of students and others have cause to be grateful to him for their initiation into so much, but particularly into a sense of world.

At the centre of his activity, there is the ongoing work, in the form of essays, poems and narrative prose. It is from this that he emerges, and it is to this he always returns. But radiating out from this central focus, in concentric circles, there has always been, as I've tried to outline, an active criticism of culture and cultural politics, a concern for education, and attempts at new organisations, with new thematics and new perspectives.

As a student, White plunged into Jaeger's *Paideia* and the Paideuma theory of Frobenius. In 1938, in *The Criterion*, Ezra Pound, with similar references behind him, published an essay "For a New Paideuma". In it he criticises both the quality and the relevance of authors taught in literary courses, and the lack of any real co-ordination and correlation between courses. This is exactly what White has always been working at, from university to university.

In a wider field, Pound – like Nietzsche before him, who spoke of a new kind of monastery – evokes the possibility of new organisations outside the university. Looking at the intelligentsia and the literati, Pound is, to say the least, not confident, saying that up to now the Anglo-Americans have not even been able to set up a viable Academy, and he leaves the question up in the air.

It is unlikely, though not totally inconceivable, that White would go for the creation of an Academy – so far he has been content with what he calls 'the Gull Academy' as in his poem: 'First Colloquium of the Gull Academy'. He has just as many, if not more, misgivings as Pound with regard to the 'literary world', and probably doubts whether an intelligentsia exists at all, which is why he has looked instead to students. It is also why his most ambitious attempt to date of this kind, the International Institute of

Geopoetics, while welcoming individual artists, writers, philosophers, psychologists and scientists, recruits extensively amongst people with no professional qualifications or artistic status, but who are deeply aware of a culture problem and eager to see the opening of a general new field.

He has worked at this, and continues to work at this, in many different ways. Many of his texts on culture, education and politics have been gathered into a book entitled *Une stratégie paradoxale* (Presses Universitaires de Bordeaux). It's perhaps in the notion of a 'paradoxical strategist' that I can sum up what I have been trying to say about White's journey as an educator.

KENNETH WHITE'S ERRATIC ITINERARY
Marco Fazzini

Kenneth White's work will be the focus of attention here to illustrate the way in which the study of the relationship between literature and environment – the main subject of a new critical approach called *ecocriticism* – can teach us how to improve our status within nature, in terms of being more aware of how we treat the earth and its inhabitants, as well as how we can achieve a closer relationship with the environment where we breathe, walk, love, etc.

When Greenblatt and Gunn felt the necessity to re-draw the field of literary studies in their 1992 volume *Redrawing the Boundaries*,[1] they paid no attention to an ecological approach to literature, and to a possible involvement of literature in the global environmental crisis. As Glotfelty suggests in one of the key volumes dedicated to ecocriticism, there is a vast area available to research and study which could be included in a multidisciplinary discourse:

> *If your knowledge of the outside world were limited to what you could infer from the major publications of the literary profession, you would quickly discern that race, class, and gender were the hot topics of the later twentieth century, but you would never suspect that the earth's life support systems were under stress... While related humanities' disciplines, like history, philosophy, law, sociology, and religion have been 'greening' since the 1970s, literary studies have apparently remained untinted by environmental concerns.*[2]

Literary studies as a discipline has completely ignored such environmental concerns. Just a few poets, writers, or individual scholars have spent years trying to construct an ecocritical discourse on that topic. One of these is Gary Snyder. Here's what Snyder wrote in 1984:

> *We can all agree: there is a problem with the chaotic, self-seeking human ego. Is it a mirror of the wild and of nature? I think not: for civilization itself is ego gone to seed and institutionalized in the form of the State, both Eastern and Western. It is not nature-as-chaos which threatens us (for nature is orderly) but ignorance of the natural world, the myth of progress, and the presumption of the State that it has created order. That sort of 'order' is an elaborate rationalization of the greed of a few.[3]*

Of his own experience, Kenneth White has observed:

> *I am not suggesting that we celebrate any mountain goddess. I am suggesting that we try and get back an earth-sense, a ground sense, and a freshness of the world such as those men, those Finn-men, knew when they moved over an earth from which the ice had just recently receded. This is the dawn of geopoetics.[4]*

It seems that moving from America to Europe, and from Europe to Africa some 'eccentric' (de-centred) writers have decided not to treat nature as a guest in our world, or act as nature's superior. Instead, they have focussed on how it can improve the human standard of living.

Kenneth White loves wilderness and desert areas, and he feels he must go and live there for short or longer periods. The journey can be difficult (like in *The Blue Road* where he travels through Labrador, slowly moving out of civilization and the urban areas of an industrialised society);[5] his efforts are often tinged with a certain ascetic quality (like in *The Wild Swans*, moving slowly towards an epiphanic movement of illumination and vision);[6] or an ironic intent is used to guide the reader towards a deeper understanding of our urban western environment (like in *Travels in the Drifting Dawn*).[7]

White discovers himself (a larger self) in nature, comes to a better understanding of his place in the world, while seeking a transcendental experience which takes him beyond himself and into the contemplation of a cosmic totality.

Georges Bataille, calling for a move away from 'actuality' and civilized cacophony, towards 'desertic man' has observed that:

> *To give an idea of the distance between contemporary man and the desert, I'd say that the desert means the total abandonment of all the concerns of contemporary man, that inane and cacophonous mixture of bits of science, idealism, sentimentality, faith, and big talk. There's no noise in the desert. Foregoing all attempts at rational mastery of the universe, the mind becomes the dream of the universe, and we move with the dream.*[8]

If ecocriticism is the study of the relationship between literature and the physical environment, advocating an 'eco-centric' criticism that rejects the anthropocentric concerns that have characterised literary studies,[9] and free of any residue of ecological imperialism,[10] it is obvious that White's work is not only highly relevant to it, but he has worked in this field so long that he has developed concepts, a vocabulary, ways of writing and thinking that go far beyond that discourse as it now stands.

It began with experience on the west coast of Scotland, was first formulated in the notion of 'white world' and later expanded considerably into the whole complex field of geopoetics:

> *That's what I called 'white world'. But maybe I'd formulate the thing differently: I wouldn't say 'communication between writing and the universe, between literature and the world', but communication between the self and the world. For a great part of the work goes on* outside *writing, outside literature. You have to worldify the self, littoralise (if I may say so) being. Otherwise you remain in the pathetic, the illusory – in 'literature' (or 'poetry').*[11]

Kenneth White's favourite literary 'persona', the 'intellectual nomad', walks the path which leads astray from the Motorway of Western Civilization. Along this path he looks for a power of synthesis which Western culture has forgotten since the building up of that 'motorway' by Platonic idealism, Aristotelian classification, Christianity, Renaissance humanism, Cartesianism, Hegelian historicism, etc.[12]

What Anne McClintock says in her recent study on race, gender and sexuality in the colonial context has also some relevance for explaining the kind of opposition White has maintained during his literary career,[13] and the research he has undertaken. She notes that all the terminology which uses the prefix 'post' in contemporary intellectual life (post-colonialism, post-modernism, post-feminism, post-marxism, post-structuralism, post-national, even post-historic) is a symptom of a 'global crisis in ideologies of the future, particularly the ideology of progress'.[14] Discussing the totalitarian U.S. Third World policies, the New World Bank projects adopted after the decolonisation of Africa, the collapse of the Soviet Union and its history-driven discourse, and the failure of alternative forms of capitalist or communist progress, the critic questions the value of that metaphor which has represented Western progress as able to guarantee security and development to certain human civilizations. McClintock's desire for a new intellectual era includes the birth and the growth of innovative theories of history and popular memory, something which could replace all the words prefixed by 'post' with a multiplicity of intents and powers.

Multiplicity is certainly a primal trait in White's work. Here he is speaking about his poetic project:

> *and when a Japanese literatus*
> *speaks of the series of waka poems*
> *(sometimes as many as 100 in a sequence)*
> *written in the Kamakura period*
> *(thirteenth and fourteenth centuries)*
> *saying 'the result*
> *was often a kind of kaleidoscopic beauty*
> *with infinite variety*
> *revealed to the reader*
> *in a slowly evolving movement'*
> *I recognize my aim*[15]

There is no doubt that the 'motorway' White speaks about in many of his books and articles is the straight way of the stereotyped values of the violent or debased civilizations of our continents.[16] There is also no doubt that in the last decades the attention which has been paid to travel and to the literature produced around and about it has been broadly enlarged. Obviously, such a phenomenon has been partly produced by both the recent accessibility of travelling and the banality of its use in the politics and economics of mass tourism. This has often caused an impoverishment of the value given to travelling, especially to travelling as a means of acquiring and transferring knowledge, which is why, in his own travelling, White goes back to primal influences on the one hand, and, on the other, moves forward to an expansion of concern and thought. In one of his core books, he speaks about the first traveller-writers (early representatives of the figure of the 'intellectual nomad'), and of Bashō in particular.[17] Both exiled and rejected by their civil society, they managed to transform their exile into a soul-searching investigation and an enlarged experience.

Edward Said tells us that the exile is an outcast who is 'inconsolable about the past, bitter about the present and the future'.[18] This statement suggests a strong sense of nostalgia for the abandoned patria, a sensation of discomfort in the present, and a gloominess about the future. But nostalgia, habitually associated with the idea of exile, is, in fact, alien to both Said and White, two intellectuals who stand half-way between the position of exile and immigrant, and argue very strongly that exile need not be an unhappy condition. According to Said, the exile exists in a 'median state', neither fully integrated into the new system or society, nor totally relieved of his or her burden of cultural and personal memories. The ambiguity of the border gives such a figure a dual position which can offer stimulating advantages. This ties in with the differences between the exile and the immigrant established by Abdul R. JanMohamed in his article on the 'specular border intellectual'.[19]

One of the most remarkable figures whom Said chooses to illustrate the point is the philosopher Theodor Adorno, whose *Minima Moralia* Said takes as his representative work in this context. Adorno, who left his country because of the rise to power of the Nazis, takes a critical stand against all systems, contrasting this side or that, East and West, the housed and the unhoused, aggregation and complete privacy. His life produces a 'destabilizing effect' which manifests itself in a series of 'discontinuous performances'.[20] Consequently, as Said observes of Adorno, this intellectual's work must be 'fragmentary first of all, jerky, discontinuous; there is no plot or predetermined order to follow. It represents the intellectual's consciousness as unable to be at rest anywhere, constantly on guard against the blandishments of easy success, which, for the perversely inclined Adorno, means trying consciously not to be understood easily and immediately'.[21]

This is an interesting approach, but with White we can go further.

To give 'erratic travel' a specific cultural dimension, or an autonomous historic development, is no easy matter. After that extraordinary tradition linked to some of the most fabulous medieval travellers such as Duns Scot, one of White's closest 'companions', the accepted and canonised model for the definition of 'travel' excludes any other variation or transgression played on it, in particular those journeys which do not close their own circle, which do not return to their point of departure.[22] But it is possible to distinguish between two different figures: the traveller and the wanderer. The latter, instead of returning to or reconquering the place where he or she moved from, multiplies his or her paths and trajectories which come to be other than 'straight'. Losing, deliberately, his or her right/straight way, and indicating no obvious direction at all in his or her peregrinations,[23] White's nomad keeps outside:

> with the calling of the navigator-wanderer, the terrain of the difficult territory, and a sense of ongoing itinerary. The intellectual nomad (the term used, in passing, by Spengler in his Decline of the West, and whose scope I was to develop), is engaged, outside the glitzy or glaury compound of late modernity, in an area of complex co-ordinates. He is trying to move out of pathological psycho-history, along uncoded paths, into fresh existential, intellectual, poetic space.[24]

As is also shown in this fragment from White's 'Walking the Coast', the intellectual nomad is the one who feels the strength of a gathering force within chaos, without the necessity to surrender to the attraction of any hegemonic 'centre' to be reached or any reassuring 'meaning' to be stated. Here his poetic 'persona' seems to lose not only its control over a geographic itinerary, but also, and mainly, over some of the canonised and expected speculative, epistemological and political horizons:

living and writing at random
but knowing
that
though living at random
there is a tendency to stress
the essential in the random[25]

Nomads, tramps, the homeless, and wanderers are often considered as representatives of a mode of travelling which is often dangerous, in most cases a real pathology. Yet, what Michel Butor says about nomadism and wandering seems to give a new and dynamic status to this ontological process.[26] Michel Maffesoli thinks that nomadism translates the plurality contained in each individual, highlighting the multiplicity of existential potentiality.[27] At the same time, it expresses violent or discrete opposition to a fixed order. White never forgets that, while touching and crossing traditions and cultures which are marginal to the 'motorway' of the Western world, he must maintain both the impulse of the research (there is no end to ethnology) and the vigour of the ongoing concept:

For some years now, the word 'nomad' has been in the air. In a vague enough way at the beginning, but precision comes as one goes along, it indicates the movement towards new intellectual and cultural space. In our hyper-mediatised cultures, however, every concept, immediately sub-translated, turns into a mere fashion. What is in question in the work in hand is no mere modish fashion, but a whole world in movement. [...] The nomad leaves the motorway of civilization, as also the pathogenic cities it

*passes through or around, and moves off into a landscape
where there are sometimes no roads, no paths, no tracks, at
most a few traces.*[28]

So, what we have defined by the term 'erratic travel' is clearly
more than just a geographical move from one place to another. Any
journey can be transformed into an erratic path by a fortuitous
accident: a storm can delay or divert a ship from her course; the
sight of an exceptional animal can lead the hunter astray or into a
dark wood where he has to face unexpected experience; or the lack
of a detailed map can force the traveller to accept an occasional
guide who comes to divert routes and planned experiences. This
happens, for example, in White's *The Blue Road*, when the narrator
accepts the guidance of fortuitous acquaintances met on the way to
Labrador; or, again, when 'By a stroke of good luck that morning I'd
come across a taxi-driver who'd offered to take me to a hill-tribe
village off the normal circuit'.[29] So, even though we have still to
distinguish between a traditional journey which, by accident, may be
transformed into an erratic one, and an intentional pathless
itinerary, the two dimensions, like some of the differences existing
between the exile and the immigrant, seem to blur when one has to
admit the possibility of the presence of 'unexpected' or 'strange'
events. But what is the fundamental relationship between literature
and travelling? How does prose-narrative (travel-writing) turn into a
waybook, how does the act of moving turn into an attitude to life,
how does poetry turn into geopoetics?

White's refusal of every sort of classification or category by
which one can define literary genres, the intimate essentiality of East
and West, or the Old and the New Worlds underlines, once again,
the in-between, no-man's-landish condition of this new 'intellectual
nomad':

*walking in the stillness
half-way between the Old World and the New
trying to move in deeper
ever deeper
into a white world
neither old nor new*[30]

Part of the peculiar attraction of White's writing derives, from his total determination to experience the wilderness on his own terms. His prose writing, but also his poems, chronicle his emancipation from the category of macho tourism or solitary travelling: 'the pilgrim trip has an aim, the sacred spot. But beyond the sacred, there's emptiness. I'm not out to cover kilometres, or to reach a particular place, I'm out for a kind of spatial poetics, with emptiness at its centre. And you begin again, for the pleasure, to get at an even finer sense of emptiness-plenitude.'[31]

One of the significant features of poetry is its therapeutic quality. In the Outer Hebrides, until at least as late as the eighteenth century, the poet was considered a kind of healer. People would travel many miles on foot to the North Uist poet John MacCodrum and confide in him some difficulty they were experiencing. The remedy he offered them mostly took the form of healing words, words they could carry away with them, write down or learn by heart. 'While it is important', observes Christopher Whyte, 'to be extraordinarily tentative in ascribing a therapeutic function to poetry, there can be no doubt that, in moments of acute tension, whether this be the first experience of sexual love, a major bereavement, or dizzying ontological uncertainty, again and again isolated individuals have encountered, in a poem, normally within the space of a few lines or even in one single line, a formula, a spell almost, which helped them survive, a sort of talisman'.[32] In a similar way, but in even more physical terms, Mandelstam says of the poetry of Pasternak, compared with most poetry, that it's like drinking *koumys* after a diet of pasteurized milk, it clears the throat, gives one breathing space: 'There is no poetry more salubrious.'[33]

This is the effect the reader often experiences when reading White's books. This is the effect contemporary men and women are in dire need of because of the devalued relationship between 'human' and 'non-human' in our society. This is the language which can recall for us ancestral reminiscences and insights, serving as both a walking and linguistic yoga: writer and reader together become the field of an experimentation where the internal landscape coincides with and faces an external one for an eternal re-symbolization of *being* in the world, thus exchanging flux and energy, steps and passages, 'limits and margins'. Within a context where we have witnessed the failure of philosophical, ethical, and historical fundamentals, as Lyotard has observed, it is no longer possible to start up a new system of values: only a creative crossing will suffice, a crossing where a poetic erudition and an erratic route mingle and support each other. This is the only way to free our context of all its lines encrusted by power and corruption.

White's non-linear and non-logical language-itinerary can relocate our lives in the world, transforming our selves into active presences whose culture finally interacts with nature, and whose agility of movement and thought can become the nexus of a new network of illuminating trajectories.

NOTES

1   Stephen Greenblatt and Giles Gunn (eds), *Redrawing the Boundaries: The Transformation of English and American Literary Studies* (New York: MLA, 1992), pp.1-3. See also Cherryl Glotfelty's attack on Greenblatt and Gunn in her introduction to Cheryll Glotfelty and Harold Fromm (eds), *The Ecocriticism Reader* (Athens and London: The University of Georgia Press, 1996), p. xv.
2   Cheryll Glotfelty and Harold Fromm (eds), *The Ecocriticism Reader*, p. xvi.
3   Gary Snyder, *Good Wild Sacred* (Hereford: Five Seasons Press, 1984), p.24.
4   Kenneth White, *On Scottish Ground: Selected Essays* (Edinburgh: Polygon, 1998), p.48.
5   See Kenneth White, *The Blue Road* (Edinburgh: Mainstream Publishing, 1990).
6   See Kenneth White, *The Wild Swans*, in *Pilgrim of the Void: Travels in South-East Asia and the North Pacific* (Edinburgh: Mainstream Publishing, 1992), pp.177-254.
7   See Kenneth White, *Travels in the Drifting Dawn* (Edinburgh: Mainstream Publishing, 1989).
8   See Georges Bataille, *L'Expérience intérieure* (Paris: Gallimard, 1954). Quoted in Kenneth White, *The Tribal Dharma: An Essay on the Work of Gary Snyder* (Carmarthen: Unicorn, 1975), p.11.
9   See Glen A. Love, 'Revaluing Nature': Toward an Ecological Criticism, *Western American Literature*, 25.3 (1990), pp.201-15; and Steven Rosendale (ed.), *The Greening of Literary Scholarship: Literature, Theory, and the Environment* (Iowa City: University of Iowa Press, 2002), pp.xv-xxix.
10   This term has been coined by Alfred W. Crosby to indicate all the forms of imperialism which have physically transformed the environments of colonial societies. See A.W. Crosby, *Ecological Imperialism: The*

Biological Expansion of Europe, 900-1900 (Cambridge: Cambridge University Press, 1986); and R. Grove, *Green Imperialism* (Cambridge: Cambridge University Press, 1994).

11 Kenneth White, *Coast to Coast: Interviews and Conversations 1985-1995* (Glasgow: Open World in association with Mythic Horse Press, 1996), p.34.

12 Kenneth White, *Le Plateau de l'Albatros: introduction à la géopoétique* (Paris: Grasset, 1994), pp.21-42.

13 See Anne McClintock, *Imperial Leather: Race, Gender and Sexuality in the Colonial Contest* (New York and London: Routledge, 1995), pp.391-96.

14 Anne McClintock, *Imperial Leather*, p.392.

15 Kenneth White, *The Bird Path: Collected Longer Poems* (Edinburgh: Mainstream Publishing, 1989), p.59.

16 See Kenneth White, *Geopoetics: place, culture, world* (Glasgow: Alba Editions, 2003).

17 Kenneth White, *L'Esprit nomade* (Paris: Grasset, 1987), pp.17-76.

18 Edward Said, *Representations of the Intellectual: The 1993 Reith Lectures* (London: Vintage, 1994), p.35.

19 Abdul R. JanMohamed, 'Worldliness-without-World, Homelessness-as-Home: Toward a Definition of the Specular Border Intellectual', in Michael Sprinker (ed.), *Edward Said: A Critical Reader* (Oxford: Blackwell, 1992), pp.96-120.

20 Edward Said, *Representations of the Intellectual*, pp.40-44.

21 *Ibid*, p.42.

22 In one of his recent books White himself has observed: 'There's an erratic logic in it all, as well as what you might call erotic research work, if you're ready to give the word 'erotic', its full scope – remember that in Greek mythology, *eros* is the son of *penia*, necessity, and of *poros*, the maker of passageways. There's flight in it also, in the sense of fleeing from, but also in the sense of the plenitudinous deployment of energy.' See Kenneth White, *The Wanderer and His Charts: Essays on Cultural Renewal* (Edinburgh: Polygon, 2004), p.5.

23 See Gianfranco Rubino (ed.), *Figure dell'erranza: immaginario del percorso nel romanzo francese contemporaneo* (Rome: Bulzoni, 1991), pp.7-8.

24 Kenneth White, *The Wanderer and His Charts*, p.vi.

25 Kenneth White, *The Bird Path*, p.68.

26 Michel Butor, 'Le Voyage et l'écriture', *Romantisme, 4* (1972), p.7.

27 See the Prologue to Michel Maffesoli, *Du nomadisme: Vagabondages initiatiques* (Paris: Libraire Générale Française, 1997).

28 Kenneth White, *L'Esprit nomade*, pp.10-11.

29 Kenneth White, 'The Northern Route', in *Pilgrim of the Void*, p.163.

30 Kenneth White, *The Bird Path*, p.187.

31 Kenneth White, *Coast to Coast*, p.37.

32 See Christopher Whyte, *Modern Scottish Poetry* (Edinburgh: Edinburgh University Press, 2004), p.27.

33 Quoted by Angelo Maria Ripellino in *Letteratura come itinerario nel meraviglioso* (Turin: Enaudi, 1968), p.278.

WALKING THE EDGE: KENNETH WHITE'S LANDSCAPE-MINDSCAPE
Olivier Delbard

Scot. I like the etymology of that word as 'wanderer'. Yes, that's it. The extravagant (extra vagans: wandering outside) Scot. Scotus vagans. Wandering, more or less obscurely, in accordance with a fundamental orientation.[1]

The invisible lines that crossed and criss-crossed the emptiness [...] It's those 'invisible lines' I'm interested in, it's those I'm going to try and follow out.[2]

... where the lines break, sinuosities develop and intertwine, where physical experience attains such a degree of density and intensity that we can almost call it 'metaphysical'.[3]

But it's an anonymous archipelago I have in mind. White mist, blue sea. Ahhh.[4]

Wherever we go, we're going home.[5]

What follows is not meant to be an academic article, it is rather to be understood as a 'walk' into Kenneth White's landscape-mindscape, that 'topological coherence in progress', a complex logic unfolding, a vast physical and mental geography leading to the ultimate territory, that of the poem of the world, the old-new reality... That is at least how I have read Kenneth's work since I began exploring it about twenty years ago. And my wish here was to let the words mostly speak for themselves...

The focus clearly is on topology, rather than chronology, with:

Landscape as a 'field of correspondences', where the physical world and human beings meet, a network of lines, both visible and invisible, a series of signs, colours (from red to yellow to blue to white), elements (rocks, trees, water), landmarks (places, people).

Mindscape as a way of thinking, on the edge, an 'archipelago of the mind', fertile, fluid, unique. Wandering on the edge of Western culture, leaving it, as an 'intellectual nomad' writing a new map of the mind.

> *'The mind can also be seen as a landscape – with fields and streams, fluid concepts.'*[6]

Landscape-Mindscape: A mental geography following the topological logic, to reach what Gregory Bateson once called the 'necessary unity',[7] an 'ecology of the mind' beyond dichotomies, where physical intuition and mental intellectual insights interconnect, in the open world.

Diversity-Unity
Complexity-Simplicity
Chaos-Harmony

And a double coherence, an existential logic where exploration and residence combine and complement each other:

Outward Bound: from the heart of cities into a new dawn, step by step into open spaces, then farther and farther away into the white country.

Living and Dwelling on the Edge: Along the Atlantic coast, in the French desert, facing the blue mountains, along the coast again.

Outward Bound

> *The question in my mind*
> *is of going outward*
> *always farther outward*
> *to the farthest* line of light[8]

To get out of the malaise in our Western world, it is necessary to 'get ready' for the dawn. Hence, Kenneth White's personal journey 'into the light' started with a first phase of dissolution, deconstruction, drifting... From the heart of cities into more open country.

Studying the Language of Dawn

Once I lived in that city

...

I studied
the language of dawn[9]

First there was Glasgow (1954-56), then Munich (1956-57) 'where I nearly froze to death',[10] Glasgow again (1957-59), Paris (1959-63) in *Incandescent Limbo*, Glasgow (1963-67) again like a little *Season in Hell*, in the heart of the furnace, 'flinging crazily about the city'[11].

Looking for signs of the dawn... A 'dark, red sun'[12], red lights. Signs of the Open: railway stations, libraries, ports... But a lot of darkness still.

Travelling in the Drifting Dawn

From Port to Port
Then there were short journeys to ports, 'open' cities: Barcelona under the sign of Eros, Amsterdam and the 'white laughter of Shiva',[13] Antwerp on a 'raw blue morning'.[14]

Into Open Country
On the plains, 'waiting for the dawn'.[15]
Winter as Open World: 'sudden flashes of whiteness',[16] a landscape of white and blue, cold and dangerous, but sharp and clear.

Into the South
South of France: Provence, the Camargue and the mistral, a 'white wind blowing'.[17]
Signs: 'a big red sun/running mad on the horizon'...[18]

Towards the ocean; 'to the cape, along a narrow path of rocks and shrubs... I am at home in the desertic landscape'.[19]

Reaching the African Desert. Last word of *Travels in the Drifting Dawn*: emptiness.

'Passage to more than India'[20]

The seventies and eighties. Following the first phase of deconstruction-reconstruction.

In search of 'radical exoticism', of an 'aesthetics of diversity',[21] Kenneth White heads for the East, the Far East.

India: yin, the Moon, feminine territory, a girl dancing, the 'same blue sari,'[22] books, an India of the imagination, of the mind...

Into the Floating World: South East Asia

Here begins the 'waybooks' cycle: journeys that always start in the heart of a metropolis, then signs gradually lead the pilgrim outside, into the open world.

> *Hong Kong*
> *a warm white mist over the bay*
> *and an old junk making it*
> *the slow way*[23]

First the city as a gateway, then Macau, then an island... Alone on a shore, understanding the signs-ideograms: a waterfall, 'time and place gradually get lost',[24] and later 'blue glimpses of the sea', a 'cluster of blue islands'.[25]

Into metaphysical territory and the archaic Self: 'I was waves breaking on a beach, wind in pine trees'...[26]

Thailand and Taiwan: 'the face of the East Wind'

The geomental logic intensifies in Thailand and Taiwan. All this is much more than travel writing, with its multi-level coherence, taking the reader into the open world, towards abstraction, yet firmly grounded in immediate physical reality.

First the metropolises: Taipeh and Bangkok, where extremes meet, the sordid and the marvellous.

Leaving Taipeh, White goes to the very centre of the island, into wild archaic territory: the Sun Moon Lake, 'a blue paradise' opening out onto white territory where only the essential remains:

> *Up here*
> *there is neither East nor West*
> *the white heron*
> *has disappeared in the mist*[27]

In Thailand, White leaves Bangkok for the 'Blue Hills of the North'. At the end of the physical-spiritual journey, blue is everywhere, the world is nothing else but 'blue woven into blue'...[28]

With those two journeys, one leaves autumn for winter, led by the East wind.

Colours change too, from yellow (Buddhism's yellow sources), red and brown, to blue and white.

Moving further into the North, into the open world, into the white world, into White's world.

If 'to travel north is to travel into the mind',[29] then the journey is not only metaphysical or metaphorical, it has to be real... Which will lead White to Japan and Labrador.

The Northern Route

The Wild Swans on Hokkaido

The journey once again starts in a metropolis, Tokyo, then leaves it behind to travel both 'really' and 'cerebrally', following Bashō's route,[30] up north, into archaic Nipponese ground, the world of Ainu people and Shinto spirits, into winter (from rain to snow), into Pacific space (salmon and whales), into a wild, empty, open nordic and oceanic landscape, the north-eastern tip of Hokkaido, or to put it metaphysically, into 'the north-east corner of the mind'.[31]

The ultimate *sign* of the journey is that of the wild *swans* (the French '*cygnes*' is pronounced like '*signes*') by the end of the book, when White sees them landing on the water, in a scene filled with simple, intense joy:

> *Round and round they circled in the clear bright air.*
> *I followed them with my eyes and with my mind*[32]

Perception and intellect are blended in this perfect mindscape-landscape, at the very edge of Asia, so close to another continent of the mind, America.

Into Labrador

The Blue Road to Labrador closes the first cycle of the waybooks, where White 'comes full circle',[33] back into Atlantic space. Once again, the journey is a 'geomental meditation', confronting real places with the 'America of the mind', present in White's world since childhood.

From Montreal to the North Bank of the Saint-Lawrence and into Labrador where the road ends, signs multiply, blue signs everywhere, in the midst of 'Red America'.

Finally, at the end of the journey, Labrador has become a metaphysical 'stepping-over place',[34] ending a cycle, starting a new phase, work in progress, 'the Atlantic territory', past-present-future.

> *trying to move in deeper*
> *ever deeper*
> *into a white world*
> *neither old nor new'*[35]

Living and Dwelling on the Edge

Kenneth White's landscape-mindscape is obviously also made up of 'places of residence', which follow his mental itinerary and intensify the geographical logic by grounding it in time and space. What also makes White's context so unique is this constant dialectic between movement and dwelling.

White's places of residence are as meaningful as the journeys undertaken. In their own way, they are on the edge, of the ocean, of the desert, of the mountain.

Scotland

> *rock province, roots... and lights*[36]

Scotland, as native, primary, elementary space, is the central metaphor of White's exploration of the world. It concentrates all of the Whitian landscape-mindscape.

The Region of Identity[37]

First, Fairlie, the West Coast. 'Ragged'. 'Fragmented'.
Elements: the shore, mountains ('the womb of the hills'),[38] rocks ('Ice Age markings'),[39] birch trees and moors ('Birch rites/empty moors'),[40] 'a wild wave talking',[41] seagulls ('like overwhelming metaphors').[42]
The past: the 'Scot' as the Wanderer, the Eccentric. History. Geography. Geology.
Soon, exploration expands to the whole coast, up north:

a bird yell
emptied my skull.[43]

spaced out, and lost in the high open joyance...[44]

Today, Scotland has become geomental reality. Where White 'begins again'. The clear expression of 'my thought's ragged edge'.[45]

It is forever present, beyond time and space:

birthplace
of a wave-and-wind philosophy
...
pelagian discourse
atlantic poetics

from first to last[46]

Gourgounel or the 'French Desert'

Kenneth White spent the summer of 1961 in an old isolated farm in the Ardèche, France. The place was called Gourgounel.
Gourgounel in the middle of the French desert: a place to concentrate life and thought. Physical work and intellectual study.
The 'place of fire', with the bright sun, the heat, roaring thunder.
The 'fireplace'.

Like Thoreau's Walden Pond, White's Gourgounel is a unique experience of a deep sense of place, from reality to a place of the mind, everywhere and nowhere, another step forward in White's 'reinhabitation' of the world. 'Remembering Gourgounel'...[47]

The Blue Ridges of the Pyrenees

blue light breaking in the mountains[48]

From 1967 to 1983, Kenneth White lived mostly in Pau, facing the French Pyrenees.

A time of study ('I've opened one book after another/all along this winter'),[49] and writing ('Working and reworking/the same texts/over and over again').[50]

A place of silence and snow: 'the flurried fullness of/the inner murmuring of/the snowy silence.'[51]

Looking at the mountains 'in the warm white/misty light/of early Spring'.[52]

Glimpses of the white world again, walks into the 'high country', 'thinking of nothing/only the body moving'.[53]

But the ocean is never far, 'the sea and pine country': dunes, beaches, a dune carnation,[54] a blue thistle...[55]

Following the Atlantic coast, up North... towards Britanny, *Armorica*.

The Armorican Shore

Over on the headland
where the wind, from second to second
turns into light
he felt
a sense of living
at the edge of all knowing[56]

In 1983, Kenneth White settled on the north coast of Brittany, another West Coast facing the Atlantic territory, at Gwenved.

'Here I am at home!',[57] in a 'centred complex' – Celtic territory, geological chaos-harmony, 'broken coastlines', 'confused clarities', 'fracture patterns' ...[58]

A place for the gathering of elements, concentrating life, work in progress, the 'House at the Head of the Tide'.[59]

No need to add commentary. For White, living at Gwenved means:

a place to work from
(to work it all out)[60]

The maturity stage. Geopoetics in action.
The 'house of tides'...

atlantic archipelago
and a sense of something
to be gathered in[61]

Conclusion

Kenneth White's landscape-mindscape shows us one of the very few fundamental experiences of the open world in today's literature.

A geographical as well as mental exploration of the edge.

Work in progress.

NOTES

1   Kenneth White, *Travels in the Drifting Dawn*, p.133.
2   'The Wild Swans', Kenneth White, *Pilgrim of the Void*, pp.229-230.
3   'Meditations on a Chinese Island', *ibid.*, pp.67-68.
4   'The Taiwan Itinerary', *ibid.*, p.93.
5   'Preface', *ibid.*, p.15.
6   From *Une Apocalypse tranquille*, my translation.
7   See Gregory Bateson, *Steps to an Ecology of Mind* (St Albans: Paladin, 1973) and *Mind and Nature: A Necessary Unity* (New Jersey: Hampton Press, 1979).
8   Kenneth White, *The Bird Path*, p.118.
9   *Ibid.*, p.77.
10   *Ibid.*, p.55.
11   Kenneth White, *Travels in the Drifting Dawn*, p.26.
12   Kenneth White, *Handbook for the Diamond Country*, p.69.
13   *Travels in the Drifting Dawn*, p.84.
14   *Ibid.*, p.107.
15   *Ibid.*, p.89.
16   *Ibid.*
17   *Ibid.*, p.101.
18   *Handbook for the Diamond Country*, p.97.
19   *Travels in the Drifting Dawn*, pp.115-116.
20   Walt Whitman, 'Passage to India' in *Leaves of Grass*.
21   See Victor Segalen, *Essay on Exoticism: an Aesthetics of Diversity*.
22   *Travels in the Drifting Dawn*, p.85.
23   *The Bird Path*, p.130.
24   *Pilgrim of the Void*, p.41.
25   *Ibid.*, pp.62-63.
26   *Ibid.*, p.65.
27   'In the Mountains of Taiwan', *Handbook for the Diamond Country*, p.126.
28   *Pilgrim of the Void*, p.176.
29   *Travels in the Drifting Dawn*, p.143.
30   See Matsuo Bashō's *Narrow Road to the Deep North*.
31   *Handbook for the Diamond Country*, p.128.
32   *Pilgrim of the Void*, p.247.
33   'Labrador is where I come full circle', Kenneth White, *The Blue Road*, p.20.
34   *The Bird Path*, p.187.
35   *Ibid.*
36   *Handbook for the Diamond Country*, p.33.
37   Title of poem in *The Bird Path*.
38   *The Bird Path*, p.45.
39   *Ibid.*, p.128.

40 *Handbook for the Diamond Country*, p.27.
41 *The Bird Path*, p.44.
42 *Ibid.*, p.43.
43 *Handbook for the Diamond Country*, p.76.
44 *Travels in the Drifting Dawn*, p.144.
45 *Handbook for the Diamond Country*, p.47.
46 *The Bird Path*, pp.126-27.
47 Title of a poem in *The Bird Path*, pp.84-85.
48 *Handbook for the Diamond Country*, p.158.
49 *Ibid.*, p.148.
50 *The Bird Path*, p.169.
51 *Ibid.*, p.167.
52 *Handbook for the Diamond Country*, p.156.
53 *The Bird Path*, p.164.
54 'In Aquitania', *ibid.*, pp.90-91.
55 'Blue Thistle Sermon', *Handbook for the Diamond Country*, p.162.
56 *The Bird Path*, p.214.
57 *Travels in the Drifting Dawn*, p.70.
58 'Broken Ode to White Brittany', *The Bird Path*, pp.205-09.
59 Title of the last section of *The Bird Path*.
60 *Ibid.*, p.221.
61 *Ibid.*

THE DIALECTICS OF OUTSIDE AND INSIDE
Khalid Hajji

The overall sensation a post-colonial Arab intellectual is likely to have with the rise of the new millennium is one of helplessness and discontent. This is best illustrated in the case of those intellectuals who, in the haze of the decolonization experience, were craving for recognition from the part of the colonizer and for inclusion in his culture. Not until they were confronted with their own original culture again, did it occur to them that they were now homeless and traditionless castaways. It is impossible to undertake the critique of Western power without diving into the history of Western civilization, Western culture and languages, and without thereby experiencing a certain form of estrangement from the self. Despite all efforts, one is able neither to put on the skin of a Westerner, nor to live at peace with his/her own self.

For Edward Said, his British first name strangely yoked to an Arabic surname sheds in itself light on the nature of a divided self and a broken identity. His visit to Egypt in 1989 proved a significant experience in this respect. Trying to visit the old college from which he was expelled by its British administration, he found himself with his daughters in the position of trespassers and was unsympathetically invited to leave: 'The British Eton in Egypt has now become a new kind of privileged Islamic sanctuary from which thirty-eight years later I was once again being expelled.'[1] This experience typifies the case of an out-of-place Arab intellectual in our post-colonial Arab society.

Fatema Mernissi, the famous Moroccan feminist (Haremist), represents another instance of the discontent characteristic of our contemporary Arab intellectual life. After decades of attempts to debunk the nature of traditional Muslim society that nurtured the Harem culture and furthered the exclusion of Arab women from the scene of historical events, she discovers that the Western World has its own harem too, as revealed in the title of one of her recent books: *Le Harem Européen (Scheherazade Goes West)*.[2] For an Arab feminist like Fatema Mernissi, the whole world, West and East, is now an unsafe place for women. For lack of a sheltering haven, she practises a curious style of writing which betrays a typically European mode of intellectual inquiry mixed with doses of obsolete leftist Arab ideology, the result being a total failure to embody the voice of masses of women aspiring for better life perspectives within the framework of their own societies, and also a failure to live up to her oft-declared ambition of relating the narrative of Arab women.

Having once excelled in destruction, Mernissi seems now unable to build. The case of Mernissi typifies the status of daring Arab intellectuals running short of the right means to build for a new coherence, a new harmonious whole able to embrace the self and the other, the West and the East, man and woman.

In *Samarcande*, a novel in which the peregrinations of Omar Alkhayyam, the medieval Persian poet, mesh delicately with a love story between a twentieth century American lover and a princess from modern Iran, Amin Maalouf voiced through the characters his deeply ingrained sensation of the incapacity of the Arab intellectual to contain both the poetic East and the scientific West. Looking at the old manuscript of Alkhayyam on board ship, Chirine, the Persian princess says: 'The Rubayat on the Titanic! The flower of the Orient carried by the jewel of the West! Khayyam, if only you could see the beautiful moment we have the chance to live!'.[3] Unfortunately this beautiful moment is not going to last. In next to no time, the Titanic goes down and with it the dream of seeing the East and the West yoked to one another in a bond of love.

Closer scrutiny of the works and trajectories of other Arab and Muslim intellectuals brings us to realise that the discontent pervading our post-colonial intellectual climate can be traced to the nature of modern Western civilization basically predicated upon clear-cut divisions between 'inside' and 'outside', civilization and barbarity, self and other, order and disorder. To gain acceptance and admission in the modern Western polis, the Arab intellectual undergoes a process of polishing until he/she becomes a polite political creature stripped of its impolite exterior.

Bernard Lewis's book about Islam and modernity sets up a perfect example of what modernity expects Arabs and Muslims to do in order not to incur the scourge of colonization and military occupation again.[4] If they want democracy, for instance, they must learn polyphonic music as a prerequisite, because, for this 'enlightened orientalist', harmony or counterpoint would teach Arabs and Muslims how to match different voices and instruments to produce a result that is greater than the sum of its parts. Otherwise they will be denied access to democracy.

Isn't it a sad destiny to have to choose between: 1) tinkling one's life away sitting in front of a dark cupboard (sorry, keyboard), or 2) being denied entry to the age of modern democracy?

Fortunately, numerous other Westerners – here I come to Kenneth White – have undertaken a serious critique of Western civilization, the arts this civilization has produced, and the metaphysical ground upon which it is built. While reading the essays, poems and travel books of Kenneth White, I have always felt that I am in the presence of an inspiring author whose poetic thought opens a space where people from different cultural horizons can free themselves from the shackles of a linear uni-dimensional Western tradition which divides human beings into two categories: go-aheads and followers/imitators.

Nothing in the works of Kenneth White can be more appealing to the mind of a cast-away Arab intellectual than the author's insistence on quitting what he metaphorically calls the 'Motorway of Western History'. A considerable part of his essays draws on the trajectories and experiences of those solitary figures who, at an earlier stage, felt the need to roam outside the realm of Western metaphysics. No matter how different their trajectories seem to be, in sum they amount to a fundamental quest for a more real world; their mode of inquiry is 'geopoetic' according to White's terminology.

Geopoetics, as it unfolds through the reading of White's poetry and waybooks proper, points out endless possibilities for the expansion of the self through an attentive geographical exploration of the world in which we are present and an intelligent poetic articulation of genuine kinds of rapport with the Earth. What stirs beneath the surface of White's combined interest in geography and poetics is an urgent cultural need for a space of meditation:

> *outside*
> *at the end of that dark winter*
> *he saw blue smoke, green waters*
> *as he had never seen them before*
> *they were enough*
> *a black crow busy on a branch*
> *made him laugh aloud*
> *the shape of the slightest leaf*
> *entertained his mind*
> *his intelligence*
> *danced among satisfactory words.*[5]

This world outside, where the shape of the slightest leaf entertains the mind and provides intelligence with satisfactory and adequate words, is a world that enhances contemplation. While describing this world in his works, White is continually driven to accuse the world of civilization for its unrelenting infringement upon the domain of meditation:

> *little pink flower*
> *carrying the whole of history*
> *in its slender roots*
>
> *a world in miniature*
> *and religion, of a sort*
>
> *destroyed*
> *by fools on motor-bikes*
> *in the name of Sport.*[6]

In its depth, this condemnation of civilization is not the expression of an idyllic attachment to nature; it coincides in White's essays with a coherently formulated critique of a long history of philosophical activity. Western civilization is in fact the product of a centripetal mode of thinking which attempts to reduce living reality to an immutable truth, the aim being to make this truth fit into a system of classification. Nothing better than the word 'philosophy' itself betrays this centripetal tendency to bring truth from the realm of the unknown to a pre-established framework of reference. 'Philo' in 'philosophy' does not only mean love for a thing, but its collection also. A bibliophile does not only love books, but collects them as well. To say the least, Western philosophy, being essentially centripetal, lays the foundation of a sedentary civilization where the human being:

> *...lives and rots perpetually*
> *in a crowded society*
> *that teaches him*
> *nothing essential*[7]

To learn something essential, White advocates intellectual nomadism, a centrifugal mode of knowing capable of lifting our contemporaries from the uni-dimensional world of history and its accumulations where they get bogged down. We retain from White's extensive writings a sense that to intellectual nomadism corresponds a type of poetics, a poetics that still looks foreign within the great bulk of western literary production. The poetics in question has less to do with verse, a set of mechanical movements to and fro, than with a mode of being enhancing our sense of being biocosmic creatures. In order to find out accurate definitions of this poetic activity, White transcends the history of mainstream Western literature and has recourse to enlightening examples from Eastern tradition, and individuals living at the margin of Western tradition.

What Kenneth White describes as poetic sensibility, conspicuously absent from the technologised West, constitutes in fact the core of Arabic intellectual life. In one of the earliest debates, Assayrafi, arguing for the logic of sensual natural language against formal logic, expresses the following view: 'songs (knowledge) of the world are scattered / and towards them the lucid mind is constantly driven.'[8]

Assayrafi's argument carries the implication that formal logic would hamper the mind in its travelling towards scattered signs that constitute genuine knowledge. Only a mind freed from the shackles of such logic can attain to the realm of poetic thinking and be introduced to the real sensual world. Minds rigid with formalist modes of reasoning end up denying its existence and fail thus to take it as the 'House of Being', to use White's terms.

Poets are ontological heroes par excellence. The Arabic word for poet means the 'one who feels so much as to have creeping and crawling flesh': *al-mushaara*. *Shi'r*, which means something like 'to poeticise', combines both: 1) 'to have creeping flesh', and 2) 'to express oneself in poetic language'.

As for 'poem', the Arabic word for it, *qasida*, stems from *qasada*, which literally means: 1) to take the shortest way possible towards something or someone; 2) to mean something. Thus the word for poem condenses a multiple sense that involves travelling and meaning. The poem is the shortest possible way to genuine meaning. Greek logic, as numerous Arab thinkers used, with a pinch of sarcasm, to call Aristotelian logic, does nothing but 'lengthen expression and chase away signs'.

The Arabic word for verse is *bait*, which literally means 'tent'. This appellation does not refer only to features of prosody, but also suggests a way of thinking. Not any old verse, however respectful of prosody, belongs to poetic art. *Al-Bait* suggests that poetic activity consists in travelling towards scattered signs in space. This poetic activity is the product of a mind of no fixed abode, a mind sheltering temporarily under a movable tent that offers a multitude of perspectives of the cosmos with every new move. Unlike the non-poetic mind, which dwells in a sedentary place where knowledge keeps piling up indiscriminately, the poetic mind highlights cosmic moments and magnifies mankind's endless amazement at the world.

For a host of Arab thinkers anxious that Arabs should integrate themselves into the history of Western philosophy, science and technology, poetic sensibility and thinking as embodied in the above-mentioned terms and concepts constitutes an impediment to progress and development. These thinkers will argue that the Arab's rhetoric of the tongue is the cause of the inefficiency of his mind. A mind constantly on the road is unable to build systems, to impose architecture on nature. To attain to the age of modernity, to integrate into the history of development and progress, the Arab mind must get rid of its poetic sensibility and quit the state of envelopment in nature. For the forces committed to 'progress' in the

Arab world, giving credit to discredited poetic thought means sinking into regression and pre-history. In an intellectual climate where much emphasis is laid on the question of how to obtain a cosy place inside civilization and history, the idea of roaming outside is, to say the least, unpleasant and dubious. In this context, intellectual nomadism and geopoetics might be taken for disabling concepts unnecessary for the already paralysed body of the Arab world.

If, for intellectuals blindly committed to progress *à l'occidentale*, geopoetics and intellectual nomadism are two concepts that would lock the Arabs in an unreservedly irrational world, for Taha Abderrahman - a lucid thinker and a philosopher perfectly aware of the wiles and the ways of modern thought and civilization - poetry, geography and intellectual nomadism are assets that would further the grounding of concepts and dam up the process of ridiculous imitation and debilitating uprooting. While they enable the mind to envisage the edification of systems and architectures, concepts grounded in poetic intelligence, stemming from what is a fundamentally genuine contact with space and time of being, set limits to this edification. Only a civilization predicated upon the premises of a poetic mind can harmonize the fundamental human yearning for a dwelling place and the need for movement in space. Concepts grounded in a strong poetics of *almakan* or place can open a field of abstraction, where the possible is unlimited, while at the same time never losing touch with the sensual, where the possible is attached to earth (earthly).

In an excellent essay, Taha Abderrahman shakes the foundation of Descartes's *cogito*, so dear to Arab translators of philosophy (in opposition to philosophers), grounding it in the Arabic language and in the world view unfolding through its specific ways of expression.[9] Stripped of its linguistic scaffolding, Descartes's 'I think therefore I am' becomes within the framework of Arabic expression something like 'seeing and finding'. By opening the *cogito* to seeing, Taha Abderrahman connects the realm of abstract thought to a world of the senses in which mind, body and soul are plunged. His declared aim is to open up the world of mechanical philosophy and enclosed institutions of knowledge and truth to experiences of minds having immediate access to reality through seeing.

This is not the place to advance a fully detailed comparison between White's poetic thought and Taha Abderrahman's philosophic activity. The rapprochement between these two important figures of our current intellectual scene is meant simply to suggest the presence of an unsuspected affinity beyond the barriers of any fixed East/West dichotomy. In Europe as in the Arab world, established institutions of knowledge and structures of power cover up the same deep cultural impasse. Either one is an insider, as in the case of most our contemporary modern thinkers, or one aspires to turning things inside out, as is the case of most post-colonial Arab thinkers. The example of Kenneth White and Taha Abderrahman offers on the contrary the possibility of an alternative. Neither outside, nor inside, but an inside open to the outside in the case of Kenneth White, and an outside open to the inside as in the case of Taha Abderrahman. Although coming from different horizons and adopting different strategies, they are the embodiment of a sharp cosmic awareness that life cannot be reduced to either being inside an architecture or outside in nature. Whoever opts for one of these two possibilities runs the risk of being exposed either to a musty atmosphere that dulls and deadens the senses, or to the whims of a harsh capricious nature. What is at stake in the essays of both White and Taha Abderrahman is a new whole able to harmonise philosophy and poetry, architecture and nature, inside and outside, known and unknown, self and other.

This is the real space of wisdom.

NOTES

1   Edward Said, *Out of Place* (London: Granta, 1999).
2   Fatema Mernissi, *Le Harem Européen* (Casablanca: Le Fennec, 2003).
3   Amin Maalouf, *Samarcande* (Paris: Lattès, 1992), p.812.
4   Bernard Lewis, *What Went Wrong?* (London: Weidenfeld, 2002).
5   Kenneth White, *Les Rives du Silence* (Paris: Mercure de France, 1997), p.14.
6   *Ibid*, p.188.
7   Kenneth White, *Le Grand rivage* (Paris: Le Nouveau Commerce, 1980), p.118.
8   Abu Hayyan Attawhidi, *Al-Muqabassat* (Cairo: dar Al-kitab Al-islami, 1992), p.73.
9   Taha Abderrahman, *Fiqh Al-Falsafa: Al-falsafa wa at-tarjama* (Casablanca: al-Markaz at-taqafi al-arabi, 1995).

KENNETH WHITE:
THE SELF AND CREATIVITY
John Hudson

I'm going to start this text with a quotation from a well-known Scottish poet; it will, however, remain unattributed: 'White, White, White, with Kenneth White everything's white, everywhere's white, bloody white!' Despite the paradoxical 'bloody white', this fit of bad faith has some good in it, a kernel of truth that reveals, through exploration, cultural dichotomies. It will also reveal creative modus operandi and a good deal of humour. The dichotomies are those of cultural attitudes to the self, especially in the field of the creative arts, and what I would term, 'religious' versus 'spiritual' thought. The opposition typifies, albeit crudely, attitudes that apply in much of mainland Europe, including France, against those applicable in Scotland and Britain in general. Our irate Scottish poet revealed a lot more than Kenneth White's self-reference, but what was he complaining about in the first place? What's in a name?

When Marie-Claude and Kenneth moved into their new house on the north Brittany coast, they had to give their home a name:

> *We decided to call it Gwenved.*
> *That is an old Celtic word which, in Christian texts, translates the notion of paradise. But it antedates Christianity by far. Literally 'white land', it indicates a place of light and concentration. In the* Triads of the Isle of Britain, *one reads: 'Three things the soul will find in the circle of Gwenved: primal power, primal memory, primal love.'*[1]

Dipping fairly randomly into *Open World, The Collected Poems 1960-2000*, we quickly find:

A warm white mist over the bay.[2]

White beach
on a summer morning
sea surfing up through mist.[3]

The white cell almost in darkness...[4]

I stand in my own inscrutable whiteness... [...]
From Strathclyde to Whiteness lies the way...[5]

Now had Kenneth been born Black or Brown, we could undertake a similar exercise. I don't select these examples of whiteness in order to justify our anonymous Scottish poet's complaint but I select them to highlight the fact that our poet had, indeed, noticed something. Kenneth White certainly puns on the word white and all the subtleties of glance and echo that such a word offers. The interesting point is that our well-known Scottish poet should complain about undertaking an activity that writers are expected to undertake. Punning is, after all, part of the poet's resource. A touch of jealousy? Perhaps. But also a confrontation with a notion of the self as primal, 'primal power, primal memory, primal love'.

There is a strong culture of disapproval regarding the elevation of self within moral and intellectual Europe. It has a complex history, plays an important role in religious thinking and was zealously endorsed with something like paradoxical assertiveness, by individual thinkers during Europe's religious Reformation. It associates self with vanity and pride – not surprisingly in view of the vulgarity of the Western attachment to material things, including the body, its urges and its obsession with appearance:

Each his small designs achieving
Hurries on with restless feet,
While, through Fancy's power deceiving,
Self *in every form I greet.*

This is from a poem written by the Scottish physicist who lived in Galloway, James Clerk Maxwell, a genius and a conventionally and deeply religious man. The poem, 'Reflections on Various Surfaces', which equates self with deception, moves to its orthodox conclusion by way of sermonising that self is a barrier to truth. Truth comes 'crushing all that makes me proud'.

I choose Maxwell precisely because he is a 'non-literary' Scottish genius who openly states in this poem that self is a barrier to Truth, God and insight or inspiration. It is ironic, for Maxwell was perhaps the first modern physicist to move towards the unification of nature through his equating electromagnetic energy and light. His equations which hold nascent much of twentieth-century physics both at the universal macro and the micro statistical level, describe a world where the limited self is almost meaningless. But in his poem Maxwell is slave to that theological and cultural bugbear that sermonises against sin, where self, with a small 's', is the origin of our fall from Grace. Maxwell certainly does not use self in the way that say, Meister Eckhart, or Nietzsche, or Rimbaud or the Buddha or Kenneth White may mean Self: 'In my birth all things were born, and I was the cause of myself and all things... I am an unmoved cause that moves all things'.[6]

Eckhart's Self is a different thing – closer to the universal truth expressed in Maxwell's equations and certainly not the lonely and proud ego. But that kind of statement got Eckhart into trouble with the Papal authorities. It should be noted that medieval European theological sermonising rarely employed 'I' or 'my', and so such engagement with the self, as Eckhart regularly employs is almost certainly representative of a profound personal experience and it was most definitely risky and did lead to excommunication or spiritual exile. The Catholic Church could not accept God as immanent; that would, after all, make the Church's vicarious role somewhat redundant.

Rimbaud expresses the journey to Self in a more fin de siècle mood: '[a] long, immense and reasoned disordering of all the senses... [towards] the great sick man, the great criminal, the great outcast... the Supreme Sage... for he arrives at the unknown' (from 'Correspondences'). This may seem a far cry from Eckhart but the great criminal is the state of the excommunicate celebrated. For Rimbaud to be a Supreme Sage one has to go against convention and the life of Eckhart is to some degree proof of that.

The Isha Upanishad is one of world literature's great essays on Self. One can quote virtually any verse or line, for example, assertively: 'Those who deny the Self are born again / Blind to the self, enveloped in darkness, Utterly devoid of love for the Lord', or 'The Self is everywhere. Bright is the Self, / ... immanent and transcendent. He it is / Who holds the cosmos together'.[7] For the Hindu, to be born again as self, with a lower case 's', is certainly undesirable. The outcast in Rimbaud's world is transformed into he who is cast out from the round of rebirth and mechanical cause and effect. The Self, with a capital 'S', on the other hand, is the guiding force of the universe.

Nietzsche's *Ecce Homo*, written shortly before Nietzsche went insane, is subtitled 'How One Becomes What One Is', and Nietzsche, who had a strictly Protestant and self denying upbringing, reviews himself in his typically controversial manner. In it he says little that is new but recovers his critical ground and asserts the necessity of Self: '*To redeem the past* and to transform every "It was" into an "I wanted it thus" – that alone would I call redemption'.[8] Here the moved becomes the mover, and that takes us back to Eckhart.

One could continue looking at examples of the Self with a capital 'S', contrasted with self with a lower case 's'. I have beside me many books taken from my shelves: Rumi, Bashō, the Gita, and I have no doubt that these issues will be explored more fully by others. The point that needs to be made now is that references to white and whiteness are references to facets of Self, the universal Self; the punning is a bridge to transcendence of the self – lower case 's' – they are routes beyond Kenneth White. So, let's dip randomly into the bright, light world of Kenneth White once more:

> *Over the grasses*
> *two white butterflies*
> *fluttering by whitely* [9]

Back in Whiteland. The playfulness of the above extract serves to highlight an important aspect of Kenneth White the person and the writer. The puns on self are playful. Unlike our irate critic-poet at the outset, Kenneth White has a sense of humour that is based in confidence, in a secure sense of self with a big smile and a wee dig in the ribs for his audience. What's more he is quite happy to laugh at himself.

MY PROPERTIES

I'm a landowner myself after all –
I've got twelve acres of white silence
up at the back of my skull.[10]

Of course, this is double-edged. White silence at the back of the skull is Gwenved or White Land or paradise. Through the inclusion of self, the ambiguity and hence humour, contrasts with that, say of the Robert Burns of 'Holy Willie's Prayer', whose rational humanism, treats self as hubris and results in satire: 'Yet I am here a chosen sample, / To show thy grace is great and ample...'

The two Ayrshire poets, Robert Burns and Kenneth White, are both products of a European culture expanding its intellectual and spiritual boundaries; both are reasoning, educated, and both share playfulness, and playfulness to the serious-minded can be seen to be 'trouble causing'. Burns was to leave for Jamaica but stayed in Scotland, died young and satirised his nation's weaknesses on his way to the grave with an enlightened wit. White left Scotland for France, for quite practical reasons, and has enjoyed the European and the World adventure ever since. His inclusion of Self within his work offsets his native scepticism and doubt, something that Burns, due to his home culture and early death, could not achieve.

Scotland's seriousness and to some extent its lack of sophistication is demonstrated by a little story I would like to tell concerning an episode in Kenneth White's *Letters from Brittany and other lands of the West* or *House Of Tides*. In the Chapter entitled 'A Bibliophile Fantasia' the author recounts the story of his discovery of a manuscript in Latin which Kenneth duly translates 'under the title *The Unknown Territories*': 'At that time, I was living on the Promontory of the Winds, in wild Galloway, near the famous white house (candida casa) founded by Ninian.' The author of the manuscript then undertakes a nomadic journey across the Celtic Sea then returns north to the unknown territories and travels alongside Ninian. He ends up: 'on the edge, at the limits, a man of nothing, a citizen of emptiness, a pilgrim of the void'.[11] Which doesn't sound too far removed from the passage from Rimbaud quoted earlier.

Kenneth White suggests himself that this pilgrim may be an alter ego, a previous existence and we could make much of this. However, my story, which happened not long after the publication of *House of Tides*, tells of a man who came up to me excitedly in the Main Street of Wigtown in Galloway, not far from Candida Casa which is to be found in the town of Whithorn. Wigtown is 'Scotland's National Book Town' and this elderly man, a believer in books, was muttering something to me about a new discovery. I should add at this point that a believer in books does not always make a reader of books, and I gathered that this gentleman had only heard of 'a new discovery'. The new discovery related to Candida Casa and 'if only we could get the manuscript it would attract tourists to the Book Town'. This was interesting, I said, but did he know any more about the discovery? The butcher had told him about it, although the butcher had not seen nor read the piece. The butcher had heard from someone else. At the time, I left it at that and said I would do some research. It did not occur to me that Chinese whispers had been at work. Later I put two and two together. I am sure Kenneth never imagined that his 'Fantasia' might be responsible for a dramatic boost in tourism to Galloway but if he could conjure the original vellum there is a climatically controlled museum-standard display case sitting empty somewhere in Wigtown waiting for *The Unknown Territories*.

There is a serious side to this story. The universal has been reduced to the local, the spiritual to the economically profitable, the larger Self brought into the landscape of the smaller self. A fantasia takes on myth, a word laden with the potential for misinterpretation.

Here the author becomes the creator of myth, both on the page and on the lips of people. The bold statements of an Eckhart or a White confront the conventional localism of the small self. 'For locality, against localism', says White in his conversations with his close friend Jean-Yves Kerguelen. This appeals to sectors of our society that require more than the selfish materialism of our commercially driven economies. The Self, that contiguous oneness, assumes the fragments that comprise our atomised psyches and society. The myth is enhanced by Kenneth White's frequent references to hermits and being hermit-like, and this is transformed through literary device into further stories much in the manner of imaginative adventure that created *The Unknown Territories*. Living in Pau in the Pyrenees becomes a mountain retreat:

They come to this studio
to discuss reality

all I ever say is
look out there at the mountains.[12]

Gwenved is paradise, tucked away far from the human gaze, as well as very real with a front gate and a Volkswagen Golf parked outside. The subtitle to *House of Tides, Letters from Brittany and other lands of the West*, conjures distance, isolation and timelessness. Not emails but letters; it is as if the author wants to keep the world from shrinking into an electronic singularity, to keep a world where time and place, and the space for dreaming and being astonished and myth, continue to exist. The reality of each location is its poetry, and it is the nature of poetry to realise the universal, the large Self, through being grounded in the particular.

The hermit is also a nomad, treading the bird path, 'a Ch'an expression which means realizing the self-nature' (frontispiece note, *The Bird Path*). The figure of the nomad links White with another great Scottish literary figure, Robert Louis Stevenson. In his work *Isolario*, Kenneth White takes a journey around the world, leaping from island to island through writings from China, the Arab world, Spain and the work of Stevenson writing from Samoa: 'Either in or out of Scotland, I was really happy only once in my life. That was at Hyères, facing the Golden Islands. Since that moment, I've just survived, as a teller of tales.'[13] The title of this work, undertaken with artist Roger Druet, holds a kind of paradox. Isolario: the island is isolated yet the staging post on a journey, a still point in a process of movement, a place for a hermitage in an over-populated world.

This interplay of hermit and nomad takes us back to Ninian, it also links to Zarathustra and Zarathustra to Nietzsche. Ninian wanders the Unknown Territories yet builds the 'White House', and if myths are patterns played out in the cosmos through the Self, we begin to identify recurrence, we begin to see a bigger picture that is rooted in the stones around us, the beating of the waves and the movements of men and birds, always moving yet, at the centre, still.

The Self is the source of creation. Eckhart says it: 'In my birth all things were born, and I was the cause of myself and all things'.[14]

The realisation of Self is the assumption of the individual into Creation. Creativity is no longer a lonely activity but part of a huge process. Another Scottish literary figure and one allied once again to Dumfries and Galloway, is Christopher Murray Grieve. His rebirth as Hugh MacDiarmid, a new self, is the subject of a revealing essay by Seamus Heaney:

> *Grieve turned into MacDiarmid when he realized that his writing identity depended for his empowerment upon his securing an ever deepening access to those primary linguistic strata in his own and his country's memory.*[15]

The last part of that phrase reminds us of 'primal memory', one of the triad to be found in Gwenved, but there is more. The adoption of a new name is the beginning of a new journey into a new self and it is also an exile from the old self. MacDiarmid needed a new self because Christopher Grieve from Langholm would always be subject to the repression of self, 'crushing all that makes [him] proud'. For a time MacDiarmid isolated himself on Whalsay, an island off the Mainland of Shetland. He suffered poverty, became something of a hermit, lived close to the land, stripped himself down and he created a myth. Perhaps, MacDiarmid is Scotland's greatest literary myth (if you listen to the stories of some of the Whalsay folk, another connotation of the word myth may well apply – that of fabricated story). He created himself and he even created other selves to review his created self in journals he edited and published. What's true, what's false: who cares?

Kenneth White left Scotland to study and work in France and in so doing realises a whole geopoetic cosmos about himself; MacDiarmid, like Burns, remained in his homeland but exiles his old self from his newly realised Self and a terrible creativity is born. The problematic MacDiarmid wrote of himself: 'My job, as I see it, has never been to lay a tit's egg, but to erupt like a volcano, emitting not only flame but a lot of rubbish' (Letter to the BBC, 1960s). But the energy and vision remain defining, both for Scotland and literature. And so it is with Kenneth White. Where MacDiarmid's historicism spiced with anger led him into volcanic rants and political polemics that, although entertaining, leave him open to the accusation of being boorish, Kenneth White's more affable chattiness edged with self mocking humour make him fine company on the road to the unknown territories. Where Burns allows his humanist rationalism to become a tool for mockery, White will give a Gallic shrug of the shoulders. There are more important things to do than to mock, although it must be admitted he shows irritated impatience over time-wasting stupidity and boorish behaviour, especially from North Americans on the Atlantic TGV:

> *I love your country.* Tray joli! *Brittany! Tristan and Isolde, oui? I'm a Wagnerite. Exactly oui, oui... Saint-Brieuk, that's an interesting name, n'est ce pas? How do you pronounce it?*[16]

Perhaps life is not about the journey after all; sometimes it is a relief to arrive. MacDiarmid may have fulminated; Burns would have dissected with mockery; but Kenneth White allows folk to make fools of themselves.

Kenneth White's Self is to be found in the rocks that populate the coast of Armorica and the coast of America, it is to be found in Gwenved, primal power, primal memory, primal love; it is not bound but boundless within a world of limits and margins, it is concrete but connected, it belongs to the context of what White calls 'le lieu sensible' which may be translated as "the sensitive place". (Kerguelen on White). It is practical, it is poetry. It adheres to Wittgenstein's dictum: 'Whereof one cannot speak, thereof one should remain silent' (*Philosophical Investigations*), but it enjoys silence, all twelve acres of its whiteness. Finally, realising the Self is not achieved without a stripping away of all that is superfluous:

INTO THE WHITENESS

> *Now I have burnt all my knowledge*
> *And am learning to live with whiteness naked*
>
> *What I call art now is nothing made*
> *But the pure pathology of my body and mind*
>
> *At the heart of a terrible and joyous world.*[17]

It is a mark of Kenneth White's vision of Self that it is realist, indeed at times starkly so: '…the pure pathology of my body and mind…' In this respect Kenneth White adds to the ongoing adventure of the discovery of the greater Self; he adds a new dimension that is consistent with what thinkers and poets have said before. His insistence, however, on the real world, its rocks and its waves, its pathology of mind and body, is what a Scot and a poet can bring to European metaphysics.

Kenneth White's Self is also to be found in the rocks of Alba, which can be translated as 'the land of the white heights'. These white heights are a challenge and a benchmark for modern-day Scotland. Can we rise to this challenge?

NOTES

1   Kenneth White, *House of Tides,* (Edinburgh: Polygon, 2000), p.6.
2   From Scenes of a Floating World in Kenneth White, *Open World, The Collected Poems 1960-2000*, (Edinburgh: Polygon, 2003), p.230.
3   From Settling into Yet Another Place, *ibid.*, p.439.
4   From Theory, *ibid.*, p.115.
5   From At the Solstice, *ibid.*, pp. 39, 41.
6   Meister Eckhart, *Sermons* (ed. Walshe, 1979-81), Book 1, p.269.
7   *Isha Upanishad* (trans. Eknath Easwaran), verses 3 and 8.
8   From *Zarathustra*, quoted in chapter 10, part 8, *Ecce Homo*.
9   From The Bhodi Notebook in *The Bird Path, Collected Longer Poems 1964-1988*, (Edinburgh: Mainstream Publishing, 1989), p.101.
10   *Open World*, p.99.
11   *House of Tides*, pp.55-58.
12   From 'Eleven Views of the Pyrenees', *Open World*, p.292.
13   Kenneth White, *Isolario* (Editions Alternatives), p.35.
14   Meister Eckhart, *Sermons*, book 2, p.275.
15   Seamus Heaney, *A Torchlight Procession of One* (London, Faber, 1995).
16   *House of Tides*, p.172.
17   *Open World*, p.109.

SPACE, ENERGY, LIGHT:
THE SHAMANIC ELEMENT
IN THE WORK OF KENNETH WHITE
Michael Tucker

I'm sending you a map of the coast

maybe you'll hear
the rushing of the rivers
and the moaning of the wind over the snow

maybe you'll see the seals
the bears and the wolves

the missionaries make me laugh
it's all too clear from their stories
they don't understand a thing

as for me
I've got no holy name
and my soul is hairy as hell

here's some Northern air for you

and along with my words
I send you eight drum-notes

ayaya! ayaya! ayaya!

Kenneth White, 'Angakok's Letter to the Future', Open World[1]

My first encounter with the work of Kenneth White had the same impact upon me as my first encounter with the poetry of Gunnar Ekelöf and Rainer Maria Rilke, the music of John Coltrane and Jan Garbarek, the paintings of Edvard Munch and Joan Miró, or the films of Ingmar Bergman and Andrei Tarkovsky. I couldn't

get enough of the stuff (still can't). It seemed as though I had been
born to read this poetry: to engage with White's freshly turned (and
tuned) ideas concerning the working out of a new 'open world'
poetics; to relish the deeply learned – yet lightly worn – intelligence
and wit of a poet and thinker who seemed to have read any and all
of the key poetic texts of both the Western and Eastern traditions
that might interest one. The man of the blue road with twelve acres
of white silence up at the back of his skull had something at his
fingertips that spoke both freshly and deeply to me: something that
led me to want to walk much more where the wind took me, to
strike out more often along the coastlines of life, and to venture ever
further along the bird path, far up into the diamond country.[2]

If that sounds a touch gushing, well, I'm sorry, but that's how
it was one day back in 1990 in Amsterdam, when Graham Ackroyd
(the poet and painter, and father of the novelist Peter Ackroyd) first
introduced me to the many joys of the White world. And that's how
it remains today. Over the years, I've had the pleasure and the
privilege of working with Kenneth White on various occasions and
in various contexts. I've always been struck by the heartening,
inspiring combination of the tremendous, wide-ranging yet sharply
focused, luminous intelligence and complementary, Taoist-touched
quality of leavenous humour that characterises this poet and his
work. Like no other contemporary creative thinker I know of, White
helps one cut through all the tedious nonsense (academic or
bureaucratic, religious or political) that so often threatens to destroy
one's sense of the marvellous, the wonderful, in life today. Offering
us a world that is neither old nor new, neither nostalgic nor
futuristic, but simply – SIMPLY! – shot through with the enlarging
spirit of what anthropologists used to call *participation mystique*,
the work of Kenneth White can help us think and imagine, dream
and feel our way into an open-ended sense of the sort of space and
energy that encourages us to develop what White has conceived as a
freshly drawn cartography of existence, with an enlarged and
heightened sense of the power of poetry at its core.[3]

The briefest acquaintance with White's work is enough to
indicate the quality of intellectual energy by which that work is
driven: an energy fired by a further fundamental quality of native
curiosity, as extensive as it is discriminating in nature, and as

broadly synthetic in its sweeping evolutionary orientation as it is sharply sensitive and attentive to essential matters of detail.[4] Once, discussing why the space of a vast Northern landscape remained simply a frozen enigma to many Canadians, while to the Amerindian, that same space was full of live realities, White commented: 'I wouldn't want to hammer the analogy, but it's something like poetic space to the normalised mind.'[5] Extending the analogy, one might say that White has an uncanny ability to turn seemingly far-flung aspects of intellectual and artistic history into something that does indeed seem like poetic space to the normalised mind. Thanks to his particular intellectual or poetic energy, White is able to sense the living light, rather than the long-dead academic detail, in things of the mind, able to conjure a living, lively poetics of space and energy out of the bones of the past.

One enemy of such a poetics would be clutter: for all his empathy with so many fine minds of the past, White has no interest in writing biography. He has long held that one of the chief problems of art and literature today is that so much of that art and literature is weighed down by far too many concerns of the type one might describe as 'human, all-too-human'. If it's one or another variety of either so-called scientific or literary psychology or sociology you're after, White is definitely not your man. Another enemy of White's poetics of space and energy – of light – would be any all-too-laboured emphasis on a search for 'meaning' or 'transcendence', such as has so often marked the dualism of metaphysics and materialism in the Western intellectual and spiritual traditions. White, who has spoken of the development of his poetics in terms of the idea of 'supernihilism', is as far from Christ as he is from Marx.[6]

If, as he often does, White speaks of the idea of a journey, of walking one's way into a deeper, fresher sense of the pulse of life, he does so with a Zen-like awareness of the wisdom of neither overfilling the rucksack that one takes along nor exaggerating the importance of actually arriving at any destination. As he remarked in an interview with Matthew Graves, published in *Coast to Coast: Interviews and Conversations 1985-1995*, 'the pilgrim trip has an aim, the sacred spot. But beyond the sacred, there's emptiness. I'm not out to cover kilometres, or to reach a particular place, I'm out for a kind of spatial poetics, with emptiness at its centre. And you begin again, for the pleasure, to get at an even finer sense of emptiness-plenitude.'[7]

In that same interview, White explained what led him to quote from various texts, often ancient, in his own books: 'I use quotations in a way which a lot of people still don't understand. My idea in that is to gather from those old texts those moments when they reach *another dimension*. It's the other dimension I'm fundamentally interested in, and I like to see it in different languages, in different lights.'[8] The *other* dimension, approached through a spatial poetics which has emptiness at its centre – but the sort of emptiness which is at the same time a plenitude: what might such a 'supernihilism' mean? If I had to use one word to tease out some of the implications of such remarks by White, to explicate some of the many affirmative implications of the particular constellations of space, energy and light that so distinguish his work, that word would be *shamanic*.

The writer John A. Grim tells us that the word shaman is a transliteration of the Tungusic word *saman* or *hamman*, which functions as both a noun and a verb. As a noun it means 'one who is excited, moved, raised'; as a verb it means 'to know in an ecstatic manner'.[9] The hard-won ecstatic knowledge of the shaman was fundamental to cultures of the past, whether of prehistoric Europe or Aboriginal Australia, and it remains fundamental to the evolution of cultures and consciousness today.[10] Essentially, shamans are people who are either born with, or able to acquire, exceptionally high levels of visionary energy – or what White might prefer to call a fundamental poetic capacity. This is the sort of capacity that lifts one above the partiality or short-sightedness which often characterises the socio-political or historical realm, in order to reconnect one with a much more cosmically-oriented sense of *world*, of life's deepest energies and potentialities.[11]

White himself has written widely and wisely about the ancient archetypal figure of the shaman: the rain-maker, dancer and drummer, healing holistic visionary, poet and image-maker of old whose ecstatic contact with the forces of the cosmos was crucial to the health of the tribe. And as we shall see shortly, the spirit of shamanism is indeed crucial to White's work. However, it is essential to appreciate that, to speak of a shamanic element in the work of Kenneth White is *not* to speak of either any reductively atavistic or neo-academicising relation to the energies of the past.

As White observed in 'A Shaman Dancing on the Glacier', the 1990 lecture (and subsequent published essay) in which he recalled shamanic aspects of his personal experience as an adolescent exploring nature in Scotland ('I was a shaman without a tribe' he says in another retrospective essay 'The Archaic Context') and traced correspondences between that experience and many of the psycho-cosmic insights offered in Mircea Eliade's classic text *Shamanism: Archaic Techniques of Ecstasy*: 'Let me make it quite clear (caricatures are so facile – and so reassuring) – I am not advocating any kind of neo-shamanism, to be practised in and around Glastonbury or Glasgow. I am speaking of a *basis*, and a basis on which all kinds of *developments* are possible. [...] On the basis of this fundamental experience (it's the *experience* I advocate, not the imitation of forms) let us both expand and intensify – into, for example, ecology and philosophy and poetics and politics (that way, we may get depth ecology, lightning philosophy, live poetics and, who knows, even enlightened cultural politics).'[12]

Later in the lecture, White discussed the work of the politically engaged German sculptor Joseph Beuys, one of the most provocative of the many twentieth-century artists who chose to align themselves with aspects of the world-wide *ur*-shamanic tradition of an animistic and cosmically-oriented poetics: 'Once again, let me insist, I am not advocating any overt mythologising art, nor suggesting that Beuys was open to any such temptation. What I see in him is something I evoked [earlier in the lecture] with regard to my own experience: the connection with an archaic tradition, allied to an anarchic use of it – let's say an *abstract* shamanism, away outside any antiquarian reproduction.'[13]

An *abstract* shamanism: such a fruitful and telling phrase brings to mind the wisdom of Ernst Cassirer's reflections on the evolution of consciousness's capacity for self-revelation through the medium of modern lyric poetry, as developed in the 1946 text *Language and Myth*: 'Word and mythic image, which once confronted the human mind as hard realistic powers, have now [.. in the evolution of lyric poetry..] become a light, bright ether in which the spirit can move without let or hindrance. This liberation is achieved not because the mind throws aside the sensuous forms of word and image, but in that it uses them both as organs of its own, and thereby recognises them for what they really are: forms of its own self-revelation.'[14]

Naturally, any process of thinking, of creativity, involves a degree of abstraction. One recalls Picasso's observation that all art is necessarily abstract to some degree, since no art is able to offer the sort of mimesis that might even begin to approach any suggestion of the totality of life. And one is reminded of the way in which so many avant-garde artists of the twentieth century (such as Picasso) were inspired by the ideas and art of so-called primitive or prehistoric cultures, in a process which saw those artists abstracting (distilling, transforming) aspects of those ideas and art in order to shape a poetics that spoke simultaneously of the very old and the brand new. And this was a poetics that, certainly in its most consequential aspects, had nothing at all to do with any mere illustration or imitation of either image or idea (what White calls antiquarian reproduction). Rather, such a poetics had everything to do with a freshly conceived abstraction and development of image and idea, embedded in the artistic process through the pure and evolving distillation of the creative energy which fired that process. Another way of putting this is that, while so many avant-garde artists of the twentieth century sought to give their work a mythic power, few if any of them were concerned either to recall, illustrate or develop any specific detail or overall framework of any particular myth.[15]

Wassily Kandinsky, the most important originator of abstract art in the early twentieth century, and a man who on more than one occasion spoke of his paintings in terms of alchemy, was deeply interested in the cultural life of old Russia, including central aspects of shamanism.[16] But this did not mean that Kandinsky wished to paint any pictures of shamans, dancing or otherwise. It meant, rather, that he wished to give the evolving poetics of his art (which flowed from the initial generative idea of an impression inspired by Nature to firstly, a free improvisation and subsequently, a resolved composition) something at least of the power of shamanism – a power now to be conjured and communicated through purely abstract qualities of line and colour, shape and form.[17] When, in the early 1990s, White kindly sent me a copy of the original French version of what is published in the *Collected Poems* as 'The Shaman's Way', his inscription was both simple and potent: 'For Mike: these few steps along an ancient path.'[18] Such a path can be seen as two-fold in nature: the original shamanic path itself, and the path subsequently taken by so many artists of the West who have wished to reconnect with the primal and generative poetics long associated with that path.

It takes nothing away from the originality, character and power of White's work to suggest that – in the spirit of White's own wide-ranging approach to intellectual ideas – it may be fruitful to pause for a moment, and try to place that work within the context of some deep, long-running and generative currents in recent intellectual and artistic history. As already indicated (and long acknowledged and commented upon by White himself) an interest in shamanism has been a key element in the recent evolution (or re-volution) of much Western thinking and creativity. In 1992 two publications appeared, independently of each other, which together offer a convenient introduction to an especially rich subject: the (essentially shamanic) return of the Western mind to ancient ideas of *participation mystique*, to ideas of what Mircea Eliade called 'cosmic religion'.[19] The two publications are Gloria Flaherty's *Shamanism And The Eighteenth Century* and my own *Dreaming With Open Eyes: The Shamanic Spirit In Twentieth-Century Art and Culture*.[20]

After documenting the considerable extent to which interest (either scientific or fictional) in shamanism grew in Europe throughout the eighteenth century, Flaherty concentrates on the impact on the creative European mind of those reports of (predominantly Asian) shamanism – whether gathered by missionaries or explorers, scientists or proto-anthropologists – which filtered back into the advanced cultural life of European cities.[21] According to Flaherty, the shape-shifting spirit of the ecstatic shaman is clearly operative in works as diverse as Diderot's *Rameau's Nephew* and Goethe's *Faust*, as well as in Herder's concept of the Romantic artist and Mozart's sense of his (essentially Orphic, or shamanic) genius. Flaherty concludes her scrupulously documented and thoroughly argued account thus: 'perhaps we are witnessing the emergence of a new discipline, one that in its own peculiar way will combine the best of the humanities with certain aspects of the social sciences, medicine, and the physical sciences. Perhaps it is time for a shamanology.'[22]

I am not sure whether *Dreaming With Open Eyes* could be seen as an example of such a shamanology. Certainly, the book sought to restore a sense of connection between the ambitions and achievements of the European Romantics of the late-eighteenth and nineteenth centuries and the (largely, but not exclusively, European and American) Modernist aims and achievements of the twentieth century – and to do so through the chief interpretive idea, or image, of the shaman of old. Through a series of thematically distinct yet related chapters, and aided by essential recourse to the ideas of Nietzsche, Mircea Eliade and Joseph Campbell, Carl G. Jung, Gaston Bachelard and James Hillman, Jerome Rothenberg and Peter Redgrove, *Dreaming With Open Eyes* considered the innovative (and often much-contested) work of artists such as Van Gogh and Alan Davie, Paul Cézanne and Edvard Munch, Wassily Kandinsky and Constantin Brancusi, Jean Arp and Joseph Beuys, Andrei Tarkovsky and Jan Garbarek, Sun Ra and John Coltrane, Marc Chagall and Frans Widerberg, Joan Miró and Jackson Pollock, Niki de Saint Phalle and Norval Morrisseau, in the light of ancient shamanic ideas, and focusing on a holistic approach to the evolution of a poetics both ancient and brand new.

Of course, *Dreaming With Open Eyes* concerned itself with theatre, with literature, with poetry. The book considered figures as diverse as Antonin Artaud and Ted Hughes, J.R.R. Tolkien and Hermann Hesse, Federico Garcia Lorca and Octavio Paz, Rimbaud and Rilke, Gunnar Ekelöf, Hugo Ball and Vicente Huidobro. Crucial here was the work of White, which I approached largely in terms of Lorca's key observation that the contemporary poet must prune and care for 'the overluxuriant lyric tree left to us by the Romantics.'[23] In correspondence, White suggested that, while he could certainly see – and appreciate – why I should wish to view his work in relation to governing aspects of the shamanic/Orphic link I was attempting to establish (or rather, resurrect) between Romanticism and Modernism, he wished to emphasise, as gently but firmly as he could, that a significant part of the evolution of his own approach to the founding – or rather, *grounding* – of a new poetics had been his working out of a whole series of fresh terms (and ideas). Chief of these is the notion of an 'open world' approach to the inter-relations of place, culture and world within the field of energy and attention that White calls *geopoetics*.[24]

For all such necessary qualifications to my approach, a consideration of White's work took its natural place as the conclusion to the chapter on the shamanic spirit in twentieth-century theatre, literature and poetry in *Dreaming With Open Eyes*. Central to this conclusion were these words from White's 1990 lecture 'A Shaman Dancing on the Glacier': 'What the shaman, or the "dawn man" as the Ojibwa call him, is out for is an ecstasy (getting outside one's-self as well as outside history) and a de-conditioning [...] the shaman comes to know an identity larger than the one coded in the community, [...] by giving it breathing space [...] A whole mystic geography, cosmic topography, is involved.'[25]

If we now return to that 'abstract shamanism' mentioned earlier, what do we find? The various steps White has taken along the ancient path of the shaman do indeed constitute a 'mystic geography': a geography of the de-conditioned, fully energised mind which would free itself from the narrow clutches of 'politics, nationality, education, newspapers', the better to dig deep into the earth and soar high into the sky.[26] Like the Catalan Miró, White knows that, if you wish to fly high, you must first have your feet planted firmly on the ground: the abstract overtones of his shamanism are thus deeply rooted in both the concrete realities of a highly developed sensitivity to place, and a cosmic topography linking and transmuting many of the finest 'ecstatic' insights of the human mind, drawn from across continents and millennia.[27]

Recall, here, the last lines of 'The Shaman's Way', which find the poet flying ever higher with the great sea eagle: so high that, as the final line of the poem declares, *'now I'm nothing but a moving silence.*[28] Or consider these particularly moving and resonant lines from 'Labrador or The Waking Dream', which form the coda to one of White's finest achievements, the 'way-book' which is *The Blue Road*:

> *I found myself saying things like*
> *'at one with the spirit of the land'*
> *but there was no 'spirit', none*
> *that was outworn language*
> *and this was a new world*
> *and my mind was, almost, a new mind*
> *there was no such thing as 'spirit'*
> *only the blue tracks in the snow*
> *the flying of the geese*
> *the frost-bitten leaf*

religion and philosophy
what I'd learned in the churches and the schools
were all too heavy
for this travelling life
all that remained to me was poetry
but a poetry
as unobtrusive as breathing
a poetry like the wind
and the maple leaf
that I spoke to myself
moving over the land[29]

What, one might ask, makes such language, such poetry, shamanic in nature? The answer is given by White himself, earlier in *The Blue Road*, when he reflects upon the immense power of an ice-bound Northern landscape and the corresponding quality of poetic utterance in Inuit songs, such as is to be found in the following lines from Uvavnuk, a female Iglulik shaman:

The great sea
has sent me adrift
it moves me
as the weed in a great river
earth and the great weather
move me
they have carried me away
they move my inward parts with joy[30]

As White comments: 'Spaced-out poems, way beyond the person. To stand up to a landscape such as this, it takes a poetry close to the bone and open to the winds.'[31] The fundamental psycho-symbolic creative principle of shamanism is that, before shamans are able to acquire the powers necessary to fulfil their healing vocation, they must somehow die to their old, socially conditioned and limited selves. In the painful process of initiation into a new life, shamans are stripped to the bone, ready thus to be re-fleshed' with visionary, archetypal or transpersonal powers handed down from the ancestors or spirit helpers of old, and fortified by the particular animal familiar or spirit who appears to the shaman at the height (or depth) of the initiatory visionary experience. The life of such a visionary, equipped with far-ranging, essentially ecstatic powers of lyric utterance, music and dance, imagery and healing, can only be sustained by the sort of concentrated sense of energy and purpose that flows from the very marrow of life.[32]

In this context, it is at the same time 'outlandish' and perfectly natural to see the development of White's creativity – from the early days represented by the 'Caledonia Road Blues' and 'In The Backlands' sections of the *Collected Poems* , through 'Walking the Coast' and 'The Bird Path' and then on to the final 'Mountain Meditations', 'Handbook for the Diamond Country' and 'Leaves of an Atlantic Atlas' – in the light of shamanic ideas. As White himself says in his 'Foreword' to the *Collected Poems*: early on, he knew well enough that 'poetry has more to do with the ecstasy journey than with anything like an entertainment industry [..].'[33] Similarly, the seeming diversity of White's various elective affinities can be synthesised in the light of the fundamental shamanic idea of ancestral spirit helpers: such affinities, we should remind ourselves, range from Mircea Eliade and Lao-Tsu to Heraclitus and Pelagius, Meister Eckhart and the ninth-century Celtic intellectual John Scot Erigena (*sunt lumina*: there are lights, is one of White's favoured aphorisms); from Thoreau, Walt Whitman and D. H. Lawrence to Hölderlin, Nietzsche and Antonin Artaud, Hakuin and Han Shan, Rimbaud and Bashō.[34]

For all such a breadth of affinities, White's sense of form and place, poetry and power has been strongly influenced by the 'less is more' approach of much Eastern poetry and thought. The result is a rigorous avoidance of overworked generalities and redundant detail alike, and a corresponding move towards, into and through the sort of poetic 'clearing' where the eternal dialectic of the external and the internal, the natural and the cultural, is mediated by a practically musical quality of what I would call a shamanic breathing: a breathing of space, energy and light.[35]

Write poetry?

rather follow the coast
fragment after fragment

going forward

breathing

spacing it out[36]

Mindscape and landscape meet in a poetics which – once again – has been stripped to the abstract shamanic – and cosmic – bone:

I take quick notes
like this:
winter morning light
and a black-winged gull
keening over the hut -
no more than that
no metaphor-mongering
no myth-malarkey

I think of lines
like lightning flashes
lines that in their flying energy
would make things
touch and radiate in the mind

I'll have to be going farther
into this night
get further into
this new space
follow right through
the transhuman road
find, who knows, the source
of another light.[37]

In *A Defence of Poetry* Shelley declared that 'the most glorious poetry that has ever been communicated to the world is probably a feeble shadow of the original conception of the poet.'[38] Here we come full, shamanic circle (or rather, spiral) to the opening words of White's 1989 inaugural text for the International Institute of Geopoetics: 'What marks the end of the 20th century, back of all the secondary discourse and all the palaver, is a return to the fundamental, which is to say, the poetic. [...] The question now is to discover where the most necessary, the most fertile poetics are to be found, and to apply them.'[39] Eschewing any overtly academic implications of the development of what Gloria Flaherty has called a 'shamanology', Kenneth White has instead sculpted a particularly resonant poetry, grounded in a particularly resonant poetics: the backbone of which can indeed be described as an 'abstract shamanism'.[40]

In conclusion, it is necessary to recall White's earlier observation about his adolescence in Scotland, namely that he was 'a shaman without a tribe.' The point is sometimes made that it is inappropriate to speak about twentieth-century or contemporary artists, thinkers and writers such as Kandinsky, Tarkovsky or White in terms of shamanism, precisely because they had or have no immediate access to the sort of community that once validated the shaman's work in traditional, small-scale societies.[41] But such an observation seems precisely, profoundly, to miss the point. For when shamanism comes to involve the question of a mass audience in the modern world, it often risks degenerating into either the banalities of mass entertainment or the danger of fascism. The question of the network of shamanic impulse and audience reception and/or validation is a much more subtle matter today – as Kenneth White has long recognised, through the various ways in which he has chosen to present his poetics, including, of course, the idea of geopoetics, and the related development of various conferences and publications.[42]

Once again: to speak of a shamanic element in the work of Kenneth White is *not* to suggest any simplistic parallelism of past and present. The Scottish artist Alan Davie, for whose work White feels considerable empathy, once commented that he too was on his own, without a tribe. However, as the art critic Waldemar Januszczak has observed, 'But he [Davie] does. We all come from the same village. But where we go around closing all our windows, the artist goes around opening them.'[43] So too does Kenneth White. In a world increasingly threatened by one virulent fanaticism or another, be it religious or political, economic or artistic, here is a poet able to offer us an expansive vision of space, energy and light, in an open-ended invitation to breathe more deeply and freely of life's possibilities, further out along the ancient path: *ayaya! ayaya! ayaya!*

NOTES

1   From 'The Northern Archives', in *Open World: The Collected Poems 1960-2000* (Edinburgh: Polygon, 2003), (as performed with the musician Garlo on the CD *Because Mots Notes* (Edition Le Castor Astral 1998)).

2   See *The Blue Road* (Edinburgh: Mainstream Publishing, 1990), 'My Properties', in *Open World: The Collected Poems 1960-2000* p.99 and *passim*.

3   On White and simplicity, see e.g. *Coast to Coast: Interviews and Conversations 1985-1995* (Glasgow: Open World in association with Mythic Horse Press, 1996), p.42: 'But the simplicity I'm after is like a stroke of lightning. One clean gesture – but what an energy field. [...] The simplicity I'm talking about doesn't mean back to an innocence but forward to a higher development. It means disencumbering the mind of an accumulation of secondary discourse and mental cinema. It means walking in a primal space.' On poetry and the primal in a shamanic context, see the 'Epilogue' to Mircea Eliade, *Shamanism: Archaic Techniques of Ecstasy* (Bollingen Series 76/Princeton University Press, 1974), pp.508-11. For the shaman's essential role in the defence of what Eliade calls the psychic integrity of the community, and the key, ongoing function of poetry in this process today: 'Poetic creation still remains an act of perfect spiritual freedom. Poetry remakes and prolongs language; every poetic language begins by being a secret language [...]. The purest poetic act seems to re-create language from an inner experience that, like the ecstasy or religious inspiration of the 'primitives', reveals the essence of things.' See also Martin Heidegger, *Poetry, Language, Thought* (New York: Harper and Row Publishers, 1975), *passim*, for an important series of related reflections, focused upon Hölderlin and Rilke. It is typical of the intellectual amnesia that White has fought so hard against for so long that, in James Fenton's recent study *The Strength of Poetry* (Oxford: Oxford University Press, 2001), there is not one sentence devoted to the shamanic roots of poetic utterance, not one mention of either Eliade or Heidegger – despite chapter titles like 'The Orpheus of Ulster' (on Seamus Heaney) and 'Men, Women and Beasts' (on D.H. Lawrence). White is equally – one might say, predictably – absent from Fenton's deliberations.

4   See *Open World: Collected Poems*, especially 'Walking the Coast' (pp.125-179) and the range of distilled reference in the concluding Notes (pp.603-624).

5   *The Blue Road*, p.111.

6   See *Coast to Coast*, pp.27-28.

7   *Ibid.*, p.37. As the legendary Afro-American (and highly shamanic) musician Sun Ra put it, in another context, 'Space is the Place'.

8   *Ibid.*

9   *The Shaman: Patterns of Religious Healing Among The Ojibwa Indians* (Norman and London: University of Oklahoma Press, 1987), p.15.

10   See Michael Tucker, *Dreaming With Open Eyes: The Shamanic Spirit In Twentieth-Century Art And Culture* (London and San Francisco: Aquarian/ HarperCollins, 1992), which includes a five-page Bibliography on these themes. Close to the shaman is the trickster figure of tribal culture, the joker and breaker of taboos who functions as a sort of creative safety valve for that culture. There is more than a touch of the trickster in White, allied to a Nietzschian quality of 'le gai savoir'.

11   The idea of 'world', approached from the cosmic rather than the historical perspective, has long fascinated White. See note 26 below.

12   *On Scottish Ground: Selected Essays* (Edinburgh: Polygon, 1998), p.42.

13   *Ibid.*, p.45. A list of examples of White's involvement with shamanic themes would be a long one: see e.g. 'The Master of the Labyrinth' in *Open World: Collected Poems*, pp.272-74, the variety of little 'shaman songs' in his work, and the references in Tucker, op. cit., pp.198-202, 390. On the theme of abstraction, see also White's lines in the beautifully illustrated *Mémoires Pyrénéens* (Vallongues: PUP, 1995), p.27: 'trying to get in touch with the territory/always the love for locality/outside all the localisms'. Reprinted as 'Pyrenean Passage', in *Open World: Collected Poems*, pp.251-65.

14   Ernst Cassirer *Language And Myth* (New York: Dover Publications Inc., 1953), p.99.

15   See Tucker, op. cit., *passim*, and Markus Brüderlin (ed.), *Ornament and Abstraction* (Basel: Fondation Beyeler/Dumont, 2001).

16   See Peg Weiss, *Kandinsky and Old Russia* 1995, referenced in Brüderlin (ed.) op. cit. See also Tucker, op. cit., pp.122-26.

17   *Ibid.* (Tucker).

18   *Le Chemin du chaman* (Lausanne: PAP, 1990). This beautiful edition contains many black and white reproductions of shaman drawings drawn from Altaic, Inuit, European and African hunting cultures from around the world, integrated into the text. White has told me that when he wrote the book, he thought of it as 'a kind of ballet' and the saxophonist Steve Lacy set *Le Chemin du chaman* to music.

19   By 'cosmic religion' Eliade meant religion sensitive to animistic, earth-oriented pantheistic values, as opposed to what he considered to be the unhealthy abstractions of the monotheism of the so-called advanced religions of Judaism, Christianity or Islam. I consider that White's 'abstract shamanism', with its strongly concrete and earth-oriented quality, ties in with Eliade's sense of 'cosmic religion' – even as it proposes a poetics free from the idea of God, and unencumbered by any all-too-soul-laden notion of animism. See *Open World: Collected Poems* p.43: 'No metaphysical solemnity, no encumbering religiosity. A great emptiness – broken now and then by exclamations, like the cry of a Laughing Gull.' See also White's poem 'Labrador or The Waking Dream', quoted below (see note 29). For an introduction to Eliade and perspectives on the meaning of the word cosmos, see Tucker, op. cit., *passim*.

20   Flaherty's excellent book was published by Princeton University Press,
      Princeton New Jersey.
21   Flaherty, *passim*.
22   *Ibid.*, p.215.
23   Quoted and referenced in Tucker, op. cit., p.178.
24   The inaugural text on geopoetics by White was published for the
      International Institute of Geopoetics in April 1989. Since then there has
      been a considerable amount of activity, including various conferences in
      France and Scotland and various related publications. See Kenneth White
      Geopoetics: Place, Culture, World (Glasgow: Alba Editions/Scottish
      Centre For Geopoetics, 2003), and note 39 below.
25   *On Scottish Ground*, p.38-39.
26   *Letters from Gourgounel* (London: Jonathan Cape, 1966), p.9. See also
      p.144: 'The world is open before you. All you need to do – and want to do
      – is walk through it.' See 'Remembering Gourgounel', in *Open World:
      Collected Poems*, pp.215-16.
27   On the implications of Miró's belief here, see Tucker, op. cit., pp.308-15.
28   *Open World: Collected Poems*, p.191. The original French reads: 'je ne
      suis plus/qu'un silence en mouvement'. *Le Chemin du chaman*, p.32.
29   *The Blue Road*, p.159. Italicised in the original.
30   *Ibid.*, p.143. Italicised in the original. For another translation of Uvavnuk,
      see Tucker, op. cit., pp.83-84.
31   *Ibid.* (*Blue Road*).
32   For an introduction to the phenomenology and symbolism of shamanism,
      including the crucial importance of the drum, see Eliade, op. cit., *passim*
      and Tucker, op. cit., pp.76-99.
33   *Open World: Collected Poems*, p.xxv.
34   See *Ibid*, Notes, pp.603-24.
35   The idea of a 'clearing' may conjure thoughts of Heidegger – one of the
      many thinkers whose work White has thought through (his phrase) to
      fruitful purpose (another important example is Gaston Bachelard).
36   'Coastline', in *Handbook For The Diamond Country: Collected Shorter
      Poems* (Edinburgh: Mainstream Publishing, 1990), p.55. Reprinted in
      slightly different form as part of 'Broken Ode to White Brittany', in *Open
      World: Collected Poems*, p.503.
37   'Ovid's Report', in *Open World: Collected Poems*, p.514.
38   *Complete Works*, Vol. VII, p.135, quoted in L.R. Furst *European
      Romanticism: Self Definition* (London: Methuen and Co. Ltd., 1980),
      p.91.
39   Inaugural Text, April 1989. White's essays, amounting to a whole
      philosophy of culture, under the general title *The Nomad Mind*, exist in
      their entirety, for the moment, only in French. However, in recent years
      some key texts and interviews have appeared in English. See Notes 3, 12
      and 24 above.

40   This is not to criticise Flaherty, but rather to underline one of the many aspects of White's achievement i.e. his fresh approach to methodology, the combination of scrupulous, time-consuming research with an open-ended poetics. It is also to note the difference between an academic and an artist.

41   This would-be critical point was indeed made to me after the lecture I gave on the shamanic element in White at the conference on White's work held at the University of St. Andrews in October 2003.

42   It is important to remember that, strong individual figure that he is, the spirit of collaboration has long played an important role in White's work. He has worked with many artists and musicians, including Karel Appel, Steve Lacy, Tommy Smith and Garlo. The reading that White gave at the University of St Andrews in October 2003 began with the CD version of 'Angakok's Letter', which is cited at the beginning of this essay: White's words are here set to some highly effective, synthesised 'abstract' soundscapes and strong, measured drum beats, very much in the shamanic tradition. My thanks to Kenneth White and to Garlo for making this CD available to me.

43   Quoted in Michael Tucker *Alan Davie: Small Paintings 1949-2000* (Brighton: University of Brighton, 2000), p.13.

KENNETH WHITE AND RELIGION
Pierre Jamet

Etymology reveals that 'religion' is not as irrelevant a word as it might seem when applied to Kenneth White. From its Greek and Latin root (leg-) were derived notions as diverse as 'take', 'read' or 'law'. Religare is 'to bind' or 'to gather', and as a matter of fact White started on his 'geopoetical' career as a boy gathering shells on the shore. A sacrilegus was the robber of a sacred object primarily. Relegere means 'to read again' and for a poet like Kenneth White, reading and writing are closely knit together. Finally, lex is the law, and White himself actually recalls that the sense of religious law he was transmitted had an influence on him, however superficial.

This essay has a ternary organization. It attempts to explain first how White re-examined some elements of his religious education so as to emerge from theology. Attention is then drawn to Kenneth White the sacrilegus, if he may be called so, who exiled himself on anti-theistic ground, following in the footsteps of fellow barbarians and Cynics. Until is finally defined the particular kind of atheism White claims for himself. Yet again religion is called for in a way that should please the poet of the earth. For indeed the more archaic Indo-European etymology of the same leg- root means 'drip' and is to be found in contemporary words such as 'leak', 'lake' and 'loch' as shall be recalled in due time.[1]

1. Emerging from Theology (Orthodoxy and Eccentricity)
The Christian lexicon – Pelagius – Erigena – Duns Scotus

The lack of interest in Kenneth White's religious education amongst research students and academics is very striking. The fact that the poet himself disqualifies altogether any profound influence is not an argument that will deter us from enquiring a little deeper into this field. White evokes his early years among the Church of Scotland community of Fairlie in an interview with Gilles Farcet dating back to 1992: 'I had a religious education and went into it pretty deeply at one point [...]. Brought up in the Protestant religion, I was initiated very early on to a sacred literature. I didn't have to waste time on little moralising catechisms but went directly to the Bible [...]. I was even in a Bible Studies group. I seemed to be so interested in these things that the minister was sure of my vocation. I can still see him dressing up for the service and saying to me : '*Ah, Kenneth, one day you'll be wearing robes like these...*'[2]

And indeed, one of White's early poems makes extensive use of religious vocabulary. 'Precentor Seagull'[3] is the first of the white-world poems featuring in *En toute candeur*, but it is original in a deeper sense too. The 'bird-poem' is *pre-cantor*, because it does something else and something more important than simply sing. Religious vocabulary, however counterbalanced by occasional barbaric yawps or squawks, gives the poem connotations of radical otherness. And it seems reasonable to conclude that a deep yearning in the young poet was first expressed through the lexicon of his religious education – the only appropriate lexicon available at that time.

Yet the presence of Christian vocabulary in White's work is nowhere near as important as the use he makes of some Christian thinkers' works and names, more particularly those of Pelagius, Johannes Scotus Erigena, Duns Scotus and Master Eckhart. The latter will be dealt with later in this essay but let us notice that the first three were from the British Isles, if not from Scotland itself. What K. White seems to suggest is, therefore, that he is continuing some sort of age-long tradition. These theologian monks provide him with an opportunity to allude to his own work. White holds that it was such peregrine monks who made it possible for a fresh wind to blow over Europe after the fall of the Roman Empire. They were self-exiled intellectuals like him who conveyed new ideas from monasteries to universities and courts.[4] St Benedict actually disliked these monks because they might import suspicious doctrines and because their mobility made it difficult to keep an eye on them.

Pelagius was indeed extremely suspicious from the point of view of orthodox Rome. Kenneth White likes to mention his name from time to time,[5] but the poet-thinker being sometimes criticized for what his detractors call mere name-dropping, it is necessary to tackle the subject seriously here and go into a few details. Clearly, the three orientations of pelagianism have something which could appeal to White. For a start, Pelagius prized asceticism. Now White is not an ascetic but he presents himself as a hard-worker and occasionally alludes to austere discipline: 'The Celto-Christian monks work and work on themselves',[6] he writes. Pelagius also refused original sin, as White recalls: 'What is extraordinary about Pelagius is that at the time when the Pauline and Augustinian notion of original sin was becoming dogma, he denied it completely'.[7] Pelagius also laid emphasis on man's free will and held that man could achieve resemblance to God by his own exertion. He thereby became a theologian of salvation and merit and undermined grace or God's will. *De Natura* showed an optimistic conception of human nature which was to bring about the condemnation of the doctrine. And this is precisely why Pelagius must have appealed to Kenneth White: he is an icon of rebellion against the law. He is a heterodoxical figure, an eccentric. This is what must have prevailed, rather than the exact conceptual content of pelagianism. In fact, for someone like Cioran, who can hardly be accused of optimism, Pelagius's thought is threadbare in that there can be no salvation if there is nothing to be saved from: 'No free and easy deliverance', he writes, 'one must deliver oneself from something [...]. Such a theologian, in his scandalous naivety believes in redemption whilst denying original sin'.[8] The allusion to Pelagius is unambiguous.

And if Erigena appears in White's work more often than not, it is probably because he was yet another highly heterodoxical figure. Johannes Scotus Erigena lived in the ninth century AD and is famous for having transposed Neoplatonist theses into the framework of Christian thought. Étienne Gilson writes about him in terms which echo White's own vocabulary: 'This barbarian, placed on the outskirts of the world, of whom Anastasius the librarian spoke with surprise to King Charles the Bald, aroused many misgivings. To us, he appears as the Latin discoverer of the immense world of Greek theology, that is to say of a hitherto unknown mental universe whose wealth we had no time to sort out nor to assimilate. Condemned and re-condemned to destruction, his writings have nevertheless survived and they even seem to have exercised a kind of underground activity'.[9] And indeed, *De Divisione Naturae* brought about Pope Honorius III's condemnation in the thirteenth century because of equivocal formulations such as this one: '*omnia quae sunt lumina sunt*'. All things that exist are lights. There is enough in this sentence alone to be suspected of pantheism. According to Erigena, the world emanated from God (symbolized by the sun) and God is present in all that exists just as much as all things can be said to be in God. Beams of light proceed from the sun, but they are also consubstantial with the sun. And there lies the core of the problem since reality is now self-justified as a whole. It is a monist hypothesis which again comprises a few drawbacks from the point of view of orthodoxy. For it dissolves all individuality and moral values eventually. The consequences of such a doctrine are that all beliefs and all religions are equivalent, that religion itself is bound to disappear. Ultimately, Erigena's rationalist system of thought is conducive to an out-and-out sceptical philosophy, of the cult of the senses and the identification of mind with matter. Small wonder that the institution rejected it, but here is a philosophy after Kenneth White's own liking. And yet, surprisingly enough, White never quotes Erigena's exact words. Indeed, '*omnia quae sunt lumina sunt*' becomes a mere '*sunt lumina*' which he translates as 'there are lights' in *Une Stratégie paradoxale*: 'Among these individuals at work (...) I'm happy to quote the example of John Scot Erigena (9th century) with his famous phrase: *sunt lumina*, "there are lights".'[10] And if one reads what he has to say about these lights in a poem such as 'Report to Erigena' for instance,[11] one understands that he does not mean them to be theophanical in the slightest. To such good purpose that Kenneth White seems more alien to Erigena's actual thought than Pope Honorius III. Once again the aura of heterodoxy that shrouds the name of Erigena prevails.

Conversely, Duns Scotus, the finest ontological thinker ever according to Gilles Deleuze, is perhaps the closest to White of all the medieval thinkers we are discussing here. What opposes Duns Scotus to Pelagius no less diametrically than what opposes Nietzsche to Plato, is the prevalence of God's will over man's will. And as a matter of fact, such an incompatibility queries White's power of synthesis according to those who prefer to call him eclectic rather than radical. What remains is that according to Duns Scotus no individual action is meritorious unless God accepts it as such. Grace is first. And therefore beatitude, which is the awakening to one's true nature, is something that one may be granted only. And yet a man's acts are a *sine qua non* condition to obtain it. This may have sounded like Chinese thought to Kenneth White's trained ear. Duns Scotus actually manages to overcome the opposition between freedom of will and the absence of freedom. Man does have the use of his own free will, yet all he does is put himself in a situation allowing for his awakening. There is something you can do, but there is nothing you can do, says Duns Scotus in essence. That sort of paradoxical thought is in keeping with White's own. For Gerard Manley Hopkins, Duns Scotus was 'Of realty the rarest-veined unraveller / [...] Who fired France for Mary without spots'[12] He was the great decipherer of reality and the advocate of the Immaculate Conception, which takes us to the question of sexuality and religion in White's work.

2. On Anti-Theistic Ground (the Dialectics of Cynicism and Sobriety)
An argument against religion – An anti-conformist stance – A dialectical relationship to Protestantism? – The White Goddess

Religions are rather amusing when they endeavour to discuss human sexuality. Their efforts in this field are proportional to the compelling energy of their obsessions. Is the soul transmitted through the sexual act? Wise Pelagius is not having that. But luckily enough, people like Charles Baudelaire or Georges Bataille have been more daring explorers of Christianity's sexual therefore cultural meaning, in its least wise aspect. It appears that White's work has something to say about sexuality too, especially at the outset, since the matter lies at the heart of all radical human quest for knowledge. By this token, 'Knowledge Girl' is the title of one of White's poems which tells us something about this subject. The poem ends as following: 'in the presence / of your naked breasts / religion has no reality // and the smooth beauty / of your loving belly / realizes philosophy'.[13] These words rather plainly show that for White sexuality is an argument against religion, a way back to the immanence. Philosophy, which is the love (*philia*) of wisdom (*sophos*), is best achieved in the wisdom of love (but as *eros*).

On the face of it, when White writes about sexuality he adopts an anti-conformist stance. In his first two narratives, *Les Limbes incandescents* and *Travels in the Drifting Dawn*, the first of which has only ever been published in French, sex is part and parcel of a portrait of the artist as a young dog and as a modern kind of Diogenes the Cynic. The Cynics called themselves so in reference to a dog (*kynos*) who'd stolen a sacrificed chicken from an altar. Had he done that in Rome that dog would have been the *sacrilegus* alluded to earlier in this paper. White probably views himself as a descendent of the Cynics in his early years as a writer, and he even draws a parallel between Yang-tchou, a Taoist father, and Diogenes in *La Figure du dehors*: 'Perhaps his most faithful equivalent in the West was Diogenes with his "step out of my light"'.[14] And although White did not tell Jacques Chirac to step out of his light when he met the ex-mayor of Paris, the Tao-cynic young writer did take the trouble to relate a few perky episodes that took place in his successive cosmopolitan studios: '*Fuck me! Fuck me!*' says a dark-nippled woman here,[15] '*your god is your sex and your land is women*' says another one there.[16] 'The biter of Karachi' is a little too prone to biting him,[17] and a significant French girl who is about to get married asks White to deflower her, which causes simultaneous laughter and erection.[18]

This episode is particularly interesting because for one thing it is longer than the usual epigrammatic irruption of *eros*, and for another because White deems it necessary to mention the fact that the girl comes from a 'very Catholic' family. Now here is a hypothesis that the pagan poet will perhaps deny: could it be that a dialectical relationship with Protestantism is breaking through in the very provocative way White writes about sex? To claim, as White does in an interview, that one is a Protestant who protests against Protestantism, is clearly to establish such a dialectical relationship. If one looks at it closely, a few details in White's later work are puzzling. In a book on Van Gogh, White writes about the famous painter in these terms: 'In order to work, Vincent needed a home, and to live like a monk who gets off two times a month'.[19]. And the

use he makes of a Zen anecdote is also interesting. Two monks meet
a girl but go on their way until one of them regrets it and is rebuked
by his companion for having refrained from seizing the opportunity:
White's conclusion is that the intellectual nomad goes straight to his
desire and does not care for mental elaborations or even such
artefacts as lace underwear. These views, however liberal, may
sound a little austere to a more southern temperament. But more
importantly, they give the impression that sexuality has to be
redeemed by some kind of seriousness and that the Zen monk's
black robe makes it more acceptable. Let us just recall the minister in
Fairlie here: '*Ah Kenneth, one day you'll be wearing robes like
these!*' At any rate, sexuality in White's work is far from any sort of
baroque plethora, any luscious, colourful Florentine fête. But it may
be likened to Rousseau's Genevan style on the contrary, and the
frequent use of a naturalistic imagery to express the erotic moment
provides us with much evidence here. White sometimes confesses
that he practised as a child what he calls 'arboreal masturbation',
but he was later to go deeper into this world and discover what we
might call 'chlorophyllian sex'. Now the narrator of his early
notebooks feels like the trunk of a birch-tree running with sap,[20]
now he revels in the marshlands of the flesh.[21] Now he penetrates his
partner as a ship slips into the sea,[22] now he finds her belly beautiful
as that of the earth.[23] It is hard to completely dismiss the idea that in
the field of sexuality White's Reformed origins, though vehemently
repudiated, are perhaps not as unimportant as readers are asked to
believe. And the cynicism of the early years constitutes no real
argument against this point in so far as it dialectically meshes with
the West of Scotland sobriety of the poet's education.

Yet again, in counterpoise to what has just been said, if we are
to unravel an ever complex reality cautiously too, one more nuance
is called for. Indeed the network of images linked to sexuality and
the *vita femina* in this work proceeds from a consistent anti-modern
vision of the world. It is a fact that Modernity has lived off the
Platonic-Socratic philosophy in which the mind prevails over matter
and entails the prevalence of transcendence over immanence, of the
human over the non-human world, ultimately of the male principle
over the female principle (cf. J. Derrida's *phallogocentrism*). And
according to an anti-idealistic vision of the world such as that which
White inherits from Nietzsche, this unbalanced relationship allowed

for the emergence of mechanical and particularizing thought. That very thought in its turn severed man from the former global vision of the world as *cosmos*. If we consider that the altogether rare dialectically Protestant passages are but mere details in this work, as well as the more and more chaste or monastic overtones of White's attitude towards sexuality, then we can identify his vision of the world as *cosmos* with a conscious return to the archaic great female principle: the White Goddess. Robert Graves very famously wrote about the White Goddess and was convinced that she was present in the cult of the Virgin Mary, so inseparable from the chtonian world since she appears oftenest in grottoes, caverns or stony places.[24] So, now, having moved from Mary without spots to the White Goddess, we can try and define White's professed atheism.

3. Towards a Mystic Atheism (East Meets West)
Eckhart's trans-continental intuition – The desert – The bird-path and the lake re(li)gion

When applied to Kenneth White, 'mystic' is a word that should be handled very carefully: 'There is nothing religious about [the drifter of this book]', says the preface to *Travels in the Drifting Dawn*, '(except maybe in a special a-theistic sense) and his mysticism, if mysticism there is, is strongly tinged with a laughing *gai savoir*.'[25] This special mixture of mysticism and atheism is what it is necessary to now examine.

Master Eckhart is the medieval theologian who appears the most often in White's work, along with Erigena. Our purpose is to elicit the trans-continental dimension which White says he finds in Eckhart's work. Here is a telling quotation by White from Schuon's book on the unity of religions: 'If every religion has its own colour, intellectual intuition would be "consciousness of the colourless essence of light and its purely luminous nature"'.[26] Eckhart's light being the diffuse light of dawn, unlike Erigena's beams which lead us straight back to a monotheistic sun, it is there, in this dawn, that White says he meets Eckhart. And it is also in this dawn that he says Eckhart meets a few radical Eastern thinkers. We may think of Dogen or Nagarjuna, for instance. But the subject of Eastern religion can only be alluded to here for want of time and because White's Buddhism is closer to philosophy or wisdom than to religion strictly speaking.

So on the way to this dawn-like consciousness there are a certain number of images which seem to be common to Eckhart and White such as that of the desert for example. From the start, White makes it clear that a shore, a moor, a forest or a single room will do if no Sahara is accessible: 'It is in the desert (coast, moor, forest or attic) that "it happens"'.[27] In Eckhart's *Poem*, the desert is the metaphor of something other than the mere absence of objects. It is the kingdom of paradox, the sunk carving or the footprint of a presence that one should feel when images have disappeared.[28] And White's barest poems should be read in the light of this analysis. All a poem like 'Rannoch Moor' says for instance is: 'dark heather / wisp of wool / buzzing fly'.[29] It says that the more absent the poem seems the more one should feel a presence, though not of a personal God.

After the desert comes *The Bird Path*. The British Kenneth White reader knows that this is a Ch'an expression used as a title for the 1989 'Collected Longer Poems'.[30] Extraordinarily enough, the Eckhart reader will find the very same expression in one of his sermons.[31] Eckhart's bird path is an image for what he calls *Abgescheidenheit*, namely the method to shake oneself free from the projections of one's will onto the world. To tread the bird path is therefore a paradox not unlike Duns Scotus' in so far as it means to exert one's will not to will in order to achieve a state of lightness of the whole being.[32] It seems reasonable to draw a parallel between Eckhart's thought and Eastern thought or Kenneth White's own work, but we have to content ourselves with a short enumeration here.[33] Eckhart spoke of an essential being beyond God himself in a way that pleases the poet.[34] He spoke of a "groundless place" and White of an "*a-topia*". He spoke of a timeless experience which evokes White's liking for the instantaneous intuition of the East. Above all, he professed that the meditant should start looking at the world first and reach what he called a dawn-like consciousness before withdrawing into himself.[35] It seems hardly possible to doubt that for White there is a difficult area of the being which a few individuals explore in times and places as diverse as one can imagine. It is an experience of place leading to a no-where and bringing back to places: *topos, a-topia, pan-topia*. 'White world' is but a name for what I call *pan-topia* here. And if I may quote the first two sections of one of White's finest poems, we shall go full circle and back to the Indo-European etymology of 'religion': *leg-* for 'drip' and present in 'leak', 'lake' and 'loch':

SCOTIA DESERTA

All those kyles, lochs and sounds...

   *

And the gulls at Largs pier:
sitting in that café
at the big window full of wind and light
reading and watching

thinking back to the ice
watching it move
from the high middle spine
out into the Atlantic

feeling it gouge out lochs
and sculpt craggy pinnacles
and smoothe long beaches

the land emerges
bruised and dazed
in the arctic light

gannets gather on the islands
eagles on the piny hills
cotton grass tosses in the wind

men come
gazing around them
what name shall be given it?
Alba[36]

It is imperative to remember here that *Alba*, which means 'white' in Latin, once was the name of Scotland itself.

To round things up a little we need to point out the fact that medieval theology as it is represented by theologian monks from Britain plays an important part in White's intellectual development, though he chooses references preferably among heterodoxical figures, nothing daunted by the inevitable costs in terms of conceptual coherence.[37]

The religious fact is closely linked to the sexual fact and some of White's poems bear the mark of this close relationship. Sexuality even provides a sort of cynical weapon against the bourgeois *lex* or norm, and establishes the young White on anti-clerical ground. A few puzzling details tend to suggest though that White still remains dialectically attached to what he professes to have emerged from long ago.

Yet there is largely enough in the work to undermine any categorical assertion in this respect and this paper has tried to define the kind of atheism White claims for himself. Master Eckhart provides the model of a possible mystic atheism. Of course Eckhart was not at all an atheist himself but he elaborated a poetic thought which can be paralleled with White's work.

But let us make one last point. Kenneth White recurrently insists on the necessity to see the moon and go beyond the word, to see the face and go beyond the name. Comparing this stance with the most exact definition of theology will show a striking resemblance, though. One of the Christian thinkers who continues the dialogue with Heidegger the most cogently, Jean-Yves Lacoste, puts this argument forward: theology did borrow the metaphysical vocabulary at the outset (when the *logos* became the Verb), but it escapes metaphysics (and at the same time Heidegger's definitive criticism of metaphysics) because it must be understood as a will-to-say which outdoes all philosophical wording: 'In this discipline, for one, the will-to-say is more meaningful than the actual spoken words'. (Le vouloir-dire excède le dit en ce domaine plus qu'en tous.')[38] For a theologian too then, seeing the face is more important than hearing the name. In which case White's thought may seem closer to mysticism than to atheism.

NOTES

1   *Dictionnaire des racines des langues indo-européennes*, R. Grandsaignes d'Hauterive éd. (Paris: Larousse, 1994), pp.104-05.
2   'La Saveur d'un monde flottant', in *Nouvelles Clefs*, juin 1992, pp.14-23 (p.14).
3   'You up there in the lurching church of the elements / mover and moved / (…) would waken wide if there was one / the sleeping gate to paradise / […] give us the sound at least the note / the initial noise / and it's we that will make the psalms we need / […] o you beginning / archangel of language we continue / […] no voice of dumb eternity yours…', *En toute candeur* (Paris: Mercure de France, 1989), pp.77-8.
4   Cf. *Déambulations dans l'espace nomade* (Arles: Acte Sud, 1995), pp.34-35.
5   As in the poem called 'The Chaoticist Manifesto' for instance: 'They're all there / the thinkers / those of the *Anfang* / Pelagius / steps out of a hollybush / Erigena / walks quiet along the shore / *sunt lumina*'. *Atlantica* (Paris: Grasset, 1986), p.226.
6   *Une Stratégie paradoxale* (Bordeaux: P.U. de Bordeaux, 1998), p.152.
7   *Ibid.*
8   *Le Mauvais démiurge*, in *Œuvres complètes* (Paris: Gallimard, 1995), pp.1224-25.
9   *History of Christian Philosophy in the Middle Ages* (London: Sheed and Ward, 1954), p.120.
10   *Une Stratégie paradoxale*, op. cit., p.153.
11   *Terre de diamant* (Paris: Grasset, 1985), p.10.
12   'Duns Scotus's Oxford', in *Le Naufrage du Deutschland, suivi des poèmes gallois et sonnets terribles* (Paris: La Différence, 1991), p.66.
13   In *Terre de diamant*, op. cit., p.200.
14   *La Figure du dehors*, op. cit., p.179.
15   *Les Limbes incandescents* (Paris: Denoël, 1976), p.52.
16   *Ibid.*, p.167.
17   *Ibid.*
18   *Ibid.*, p.95.
19   *Van Gogh et Kenneth White* (Charenton: Flohic, 1994), p.34.
20   *Les Limbes incandescents*, op. cit., p.54.
21   *Ibid.*, p.70.
22   *Ibid.*, p.75.
23   *Ibid.*, p.85.
24   *Les Mythes celtes (la déesse blanche)* (Monaco: Éditions du Rocher, 1991).
25   *Travels in the Drifting Dawn* (Edinburgh: Mainstream, 1989), p.7. See also: 'The mystic is a man who lacks meaning', *En toute candeur*, op. cit., p.68. And also: 'We must shut the door on fake mysticism', *Les Limbes incandescents*, op. cit., p.14.
26   *Une Apocalypse tranquille* (Paris: Grasset, 1985), p.24.

27 *Ibid.,* p.25.
28 'If you follow no way / on the narrow path / you will reach the imprint of the desert', in Jarczyck G. et Labarrière P-J., *Maître Eckhart ou l'empreinte du désert* (Paris: Albin Michel, 1995), pp.10-14 (p.14).
29 *Terre de diamant*, op. cit., p.74.
30 The French reader of Kenneth White knows that White borrows the expression from Oriental texts (notably in *La Figure du dehors*, op. cit., pp.177, 122).
31 Quoted by Rudolf Otto, *Mystique d'orient et mystique d'occident*, (Paris, Payot, 1996), p.37.
32 Cioran again describes it so: 'To intitate yourself into the art of detaching desire and action - a baneful operation for restless minds, but indispensable for the contemplative.' *La Chute dans le temps*, in *Œuvres complètes*, op. cit., p.1200.
33 Here is one example: 'To tread the bird path is a Ch'an expression which means realizing the self-nature. A flying bird leaves no tracks in the air, like the self-nature which leaves no traces anywhere.' Epigraph to *The Bird Path* (Edinburgh: Mainstream, 1989). The last lines of White's only poem written in French, *Le Chemin du chaman*, also obliquely evoke this detached state of being. After having been drawn away from the social community, the shaman turns into a bird and spirals up into the ether saying: 'plus haut, toujours plus haut / je ne suis plus / qu'un silence en mouvement.' *Le Chemin du chaman* (Lausanne: PAP, 1990), p.32.
34 'For Eckhart, to reach this 'essential being', is to go beyond God, to become *ledig*, or unencumbered', *La Figure du dehors*, op. cit., p.210.
35 There is a tension between two forms of mysticism which is central to medieval theology. The way in is called Augustinian and the way out Dionysian (in reference to Pseudo-Dionysius). In so far as Eckhart can be said to belong to the second stream of thought, White is definitely one of his kin. Although specialists say Eckhart rather achieves a synthesis of both.
36 *The Bird Path*, op. cit., p.123.
37 It seems urgent that oncoming research examine the differential nature of references in this work. Where does the actual influence start and where can one merely speak of a reference in passing? Hugues Robaye did not broach this particular aspect of the question in the 'Dynamique des Modèles' he read at the Bordeaux White conference in February 2003.
38 'Être', in *Dictionaire critique de théologie*, J-Y. Lacoste éd. (Paris: PUF, 1998), pp.416-28 (p.419).

BUDDHISM AND THE WHITE WAY
Padmakara

I was recently in the Swiss Alps for a week's walking with a friend. It just so happened that the trip coincided with my birthday, and so we decided to celebrate by taking a mountain train journey up to the Jungfraujoch, an observation point just below the Jungfrau peak itself, at 3,454 metres.

The electric cogwheel train slowly wound its way up from Lauterbrunnen, down in the valley, up to Kleine Scheidegg at about 2000 metres. From there we changed trains and at Eigergletscher the train disappeared into the massive bulk limestone of the Eiger and the Monch to make the final 1000 metre, half-hour climb inside a tunnel engineered by some mad visionary back in the 1890s.

At the top, and at the highest railway station in Europe, we stepped out and walked onto the dazzling snow under clear bright blue skies. Instinctively we walked away from the tourist observation tower and off into the stunning bowl of broken snow. It is too cold to think and when thoughts arise they come as poetry:

Stillness and grandeur of thin-aired altitude.
The sense of trespass.
Breathless, intoxicated, dizziness.
Delusion of safety on this high clear late-summer day.
The mind flood of clichés.
But ultimately, the sheer inexpressibility of it all.

We grin and laugh a lot,
And then go quiet and serious:
No need to say out loud
It is to do with death and human briefness.

This is diamond country, thunderbolt country, vajra country. The vajra is a diamond or a thunderbolt, an Indo-Tibetan symbol for the incandescent purity of it all: primordial whiteness. All is fundamentally fine; all is fundamentally exactly how it should be. But getting there takes the breath away, freezes the lungs, and demands a certain crazy errancy:

> *Footpath*
> > *Flight path*
> *Bird path*
> > *White path*

Vajrasattva is the diamond being, Indo-Tibetan icon, the white adi-Buddha simultaneously at the centre, at the edge and behind the mandala. He is pure lucent white, holding a vajra and a bell. 'Adi' means highest, best, ultimate, but not in any crass hierarchical sense - more a here, now, waiting, potential perfection everywhere. He smiles down and up out of the crystal glacier underfoot. We put on our sunglasses. We are too staggered to dance but we are up there somewhere.

A friend once said to me 'give yourself a break – be someone else'. I don't normally take much notice of others' advice but that one has always stuck. And when you think about it, it is playfully tantric-shamanic. Tantric-shamanic in the sense of anything which breaks us out of our narrow minded selfishness and petty concerns, anything which takes us from the closed world into the open world, anything which pushes us over the edge of insularity into the emptiness of the unknown ocean.

Kenneth White has an essay in *On Scottish Ground* called 'A Shaman Dancing on the Glacier' – here is a quotation from it:

> *What the shaman, or the 'dawn man', as the Ojibwa call him, is out for, is an ecstasy (getting outside one's self as well as outside history), and a de-conditioning. Starting out from a reduction [...], the shaman achieves a transcendence, a capacity for experiencing (and also expressing) total life. By separating himself, at least temporarily, from the community [...], the shaman comes to know an identity larger than the one coded in the*

community, and it is precisely this which enables him to do the greatest good to the community, by giving it breathing space. (p.38)

I am not advocating any kind of neo-shamanism, to be practised in and around Glastonbury or Glasgow. I am speaking of a basis, *and a basis on which all kinds of* developments *are possible. Even within the specific context of shamanism, election is followed by instruction, the ecstatic is followed by the didactic. I'd extend that on to a larger scale. On the basis of this fundamental experience [...], let us both expand and intensify - into for example, ecology and philosophy and poetics and politics (that way, we may get depth ecology, lightning philosophy, live poetics and, who knows, even enlightened cultural politics). This has already happened in the history of world culture. The rock crystal in the shaman's body becomes the 'diamond body' of tantric Buddhism. The 'bird path' of the shaman, which was originally a line of bird-crested birchtrees, becomes the 'bird path' of Zen. (p.42)*

The bird path is ungraspable yet it is a path. In the *Dhammapada* it is written: 'That Enlightened One whose victory is irreversible and whose sphere is endless, by what track will you lead him astray, the Trackless One?' (chapter 14, v.1); a fragment from Heraclitus reads: 'If you do not expect the unexpected, you will not find it, for it is trackless and unexplored' (Heraclitus, B18); and in Kenneth White's poem *The Bird Path* we have this:

Up here in the white country

any tree for a totem
any rock for an altar
discover!

this ground is suicidal

annihilates everything
but the most essential

poet – your kingdom

From my glacial Swiss peak I look over to the South West: Swiss Alps, French Alps, somewhere Mont Blanc and beyond that the Tanargue.

The Tanargue Mountains overlooking Gourgounel where a young Scottish poet is writing letters to himself, to the mountains, to Thor, to it all, to us. He tells us the word Tanargue is from Tanarus who is Thor, and Tanargue is thus the field of thunder. Thor wealds the thunderbolt – yes he is another vajra being who wakes up the night, crashes into sleeping ignorance, like Vajrapani, the dark blue wrathful Vajra-holder of Tibetan Buddhism. Vajrapani stamps, he has a necklace of skulls and an aura of fire, he is pot-bellied, sharp-toothed, and he is raging: WAKE UP! Another transcendental thunderclap, another bad night's sleep. And people think Buddhism is a peaceful religion.

The ubiquitous Stupas of Asia are not just reliquaries for the bones of saints. No, they are lightning conductors. Some sit inside them meditating, waiting. Some walk round and round whirring prayer wheels chanting

OM MANI PADME HUM OM MANI PADME HUM OM MANI PADME HUM

To be non-literal and to claim full poetic licence, it might mean 'may I be struck by lightning, if not in this lifetime then at least in the next'. It doesn't always have to be about lotuses and jewels. I am all for peace and compassion, it's just that sometimes stillness has to come after a storm; coolness after a fire. Behind every peaceful mantra is a wrathful mantra. It's why Rilke realised that 'every angel is terrifying'.

In the Tanargue it has been raining and storming for eight days. Kenneth White has just found out that the camp-bed that he has been expecting is due to arrive on the local bus. He has to set out in the worst of the weather having to tramp across the soggy meadows the long way round because the nearest bridge has broken from its moorings. He sets the scene in one of his *Letters from Gourgounel*:

The thunder was roaring, the lightning flashing, and the rain was pelting down. I ran up to the roadway.

The Tanargue road was cut through rock, and the rock rises all along it. At the moment this rock was covered with waterfalls. The road has deep ditches, but they were overflowing. I stood beside Ribeyre's shack and waited for the bus.
It did not stop for long. The driver came to the back doors of the van-bus and handed me out the bed:
'Pardon,' he grimaced, 'ça continue.'
'Incroyable,' and I gave him a quick thanks.
I decided to wait there in the doorway and looked out through the rain...
I had brought a book down with me for reading in the shack while waiting for the bus: a collection of Buddhist texts from India, China and Japan. I opened it at random. The text I came across was from the Mahayana school and was called 'The Tathagata as a Raincloud'. (pp.71-72)

This sutra is more generally known as the 'parable of the plants' from the Lotus Sutra, sometimes known as the White Lotus Sutra. As he sits there sheltered from the rain he goes on to quote a substantial section from the anthology he has. I would like to quote it in a different translation of my own personal preference. This is from the 1987 translation of *'The Lotus of the Wonderful Law'* (London: Curzon, 1987) by W.E. Soothill:

It is like unto a great cloud
Rising above the world,
Covering all things everywhere,
A gracious cloud full of moisture;
Lightning-flames flash and dazzle,
Voice of thunder vibrates afar,
Bringing joy and ease to all.
The sun's rays are veiled,
And the earth is cooled;
The cloud lowers and spreads
As if it might be caught and gathered;
Its rain everywhere equally
Descends on all sides,
Streaming and pouring unstinted,

Permeating the land.
On mountains, by rivers, in valleys,
In hidden recesses, there grow
The plants, trees, and herbs;
Trees, both great and small,
The shoots of the ripening grain,
Grape vine and sugar cane.
Fertilized are these by the rain
And abundantly enriched;
The dry ground is soaked,
Herbs and trees flourish together.
From the one water which
Issued from that cloud,
Plants, trees, thickets, forests,
According to their need receive moisture.
All the various trees,
Lofty, medium, low,
Each according to its size,
Grows and develops
Roots, stalks, branches, leaves,
Blossoms and fruits in their brilliant colors;
Wherever the one rain reaches,
All become fresh and glossy.
According as their bodies, forms
And natures are great or small,
So the enriching rain,
Though it is one and the same,
Yet makes each of them flourish.

In like manner also the Buddha
Appears here in the world,
Like unto a great cloud
Universally covering all things;
And having appeared in the world,
He, for the sake of the living,
Discriminates and proclaims
The truth in regard to all laws.
The Great Holy World-honoured One,
Among the gods and men

And among the other beings,
Proclaims abroad this word:
'I am the Tathagata,
The Most Honoured among men;
I appear in the world
Like unto this great cloud,
To pour enrichment on all
Parched living beings,
To free them from their misery
To attain the joy of peace,
Joy of the present world,
And joy of Nirvana....

Upon all I ever look
Everywhere impartially,
Without distinction of persons,
Or mind of love or hate.
I have no predilections
Nor any limitations;
Ever to all beings
I preach the Law equally;
As I preach to one person,
So I preach to all.
Ever I proclaim the Law,
Engaged in naught else;
Going, coming, sitting, standing,
Never am I weary of
Pouring it copious on the world,
Like the all-enriching rain.
On honoured and humble, high and low,
Law-keepers and law-breakers,
Those of perfect character,
And those of imperfect,
Orthodox and heterodox,
Quick-witted and dull-witted,
Equally I rain the Law-rain
Unwearyingly.

I think this is a good text for those looking to find geo-poetic links within the Buddhist canon. The Mahayana tradition from which this passage comes is remarkable in its visionary elaboration of cosmic imagery. And perhaps this is fine – a reaction to the scholarly dryness of earlier monastic tradition. However, for me, the metaphysical symbolism can get a bit too alien, too off the planet: Baroque and rococo Bodhisattvas in palaces of exotic splendour. That is not a criticism, just a statement of personal preference for the moment. This passage from the White Lotus Sutra touches me with its simpler natural images – it has immediacy and hence greater meaning for me. Rain, thunder, clouds, herbs.

Perhaps this is a launching point for what we might call dharma-geo-poetics. Dharma-geo-poetics strikes me as something resonant with the Buddhist teaching of the Middle Way. It is a way of looking at life that avoids the extremes of metaphysical abstraction on the one hand, and worldly materialism on the other; or put more philosophically dogmatic transcendentalism as against dogmatic 'immanentism'. The transcendental taken too literally is an always unattainable ideal, out there, way along the path, over the horizon, attainable over many, many lifetimes. Dispiriting, depressing.

The notion of immanence taken too literally leads either to stagnation or delusions of grandeur. Buddhahood is here and now, we are already enlightened, all striving is pointless and even a hindrance. But it quickly descends into a spiritual platitude and a screen for the avoidance of deeper thought and real personal change.

Somehow the transcendental has to be glimpsed in the immanent; what can be possible has in some sense to be grounded in our everyday, workaday, holiday life. The rain-cloud of the dharma falls on all equally, but all have their own unique and particular unfolding shapes and rates of growth. The potential of Buddhahood is always here and now, the attainment is not so simple.

Time for more White poems:

INTO THE WHITENESS

Now I have burnt all my knowledge
and am learning to live with the whiteness naked

what I call art now is nothing made
but the pure pathology of my body and mind

at the heart of a terrible and joyous world[1]

Yes, we have to admit we are pathological beings, even the Buddha hinted that we are all twisted in our perceptions of the world. But it is about bringing our madness into the 'whiteness naked'. Without the whiteness, neurosis and psychosis; with the whiteness, we are still mad, but mad in the crazy Zen sense dancing frenetically up in the snow-capped mountains:

MOUNTAIN AND GLACIER WORLD

Arrived at this point
where the whiteness is manifest
here in the mountains
where the coldness my element
surrounds me with eternity

arrived at this point
the high crest of nothingness
where the "I" has no meaning
and the self is ecstatically
alone with its aloneness

shall I blow out my brains?[2]

Well of course, Ken. 'Nirvana': from the Sanskrit root meaning to 'blow out'.

And one more from *Handbook for the Diamond Country*:

A HIGH BLUE DAY ON SCALPAY

This is the summit of contemplation, and
* no art can touch it*
blue, so blue, the far-out archipelago
* and the sea shimmering, shimmering*
no art can touch it, the mind can only
* try to become attuned to it*
to become quiet, and space itself out, to
* become open and still, unworlded*
knowing itself in the diamond country, in
* the ultimate unlettered light*[3]

I'm trying to throw out snippets and snapshots of what this dharma-geo-poetic path might feel like. It is work in progress; work in process. Maybe it is best like that – the White Path is a road of flux, snowflakes, blue sky, and whiteout. Whatever – the brains have to go – for certain – at least in the limited rationalistic sense. Genuine intelligence is necessary all the way.

Another mountain hop: this time East, and Chung-nan Mountain in China. It is the seventh century and a young monk called Shan-tao is, in time-honoured fashion, wandering throughout the country looking for advice on the Way.[4] He stayed in the mountains for around six to seven years, gaining the reputation of 'mountain monk' before going on to teach in the capital city of Ch'ang-an for over thirty years.

Shan-tao was an impressive meditator and master lineage holder in the Pure Land school of Buddhism. This is the form of Buddhism that teaches salvation through devotion and extensive mantra repetition in the direction of the Buddha Amitabha, with the goal of being reborn in Amitabha's enlightened pure land paradise called Sukhavati. The point of it is that we are so deluded that we can only rely on the external powers or as it is known 'other power' of the Buddhas. All so called 'self power' is impossible because it is always flawed by ego and self-centredness. Maybe it is a bit too close to some of the Christian dogmas that I have rejected as unhelpful. But it does raise a good question: to what extent can we really save ourselves? Can the ego be overcome by the ego?

The White Path School is named after one of Shan-tao's striking parables. He describes our existential situation in an image. The pilgrim in the wilderness is attacked from behind by robbers and wild beasts who furiously rush towards him. He runs away but comes to a strange double river: part of the river is a river of fire flowing south; the other part of the river is a raging torrent of water flowing north. Across the river to the West is a very narrow path, only a few inches wide - the White Path between the fire and the water. The traveller is paralysed by the crisis and unable to move, his position seems impossible. But then he hears an urging voice from across the rivers on the other shore. It is the Buddha calling and telling him he can get across. His doubts drop away and he makes the dangerous crossing safely to the other side.

But maybe this thin white path is even thinner than a few inches. The White Path has to be the path of emptiness: a tightrope, the edge of a sword. It is dangerous.

Kenneth White has this to say in his essay 'The Birds of Kentigern':

> *This is the sword's edge. It's the* sunyavada, *the path of emptiness, which is central to Buddhism and hence to Zen. In fact it would be better to speak no more either of Buddhism or of Zen, and speak only of the* sunyavada – *or better still, travel it, but the travelling doesn't work without the understanding (you've got to get your* mental *feet on it).*[5]

And Gary Snyder says the task is 'to simplify the mind - like a blade which sharpens to nothing'.[6]

The White Path is an empty path. The White Path is a no path because the bandits and the animals do get you; they come with you on to the sword's edge. But then the fire on one side burns everything up and the water on the other washes the ashes away. And the Buddha on the other shore laughs and dives in too.

The White Path is a path to an Open universe. The animals that chase us are the beasts of dogma and rigid literalism. The fire of one river is the fire of fundamentalism; the water of the other is the water of religious and moral certainty. These forces are raging, as we all too well know, in the world, in the Middle East, in Iraq, fuelled by the Blair-Bush moral high ground and the global surging of terrorist frustrations. These are the fuelling forces of contemporary *samsara*.

Kenneth White in an article called 'Poetics of the Open Universe' (*Cencrastus*, 22 (1986)) quotes the American poet Robert Duncan:

> *Our engagement with knowing, with craft and lore, our demand for truth is not to reach a conclusion but to keep our exposure to what we do not know, to confront our wish and our need beyond habit and capability, beyond what we take for granted, at the borderline, the light finger-tip or thought-tip where impulse and novelty spring.*

A few years before his death, Tony McManus, in response to my request for information about Kenneth White, very generously sent me a large package of photocopied articles and references. One of the articles was by Tony himself from *Cencrastus* magazine (35, (1989). The article was called 'Entering the White World' and in it he gets to the heart of the matter:

> *The central idea in Kenneth White's work, from very early on, is the notion of a space opening out, new world, a new 'landscape/mindscape', a new cultural space beyond the fracas of what we understand now as the cultural, social, political. It is a space which requires to be cleared of all that rubbish accumulated by modern society to attain to a purer consciousness of being. The responsibility for this work is devolved on the 'poet-thinkers', like White who, typically, in his work is either about the task of clearing the rubbish, or evoking the new world, 'le monde blanc...'*

That was written back in 1989. And now there is more rubbish than ever, more space to be cleared, more dharma-geo-poetics to be practised, more white-path urgency but also more crazy-planet humour and playfulness.

I have been mostly up in the mountains. I don't know if I have brought anything down to the plains. Maybe I got lost. But even the great Chinese mountain poet Han Shan did that:

> *Here in the mountains – so very cold;*
> *It's been this way from of old – it's not just this year.*
>
> *Peak piled upon peak – constantly clotted with snow;*
> *Dark, secluded woods – every day spewing forth mist.*
>
> *Here things start to grow only after the Grain is in Beard,*
> *And the leaves are coming down, even before the Beginning of Fall.*
>
> *And here – here is a traveller hopelessly lost,*
> *Who looks and looks but can't see the sky.*[7]

I would like to conclude with another Kenneth White poem. It indicates something essential about the White Path and about the Buddhist path: the principle of freedom. In traditional Buddhism freedom is what arises when two veils or coverings are lifted from the mind.

The first covering, the *klesāvarana* is the 'veil of passions'. The *kleshas* are also known as 'the poisons', such as greed, jealousy, envy, hatred etc. This veil is that which prevents us from seeing things in terms of the truth and causes us to see in terms of self-grasping, for our own ends and gratification.

The second covering the *jñeyāvarana* is the 'veil of (false) assumptions'. *Jneya* refers more to the limiting ideas that we identify with. It is the tendency to create rationalisations for our selfish desires. Our fear of death causes us to create a dogma of immortality. Our dogma of immortality is a veil to the truth of impermanence. But on a deeper level it is all our assumptions, speculation and theories about Reality which simply obfuscate the true clear light of the mind.

So the rending of these veils at enlightenment is described as a great release. The Buddha describes it as a man coming out of a dangerous jungle, or one who has been freed from a debt, or one who is released from prison.

In many of the old canonical texts the enlightenment experience is spoken of in terms of *vimukti* or *mokha* – freedom or emancipation. In the early Pali text, the Udana, there is a famous passage where the Buddha uses the analogy of the sea as having one taste, the taste of salt. The same is true for the Dharma, for it to be anything it has to have one taste, the taste of freedom.

Here is the poem: it is a section from 'Mahamudra':

*'As soon as the conscience
is rid of its covering
it stands out naked
and energy shows its essence'*

the lotus and the lightning

*'just as salt is dissolved in water
so the mind that takes its woman'*

in the arms of the knowledge-girl

earth water fire wind
and space too - honour them

'so he comes into relation
with every kind of creature
and knows the path of freedom' [8]

NOTES

1   Kenneth White, *Handbook for the Diamond Country* (Edinburgh:
     Mainstream, 1990), p.52.
2   *Ibid.*, p.49.
3   *Ibid.*, p.77.
4   Kenneth White, *On Scottish Ground* (Edinburgh: Polygon, 1998), p.82.
5   Shan-tao (613-681). Shan-tao was one of the most successful of the
     Chinese Pure Land promoters. Traditions differ as to whether he was born
     in Ssu-chou in An-hui province, or Lin-tzu in Shan-tung Province; his dates
     are given as 613-681 CE. He became a monk at a young age and was
     trained in the study of the major Mahayana sutras. Eventually he became
     drawn to Pure Land theory and studied at Mt. Lu and Mt. Chung-nan,
     where he practised contemplative visualization of Amitabha Buddha and
     Sukhavati. At the age of twenty, he became a disciple of Tao-ch'o. Later he
     preached in Ch'ang-an. He was so effective in his preaching that
     subsequent Pure Land masters were often regarded as incarnations of
     Shan-tao, and his teachings spread across China and were eventually
     transmitted to Japan. Shan-tao's most significant contributions to the Pure
     Land tradition include his focus on the recitation of the nien-fo as
     sufficient practice to realize birth in Sukhavati, and his parable of the two
     deadly rivers and the narrow path. The bandits and wild animals represent
     the dangers of *samsara* and the defilements that bind people to the world.
     The river of fire is anger, and the river of water is greed. The narrow path
     is faith in the saving power of Amitabha Buddha. The voice on the near
     bank is that of Shakyamuni Buddha, the voice on the far bank is that of
     Amitabha Buddha, and the other shore is the Western Pure Land.
6   From 'First Time Round', in Gary Snyder, *Zen Retreat Diaries*. Cited in
     Aspen Magazine, 10 ('The Asia Issue').
7   *The Poetry of Han Shan*, trans. Robert Henricks (SUNY Press, 1990), No.
     67.
8   Kenneth White, *The Bird Path*, (Edinburgh: Mainstream, 1989), p.150.

A GEOGRAPHER OF THE MIND: KENNETH WHITE AS READER AND WRITER
Anne Bineau

In 'The Road and the Library', an interview given to Frédéric de Towarnicki not long after he settled in Brittany in the early 1980s, Kenneth White makes the distinction between five ways of reading: skating-reading and gobble-reading devoted respectively to newspapers and most novels; study-reading, which we do when we want to learn something; meditation-reading which entails 'texts of high specific density'; and finally illumination-reading, which he describes as 'almost a state of grace'.[1]

The fact is that Kenneth White reads like he walks and breathes, daily and constantly. 'When the removers came here with my boxes of books', he went on to say in the interview, 'they told me there were three tons of them'.

... Three tons!

By now, the weight has probably more than doubled and yet, there has never been any question with White of amassing books just for the pleasure of accumulating and collecting. White is no complacent bibliophile, he is rather what he calls a 'bibliomaniac'. What he has built up is a 'working-library', composed of several sections like so many geographical zones of a mental space in the process of exploration: various languages and literatures (Russian, Scandinavian, etc); French literature; English and American literature; India; China; Japan; Celtic nations; social sciences; exact sciences. 'What I see in this place is the confluence of several currents', he asserts, the organisation chosen allowing 'interesting conversations', and 'the joyous exercise of mental energy', conducive to the emergence of a new cultural field.

For that is indeed the aim of this poet: 'to bring together poetically various elements in a new context ',[2] 'find the coherence of scattered elements'[3] in order to propose 'a living synthesis'.[4] His wide range of reading aims to gather, wherever he finds them, elements able to contribute towards the constitution and cartography of a new cultural world. 'It's only in the bygoing I do anything like criticism', he says in another book of interviews, *Le Lieu et la Parole* (Place and Language).[5] 'I'm not out either to contribute to an established system of knowledge. I gather in elements from diverse sources and horizons. In this sense, I'm a cartographer, a cosmographer.'

1. Opening a world: on the use of quotations

What strange kind of an author is this who spends his time studding his books with quotations from the most diverse texts and authors, continually mixing his words with those of others, his thought with theirs? For some, who consider that a writer must produce texts which are the expression of his ego or the reflection of his individuality, this is the sign of a lack of personal and original thinking. For others, whose field of reference is undoubtedly more limited and their practice of quotation non-existent, it is a professional distortion (the professor who quotes his sources), if not the sign of presumptuousness, when it is not one of pedantry. Hence the many past reproaches made to Kenneth White for his, it is considered, abusive use of quotations in his books.

It goes without saying that these are fallacious interpretations, for this practice, far from being a palliative for some weakness of the ego, is symptomatic of the way in which Kenneth White sees reading: as the possibility of going beyond his person to create a new transpersonal context.

It is often and wrongly believed that writing consists of 'personal expression of the treatment of a problem'. For White, what matters on the contrary is 'the explosion and the expansion of the person' and the 'penetration into a space'.[6] This space exists outside the pervasive and much abused myth of personal genius, and beyond any preoccupation with so-called and often illusory 'originality'. What is ultimately interesting is the 'cultural network that someone can create, reveal and radiate'.[7]

White is neither naive nor megalomaniac. He knows full well that we only think because others have thought before us. Certainly, as a convinced individualist, he believes only in 'the singular and complex intelligence, the creative process in which it is involved and the fields it can open'.[8] But he is quick to add that such intelligence cannot exist alone: it needs fellow travellers to converse with in order to create a context favourable for the development of cogent thought and of an emerging field of convergence.

To explore the field of world culture in search of inspiring figures with which to dialogue – those 'explorer-writers who bring with them a new world-thesis' –,[9] and to prospect this field for elements that will become 'the humus of a new culture'[10]: this is the first aspect of the ground-work envisaged by Kenneth White in the course of his readings and which is attested to by the quotations that run through the whole of his work.

'I'm looking for a world', he explains. 'and if someone seems to me to have approached this world in an admirable way, I salute him and quote him, not content to just borrow ideas on the sly and boil them down into some homogeneous soup.'[11] This comes from a certain intellectual honesty: to recognise that one is not the inventor of everything, all by oneself. But it is also an integral part of a cultural strategy: 'When a voice is alone in the desert, it will not have much influence, but when it presents a whole current...'[12] It also involves a certain mental topology: 'like abrupt landscapes and mindspaces, with a quotation set in it like a rock in the sea.'[13]

2. Venturing into uncharted zones

This polyphonic network naturally finds its privileged form in the books of essays where Kenneth White tries to draw up a new mental and cultural cartography, by re-reading, with a view to re-working, the work of certain figures who are particularly inspiring in his eyes because of their world-views and their attempt to open, through them, a space of living and thought.

This is the second feature of the polymorphic activity of Kenneth White as reader and author, poet and researcher:

Another aspect of the basic work consists in the re-examining, the re-working of the terrain of certain figures that have been filed and classified, but which retain a highly charged energy-field way outside the times and contexts in which the history of art and literature encloses them. I'm thinking in particular of certain late-nineteenth century figures who experienced a deep crisis and who sought for 'something else'. The context being limited, their lives often entailed error and aberration, fury and folly. The names I have in mind are Nietzsche, Rimbaud, Van Gogh – later, Artaud.[14]

How in fact can we not be revolted by 'the way in which minds are defined in the manuals of literary history or in the history of ideas'?[15] Their ideas are flattened out, forced into reductive schemas, inserted into a hold-all humanism, whereas for White the context is both wider and sharper. In a general fashion, 'the tendency is to see man only facing man, and to enclose him into human language. What has been forgotten is presence in the universe'.[16] It is this presence in the world, this contact with the universe which is fundamental in White's eyes and which he finds present in all those he is interested in. Often it has been covered over by literary, artistic or philosophical history. Hence the need to 'rediscover' those figures, to re-read and re-work them, to restore them 'to their movement and their geography',[17] in order to reveal the relationships they had with the outer world, the contacts they established with space.

We are dealing less with literary or art history than with a 'geography of the mind',[18] that brings in 'social world and solitary world, human and non-human world'.[19] We are concerned with a gathering in one single timeless archipelago of minds that may be separated historically or nationally, but who remain very close mentally because they have all worked, more or less directly, for a poetic idea of the earth. 'What, among other things, a book like this can do', says White about his book on Antonin Artaud, 'is to bring together minds and energies that never met, or hardly met, in actual life, but which can come together in the space of a new integrative thinking, the whole action leading to more movement, more power'.[20]

This amounts to an indictment of a world reduced to its contemporaneity:

> *Within the contemporary context one can feel not only distance, but disgust – the desire arises to frequent individuals of all ages with whom one feels elective affinities: minds that go beyond their age and context, and who have an original relationship to the Earth, a fresh vision of the world.*[21]

If White has a notion of contemporaneity, and he does, it is of an 'absolute contemporaneity of culture' that transcends space and time.[22]

To this must be added White's firm conviction that a lot of artists or authors never reached the horizon they apprehended because of restricted conditions and, in certain cases, premature death: 'Most artists never had the living conditions that would allow them to develop their capacities to the full and thus give society the full reach of their possibilities.'[23] Instead of dismissing them as madmen, drunks or unfortunates, instead of on the contrary 'complacently delighting in their madness and sickness', the 'real work' consists in 'trying to see where they were endeavouring to get to, removing the dross in their work',[24] so that an extra step can be made along the path they were beginning to open up. 'Crocodile tears are shed about poor misunderstood poets and thinkers – but still no effort is made to understand.'[25]

It is with such ideas in mind that White invites us to revise fundamentally our received ideas about Antonin Artaud: 'Right from the start, I want Artaud to be seen, not as some kind of anomaly: a more or less interesting artist, a more or less amusing lunatic, but as a man engaged in a general revision of concepts and values.'[26] Beyond all the pathology and pathos that surrounds and covers his person, let him, says White, be considered as an 'outgoer' – someone who has always striven to evolve outside the 'closed little world' of literature; as a 'nomadic intellect' who, throughout his life-work, tried to open out, in our shattered world ('the world has become abnormal', writes Artaud), a space for life and thought; finally as an author who not only worked upon himself ('The thing is to make oneself over again'), but who constituted a body of work 'able to propose a way out of the quagmire'.[27]

For Kenneth White, it is not a case of adhering to everything said by those authors and artists he may devote an essay to. 'In general, I pick up elements of energy and light where I find them. This never implies total acquiescence or any kind of facile solidarity.'[28]

The intention is, on the one hand, to explore physical and mental territories in order to draw up a map: to follow physical and geographical paths, and to trace intellectual and spiritual journeys by identifying the lines of force in any life-work. This discovery of new mental territory constitutes a veritable intellectual adventure: 'When you're confronted by a landscape so powerfully grotesque and contorted as that of Artaud, a landscape littered with elements so darkly clear, you can't (unless you're what Artaud calls a literary pig) reduce it all to some kind of infantile pap, served up, of course, "with style". You have to take the time to go from crest to gully, from path to track.'[29]

The other intention is to find the place they wanted to reach, to open up the space towards which they obscurely moved, in order to attain it in the here and now.

In other words, the aim is to venture into zones left white on the map.

White writes about Segalen: 'The question is to know exactly what in his experience can be not only transmitted but extended beyond what he himself envisaged.'[30]

In proceeding in this way, it is his own territory that Kenneth White is working on, beginning it at those very limits where others stopped.

Here one is inevitably reminded of Arthur Rimbaud and his famous letter of 1871: 'Author, creator, poet – they've never existed [...]. Let him drop in his tracks as he moves towards unheard of things. Other horrible workers will come. They'll begin on the horizons where the others stopped!'[31]

But what then are these horizons that such inspiring figures have caught sight of without managing to reach and which constitute for Kenneth White the great work-field?

This is the moment to look at White's narrative poems.

3. Correlations and alter egos

There are two types of narrative poem in the work of Kenneth White, which take as their subject people who have truly existed. Less figures on the scene of history than inspirers of thought. These poems care little in fact for specific historical context, either because the people in question had a life-work which, in its content, scope and implications, went well beyond the historical context that was theirs, so much so that they reached a timeless dimension; or because there are such obvious analogies between their context and our own situation, that we can consider them as our contemporaries.

The first type of poem is written in the third person singular, a sign that White wants to keep his distance, even if there is an obvious identification to which I will return.

In these poems, White is less interested in history than in geography: the movement of these figures in space and their geographical situation at a particular moment in their lives. It is on this moment that the poem concentrates. For example, the moment when the monk Brandan leaves on his 'last voyage',[32] after building for himself a boat with seventeen places on which to embark, with others, on 'a peregrination in the name of God'. Or when Hölderlin, tutor in 1802 at Bordeaux, walks through the streets of the town 'in the red days of September'.[33] Then there is 'Melville at Arrowhead', when he had retreated with his family after the 'total flop' of the *Ambiguities*, turning over in his fingers a harpoon head or gazing at the faded colours of a map – that Melville who loved the days when it snowed at Arrowhead, since they 'removed any temptation / to try and go somewhere else'.[34]

What Kenneth White seeks to identify in these poems where he dramatises, on the basis of a meditation-reading of their life-work, those figures who have inspired him, is the precise moment when they catch sight of another dimension. It is the moment when a transition takes place from the purpose to which they were devoted up until then to a poetic project towards which they suddenly feel irresistibly attracted.

Thus we see Brandan turn towards poetry after having first been involved in theology, the preoccupation with a divine figure that, for him, was not only 'the great gesture', but 'a great idea sailing through space'. The transition from one to the other, sketched out quickly and subtly by White, takes place after Brandan has lived through a radical experience of the world. This new poetic ambition requires however some definition, because it is not a question of writing *any* kind of poetry, but rather a poem 'full of the rough sea and the light'. It is here that the identification between White and Brandan becomes obvious, with White making the persona of the monk a sort of alter ego in search of a new poetics, full of strength and rugged beauty, having understood that he did not belong to those 'literary folk' with 'polish and finesse'. Certainly, White makes it clear that Brandan did not advance as far as this poetic horizon he has him catch sight of. In the notes that accompany his poem in the French edition, he says this 'last voyage' is an invention by him, and that he 'reworked the character'.[35]

We find the same re-working and an analogous strategic moment with Hölderlin. While he lived in Germany, Hölderlin had become interested in Greece and had translated the ancient tragedies. But when in France, he realises that the mental landscape has changed and that it is time for him to try something else, because the ancient model no longer corresponds to the demands of the new context. The moment has therefore come for him to ask himself: 'Why be a poet in such wretched times?...' However, although White attests that he inserted in his poem words by Hölderlin dating precisely from the year 1802, and if the thoughts he attributes to him come from the same source, that is the letters that Hölderlin sent from Bordeaux, he recognises in his notes: 'I push him in a direction he himself couldn't really take.'[36]

And finally we have Melville who, stung by the lack of success of the *White Whale* and of *Mardi*, and then by the total failure of the *Ambiguities*, retires to the countryside where White depicts him smoking by the chimney, lost in his thoughts, wondering what his fellow citizens and 'parlour poets' could possibly make of white whales and unmapped archipelagos. We have White imagining Melville, after he had written metaphysical novels of an intense physicality, but misunderstood by the public, feeling that only 'the vision of some unheard of poet' could embrace the totality of what inhabits his brain.[37]

Parallel to these narrative poems written in the third person singular and dedicated to inspiring thinkers, Kenneth White has written a long poem devoted to Ovid: 'Ovid's Report', where, as is shown by the use of the first person singular, a closer identification takes place.[38]

In this long poem in the form of a testament, Ovid recounts what became of his person and his poetics after he was banned from Rome and sent into exile on the barbaric shores of the Black Sea. At the beginning, he finds it difficult to settle: abandoned, humiliated and feeling utterly isolated, after having known glory, social success and peer-recognition, his first reaction is to protest, and plead his cause in 'finely wrought discourses'. But in time, exile becomes for him like a second chance, an opportunity to explore the depths of his mind, far from the self-satisfaction that public success had procured him. A chance also to strip himself of the superficial shell that was his social persona. A chance finally to discover a world more vast and interesting than the one he could see from Rome.

The change is total.

He who, at the beginning, felt lost and bewildered 'on the cold and foggy banks' of the Scythian coast, now begins to appreciate 'the limits of the world', filling his 'expanded lungs/with a sharper air', while the Mediterranean seems from now on to be 'wearisome, polluted, overpopulated', its *dolce vita* 'insipid'. A new life opens up to him, a primal life:

> *Outside the pale*
> *rusticated once and for all*
> *I went (abstractly) native*

Now far from the all-too-human, tired of places, 'that stuffy theatre', he listens to the universe and experiments with a new presence in the world:

> *what I'm interested in now*
> *are the silent fields*
> *I feel spreading all around me*
> *the movements of the sea*
> *the star-bespattered sky*
> *the relation*
> *between a body and the universe*
> *the nebulae and a brain*

And when he takes up his pen again, after having felt, parallel to his philosophy of life, that he also had to change 'the tenor and the spirit of his writings', he discovers a new poetics.[39] A poetics in the image of the place in which he lives, a rugged area, devoid of the frippery of the civilised world, but full of a 'new roughness' and a 'new clearness':

> *I take quick notes*
> *like this:*
> winter morning light
> and a black-winged gull
> keening over the hut –
> *no more than that*
> *no metaphor-mongering*
> *no myth-malarkey*

It is this dual process, set off by exile, of transformation of the personality and of a profound transmutation of poetics which, in Ovid, captivates Kenneth White and on which he concentrates. An embodiment of the transformation of the self, of openness to the world and of the search for words to say this new presence in the world, a metaphor of the poetic process as Kenneth White sees it, the figure of Ovid occupies a special place in his work and represents the most complete example of that illumination-reading evoked at the beginning of this essay.

It remains to ask, as White himself does: 'Is this process justifiable? Has one the right to put oneself in the skin of historical figures and do with them as one likes?'[40]

Let us say firstly that if White chose the figure of Ovid both as 'alter ego' and precursor of a new concept and new poetic practice, the reasons for this identification are many. On the one hand, White invokes the situation of Ovid, a situation that has analogies with his own situation: 'Poets and poetry have been exiled for centuries in the West'. This situation is worsened still in our day by a prevailing 'mediocracy', as White calls it, bent on 'stifling any long-term work'.[41] Add to that a socio-historical context which is strangely similar to our own: 'Our society is marked more and more by the least interesting, the most degrading aspect of Roman society, *panem et circenses*.'[42] On a more personal level, White evokes his move from Pau, where he had been living for fifteen years, to Trébeurden where he settled in 1983, from the gentle, protected South-West of France to the rugged and exposed north coast of Brittany, parallel to the removal of Ovid from the mildness and luxuriance of the Roman climate to the then inhospitable shore of the Black Sea. As White writes, the Breton coast is 'strangely similar, from several points of view, to the *terra remota*, the *fera littora Ponti* (the wild shores of the Black Sea), Ovid's *ultima tellus*'.[43] Hence, in 'Ovid's Report', White takes the liberty of including 'more than one description of North Brittany'. We find evocations of 'cold and foggy banks', 'thick fog', 'the stench of swine and seaweed', gulls, stormy winds and difficult sailing conditions. One can adduce also an analogy between the political and epistemological position of Ovid at the end of his life, and that of Kenneth White: 'Ovid stands at the extreme edge of the Roman empire, at the north of the known world, also at the limits of its knowledge and competence, where annals and genealogies yield to geography and poetics.' The parallel is obvious.

Thus, when in 1983, White begins to write about Ovid, or more precisely, 'with him', it is quite natural for him, through identification with this character, to revert to the first person singular. It is also logical that he should use the work of Ovid as a 'ground for synthesis'.[44]

White, as we know, shows little taste for historical novels and fictional biographies. What interest him are documents. Nevertheless, a poem-fiction like 'Ovid's Report' has its own justification and legitimacy, so long as the fiction does not turn into a pure aberration and so long as it respects the direction followed by the character, while prolonging it. There is no flight into the imaginary, but respect for the logic and the poetics of an author. Thus, when White 'pushes Ovid beyond Ovid', that push was not only 'latent in Ovid's work at the end of his life on the shores of the Black Sea, it actually came to the fore'.[45]

Finally, a poem-fiction such as this offers the advantage of resolving the problematics of Kenneth White consequent to his rejection of 'personal poetry': how to write a poetry that is transpersonal, without making it impersonal? By identifying with a historically defined figure, White leaves his own ego, and has recourse to an ambiguous 'I', which is simultaneously 'I' and another. And by making this figure the metaphor of the poetic process as he sees it, he avoids the trap of impersonality: it is his very own vision of poetry that he presents to us. White explains: 'I'm thinking of an idea of Nietzsche's, according to which, if one wishes to have "a universal I", one must use one's predecessors as functions, establishing, via persons, beyond persons, a complex equation. This ties in with the Taoist idea according to which predecessors are to be employed as metaphors.[46]

By using the authors who preceded him as 'functions' or 'metaphors', White seeks to present 'a new anthropological type':[47] *homo poeticus*, and by using their works as a field to be re-worked, he seeks to bring out a new conception and a new poetic practice: geopoetics.

NOTES

1   *Le Poète cosmographe*, pp.115-19. Full bibliographical details may be
    found in the bibliographies at the end of this volume.
2   *Une stratégie paradoxale*, p.204.
3   *Le Lieu et la Parole*, p.93.
4   *Une stratégie paradoxale*, p.58.
5   *Le Lieu et la Parole*, p.112.
6   *Ibid.*, p.45.
7   *Le Poète cosmographe*, p.118.
8   *Une stratégie paradoxale*, p.203.
9   *Le Poète cosmographe*, p.35.
10 *Une stratégie paradoxale*, p.174.
11 *Ibid.*, p.131.

12 *Incisions III,* Winter 1981, p.77.
13 *Le Poète cosmographe,* p.131.
14 *Une stratégie paradoxale,* p.175.
15 *Le Lieu et la Parole,* p.14.
16 *Ibid.,* p.14.
17 *Ibid.,* p.14.
18 'Notes nomades', in *Déambulations dans l'espace nomade,* p.36.
19 *Le Lieu et la Parole,* p.14.
20 *Le Monde d'Antonin Artaud,* p.73.
21 *Van Gogh et Kenneth White* (Charenton: Editions Flohic, collection 'Musées secrets', 1994), p.74.
22 *La Plateau de l'Albatros,* p.127.
23 *Le Poète cosmographe,* p.176.
24 *Une stratégie paradoxale,* p.175.
25 *Le Plateau de l'Albatros,* p.27.
26 *Le Monde d'Antonin Artaud,* p.26.
27 *Ibid.,* p.156.
28 *Le Poète cosmographe,* p.106.
29 *Le Monde d'Antonin Artaud,* p.49.
30 *L'Esprit nomade,* p.222. See also *Segalen,* p.60.
31 Arthur Rimbaud, 'Lettre du Voyant', in *Œuvres complètes,* pp.270-71.
32 'Brandan's Last Voyage', in *The Bird Path: Collected Longer Poems* (Edinburgh, Mainstream, 1989), pp.188-93.
33 'Hölderlin in Bordeaux', in *ibid.,* pp.91-93.
34 'Melville at Arrowhead', in *ibid.,* pp.193-95.
35 'Quelques notes sur les poèmes', in *Atlantica,* p.221.
36 'Quelques notes sur les poèmes', in *ibid.,* p.221.
37 'Quelques notes sur les poèmes', in *ibid.,* pp.154-155: 'l'œuvre inouïe de quelque poète visionnaire'.
38 *Le Rêve d'Ovide,* with silkscreen prints by Boulay and Bracaval, *Cahiers du Pré Nian,* 7 (1986). After having been published initially under this title, the poem was then republished, with a few modifications, in *Les Rives du silence* (pp.198-211), under the title: 'Ovid's Testament' . In the Collected Poems, *Open World* (2003), it appears under the title 'Ovid's Report'.
39 'Ovide: politique, géographie, poétique', in *Le Plateau de l'Albatros,* p.136.
40 *Ibid.,* p.136.
41 *Ibid.,* p.126.
42 *Ibid.,* p.126.
43 *Ibid.,* p.126.
44 *Ibid.,* p.126.
45 *Ibid.,* p.127.
46 *Ibid.,* p.127.
47 *Une stratégie paradoxale,* p.218.

KENNETH WHITE
AND VICTOR SEGALEN
Charles Forsdick

> *As for Segalen, he is a secret companion. For a long time I*
> *have accompanied him among Polynesian islands, through the*
> *yellow lands of China, and in the forest of Huelgoat.*
> *The dialogue is ongoing, and increasingly subtle.*[1]

When, in the early 1990s, Kenneth White was briefly associated with the emergent *Pour une littérature voyageuse* movement, his work was included in the bibliography with which the group's *livre-manifeste* closes.[2] The volume's editor – unidentified, but almost certainly the Breton author, critic and cultural activist Michel Le Bris – uses this list of publications creatively, drawing together a series of texts published between 1975 and 1992 to suggest the emergence of a major post-structuralist, post-Marxist literary phenomenon in late twentieth-century France, 'une littérature qui dise le monde': i.e. a literature that no longer bracketed off external existence for the sake of textual experimentation, but one that instead rooted itself in lived experience and underlined the consubstantial links connecting world and word. White's own search for 'a world literature, with an internationalist dimension, that transcends at the same time both conventional frameworks and old national boundaries' seems to coincide with such an aspiration,[3] and his association with the nascent movement is accordingly motivated by a sense of shared objectives.

The bibliography in which White figures remains, however, a striking instance of a literary movement's self-performance, since it simultaneously delimits contemporary affiliations whilst suggesting a more complex genealogy of previous authors to which these are linked. Despite his subsequent decision to distance himself from such active involvement with the *Pour une littérature voyageuse* authors and their annual Saint Malo festival, Etonnants voyageurs, White figures prominently in the early 'manifesto', both through key works cited in the concluding 'repères historiques' (in which he is, in terms of the number of individual works included, to be seen as the movement's most prolific author) and in his contribution of one of the texts ('Petit album nomade').[4] White's inclusion is doubly striking: not only, synchronically, is his work accordingly associated with that of a number of his contemporaries prominent in the field of travel literature (such as Nicolas Bouvier, Jacques Lacarrière, Gilles Lapouge and Jacques Meunier); but also, diachronically, it is located in relation to an earlier tradition of writing travel represented by such diverse key figures as Ella Maillart, Victor Segalen and R. L Stevenson, with a number of whom White has regularly outlined his very clear elective affinities.

White's association with the *Pour une littérature voyageuse* phenomenon evidences its eclectic, catholic nature and associated efforts to avoid any sense of a 'guild' identity. Ultimately, however, it was perhaps the movement's progressive commercialization and drift towards an emphasis on conventional 'travel writing', as well as its continued tendency to define itself negatively, that led to White's steady distancing.[5] The early links reflect, nevertheless, his affiliation to and long-standing interest in a certain strand of French-language travel literature, committed not to the journalistic documentation of journeys but to an ontological and even epistemological reflection on what travel suggests about the presence of the individual in relation to the wider context of the world (and that of the word by which it is transcribed). This is the strand represented by contemporaries such as Nicolas Bouvier (1929-1998) and earlier writers such as Victor Segalen (1878-1919), with whom the present study is concerned.[6] As the extensive yet selective bibliography of texts devoted to Segalen included at the end of this article suggests, White's engagement with Segalen is a complex and extended one, now spanning four decades. He has given a series of public lectures and papers on the author,

and is a long-standing member of the Association Victor Segalen's
Comité d'Honneur.[7] Although not one of the French authors with
whom he came into contact during his early years – such as Hugo,
whose *Travailleurs de la mer* White read as an adolescent in Fairlie;
or Rimbaud, encountered while an undergraduate at the University
of Glasgow; or other members of what Norman Bissell dubs in this
volume his 'spiritual family' (e.g. Breton and Michaux), taught while
he was briefly a lecturer in the same institution – Segalen
nevertheless haunts White's work as a privileged 'outgoer', forming
the central focus of a number of key volumes and essays, or
wandering regularly and often unexpectedly across the pages of
poems or waybooks.[8]

   To cite several of Segalen's appearances in White's work: in
'The blue gates of January' (originally published as *Dérives*), a
detour to Huelgoat allows an encounter with 'Segalen, travelling
through the yellow lands, along the Blue River, into the Empire of
himself' (p.78); in *The Wanderer and his Charts*, the same author
serves as a key point of reference in White's elaboration of 'Elements
of a New Cartography';[9] and in 'The Road to Rangiroa', the
waybook of a journey in the Tuamotu archipelago, White connects
with Segalen's own travels in Polynesia a century before, comparing
his plans for a 'Fondation sinologique' with the Museum of Tahiti
(p.212), and contrasting Stevenson's response to Fakarava (where he
spent time in 1888-89) with Segalen's own reaction to the area in the
wake of a cyclone:

> *I like Stevenson well, but I'm more interested in Segalen's
> attempts to get out of human narrative entirely and really
> walk the edge. When Segalen was up here in what he called
> the Archipel des Paumotou, a place outside history, in
> January 1903, as a naval doctor aboard the* Durance, *it
> was to bring help to people whose homes had been
> devastated by a cyclone. But even in the midst of all these
> human events, he has an eye to the islands themselves, their
> topography, their topology (outside of form, deep lines of
> growth). If an island, he says, can be defined as land
> surrounded by water, an atoll, paradoxically, is water
> surrounded by land. And he describes the 'yellow line of
> coral' becoming incandescent when the sun is high. That's
> another line entirely. (p.230)*

I cite these three texts for they reflect the rare presence of Segalen in White's English-language (as opposed to French-language) publications: a fleeting presence, but one that nevertheless reveals clear evidence of his significance. Even in the present volume, however, where Segalen is only referred to explicitly (if fleetingly) on three occasions – in one of Tony McManus's footnotes, outlining White's work as an essayist; in Anne Bineau's discussion of White's uses of quotation; and in Olivier Delbard's evocation of an 'aesthetics of diversity' – the author remains latent: his self-designation is alluded to in White's self-presentation as an 'Exote de l'Ecosse', cited by John Hudson;[10] and the Segalenian terms 'exote', 'exotisme' and 'Divers' all relate to White's own preference for neologism or at least to his 'working out of a whole series of fresh terms (and ideas)' (Michael Tucker) – i.e. the search for alternatives (to 'writer', 'author' or 'poet') described in 'Grounding a World', where White comments on Spengler's notion of the 'intellectual nomad'. This relative absence of Segalen is in part associated with a lack of translations of key French-texts (three of which figure in the *Pour une littérature voyageuse* bibliography) in which Segalen plays a central role: *La Figure du Dehors* (1978), *Victor Segalen: théorie et pratique du voyage* (1979), *L'Esprit nomade* (1987), *Aux limites* (1993), *Les Finisterres de l'esprit* (1998), and *Victor Segalen et la Bretagne* (2002).[11] At the same time, however, Segalen remains a figure whose work's already restricted readership in France is further limited in the English-speaking world by his continued obscurity. Translations of his texts exist, but are not widely distributed;[12] Segalen is, moreover, associated with a certain pejorative and primarily 'Anglo-Saxon' (i.e. British and North American) understanding of 'exoticism', a term subject to systematic denigration among postcolonial critics, according to whose 'puritanical fumigation of language, terms like exotic [...] are all subject to a merciless grinding down to a single ideological edge, thereby sharply reducing the range of different contexts in which such words might retain some usefulness and some flexibility of meaning'.[13]

Whether Segalen's relative lack of Anglophone readers results from a cultural blind spot, from intellectual incompatibility, or from (an extreme case of) the time lag inevitable to the transmission of texts and ideas, what is clear is that in the same way that Kenneth White has contributed to an awareness of his work in France so he has been (and remains) instrumental in the stirrings of a similar process in the English-speaking world. The transcultural intellectual, as White quite rightly styles himself in *Aux Limites*, often operates as what the French would term a 'passeur', i.e. a smuggler who permits ideas (and the texts that freight them) to travel beyond the cultural and linguistic contexts to which they are often tied. This article may accordingly be seen as a case study of White's role in the 'travels' of the work of Victor Segalen, and more particularly in the exploration of the aesthetics of diversity with which Segalen's writings are underpinned. It aims, however, to illustrate a more complex process whereby White has drawn Segalen into a sustained and prolonged dialogue: the latter has clearly contributed to the former's transcontextual reflection (along with Francophone thinkers as diverse as Edgar Morin and Édouard Glissant)[14] on global complexity, and his subsequent elaboration of a working model of geopoetics;[15] but White's engagement with the figure he dubs in *Aux Limites* his 'neighbour', in *Le Lieu et la Parole* a 'secret companion' (p.32), in *Les Finisterres de l'esprit* a 'constant interlocutor' (p.9) or in 'Lettre de la montagne' 'my neighbour and travelling companion' (p.27) has also served to illuminate further Segalen's own early twentieth-century attempt to grapple with cultural diversity and to present a non-systematic system whereby it may be understood, represented – and accordingly preserved. Segalen's reflections on entropy, present in particular in the fragments of his *Essai sur l'exotisme*, for instance seem to underpin White's conclusions to 'Petit album nomade' relating to the implications of globalization:

> *Today, for the first time in the history of humanity, the wind sweeps across all the planet's regions at once, and everybody has access to all the world's cultures. This situation may lead to a cacophony, or to disarray, a sheer weariness when one is faced with such an accumulation of riches, but it might also lead – thanks to a labour of analysis and synthesis, thanks also to the contribution of new knowledge and new thought – to a great world-poem, open to all.* (pp.195-96)

For Olivier Delbard, Segalen's role in White's work is a culminating one, for his repeated evocation is taken to represent: 'a culminating point in White's research carried out at the limits of European modernity'.[16] The essay-books and way-books are, of course, haunted by a whole series of authors and thinkers with whose writings his work represents a sustained engagement. A number of these – such as Bashō – have a substantial reputation and consequent transcultural valency as a result of which most readers will be familiar with the relevant material to which White refers; such, however, is his ease in shifting between cultures – and in particular in straddling the divide between Britain and France – that certain points of reference familiar in one context may be less recognizable in another: White himself admits, for instance, that one of his principal interlocutors, Hugh MacDiarmid, is largely unknown to a French-speaking audience. The case of Victor Segalen is another clear illustration of this, for whereas this author's work has in France attracted increasing attention over the past five decades – a process triggered, in part at least, by the publication of his three major works, *Stèles*, *Peintures* and *Equipée*, by the Club du Meilleur Livre in 1955 – there has been no evidence of any such emergence of a readership in Britain, despite (as I have commented above) the availability of a number of works in English translation. Even in France, with the appearance of the author's *Complete Works* in an accessible two-volume paperback edition in 1995, a prominent exhibition at the Bibliothèque nationale in 1999 and the inclusion of *Stèles* and *Equipée* on the syllabus for the *agrégration* (the high-level competitive examination for teacher recruitment) in the same year, Segalen has retained the reputation of being a 'difficult' author whose texts are characterised by what Michel Le Bris has dubbed a 'refusal of the reader'.[17] As a result, Segalen has become an author associated in the general (if not popular) imagination with a hazy and primarily poetic notion of Orientalism or exoticism, but whose works have not yet attracted the wider readership that they would seem to merit.[18]

Given Kenneth White's own connections to Brittany, the Breton aspects of Victor Segalen's life and work are given prominence in White's treatment of the author. Central to these Celtic dimensions are the details of Segalen's premature death in the forest of Huelgoat in 1919, an event on which White himself focuses in a number of texts, including *Victor Segalen et la Bretagne* and 'Season's End at Huelgoat'. Segalen's death, the enigmatic circumstances and almost certain stage-management of which have been discussed elsewhere,[19] triggered a process of mythologization of the author which continues today. As such, a detailed reception history of Segalen, along the lines of Etiemble's multi-volume *Mythe de Rimbaud* (in which Segalen himself appears, as the author of 'Le Double Rimbaud'), would reveal the ways in which the various exegetes involved in this mythologization have 'instrumentalized' in their own intellectual projects Segalen's often secret purposes: to cite only some of the most recent examples, Xavier Grall has posited an anti-colonial 'Breton' Segalen, Jean Baudrillard has presented a 'postmodern' Segalen, Patrick Chamoiseau, Edouard Glissant and Abdelkebir Khatibi a 'postcolonial' Segalen, Francis Affergan, James Clifford and Jean Jamin an 'ethnographic' Segalen sensitive to the instability of identity in intercultural encounters, Tzvetan Todorov an 'ethical' Segalen central to French reflection on human diversity. In any such catalogue, a 'geopoetic' Segalen would play a key role, but although White is undeniably drawn into these processes, any involvement in them is tempered by an awareness of what he dismisses as a 'a pocket-size Segalen, reduced to the dimensions of distinct aspects ('difference', 'hybridity', etc.)' ('Aux limites de la littérature', p.28) – an awareness he complements with a detailed engagement with the whole of Segalen's work, including (and, at times, especially) those texts such as *Thibet* and *Odes* that often defy critical attention. Moreover, White counters any short-term instrumentalization by stressing 'the topicality of his untopicality' ('Un Celte en Asie', p.188), a paradoxical urgency linked to the sense of Segalen's work being permanently out of time and out of place.

　　　Kenneth White's initial engagement with the Brest-born poet, novelist, dramatist, librettist, essayist, archaeologist, travel-writer, musicologist, museologist, art historian, theorist of the exotic and (since he was obliged to earn a living) naval doctor dates back to the 1970s, the decade at the beginning of which his first publication on Segalen appeared.[20] French awareness of Segalen at that time remained patchy, with (until the late 1960s) most of the author's key works either difficult to find, out-of-print or as yet unpublished in an accessible form. The bibliography of White's *Victor Segalen: théorie et pratique du voyage* reveals the unevenness of this availability. Of the texts published during the author's life time, the Polynesian ethnographic novel *Les Immémoriaux* was still available in a 1966 10/18 paperback edition, and the prose poetry collections *Peintures* and *Stèles* (supplemented by the travel narrative *Equipée*) had been made available by Plon in 1970 in a re-edition on the important 1955 Club du Meilleur Livre version of those three works. (As with any generic labels applied to Segalen's work, those used in this sentence remain profoundly inadequate.) A definitive edition of the Chinese novel *René Leys* appeared with Gallimard in 1971, followed the next year by a Flammarion version of *Chine: la grande statuaire*, edited by the author's daughter, Annie Joly-Segalen, and a critical edition of *Thibet* (Mercure de France, 1979). In addition, two small presses committed to the dissemination of Segalen's work produced editions of a series of texts considered more minor: *Imaginaires* (Rougerie, 1972), *Siddhartha* (Rougerie, 1974), *Briques et tuiles* (Fata Morgana, 1975), *Gauguin dans son dernier décor et autres textes de Tahiti* (Fata Morgana, 1975), *Essai sur l'exotisme* (Fata Morgana, 1978), and *Le Double Rimbaud* (Fata Morgana, 1979). This flurry of scattered publishing activity (reaching a peak around the centenary of the author's death in 1979) triggered a process of interpretation, rendered all the more necessary as a result of the tendency of Henry Bouillier's monumental doctoral thesis on Segalen, presenting the author primarily as a post-symbolist figure and published for the first time by the Mercure de France in 1961, to eclipse all pre-1970s scholarship.

White was central to these processes of exegetical reorientation, and is to be seen as a result as a key figure in Segalenian scholarship over the past thirty years. Besides granting Segalen a spectral role in one of the waybooks constituting *Dérives* (1978), the English translation of which has already been cited above, and contributing articles to *Les Nouvelles littéraires* (1979) and *Le Monde* (1980), he includes a chapter on Segalen (first published in *La Figure du Dehors*) in *Regard, Espaces, Signes* (1979), the proceedings of the centenary conference held at the Musée Guimet, and in the same year produces the influential *Victor Segalen: théorie et pratique du voyage*. Just as Segalen, whose work is peopled by doubles (either figurative or clinically autoscopic), elected a restricted series of figures – in particular Rimbaud and Gauguin – to whom, in his 'journey to the depths of the self', he is continually drawn, so at times White seems to be associated with Segalen according to the ties that connect *alter egos*. Segalen and White are brought together by a series of coincidental connections and shared concerns.[21] Both figures, in reflecting closely on their own names, reveal an interest (part ludic, part serious) in onomastics;[22] the relationship of each to his respective culture of origin seems to be characterized by an initially chronic extroversion, tempered subsequently by a degree of reconnection. It is, however, in literary and intellectual practice that these ties are most striking. Writing of Segalen's engagement with Rimbaud, White claims: 'As ever in poet-to-poet readings of this type, Segalen is lining up there elements of the poetics he wants to practise himself' ('The Voice of the Desert', p.154), and White's engagement and continued re-engagements with Segalen accordingly coincide, as Jean-Yves Kerguelen has made clear,[23] with some of the major developments in his trajectory: early references to this 'Celte en Asie' occur in White's first text on Brittany, *Dérives*, in a fragment first published in *Les Nouvelles littéraires* in 1970; Segalen plays a role in the 'East-West' seminar at Paris VII in the 1970s, as well as in the 'World Poetics' seminars at the Sorbonne from which the coherent expression of geopoetics emerged during the following decade; and Segalen's work feeds creatively into White's elaboration of both the 'waybook' and the 'essay-book' (of which more below).

The relationship is not, however, as I have already suggested above, a straightforward one of influence or critical instrumentalization: defying chronology, it is more creatively reciprocal, symbiotic, even synergist. White himself, in giving *Les Finisterres de l'esprit* the provocative and apparently presumptuous subtitle *Rimbaud, Segalen et moi-même*, clearly suggests an intellectual continuity that is revealed in his own engagement with the Segalenian project, an engagement described in Kerguelen's terms as 'a task that is simultaneously one of understanding, extension and projection' (p.35). White presents Segalen's *oeuvre*, therefore, as fundamentally *incomplète*; commenting on the ontological dimensions of the Chinese cycle of his work, he states, in terms reminiscent of Segalen himself:

> *Let's try to move forward a little into this area – without forgetting Segalen who, dying aged forty, in his prime,*

reached its boundaries, without entering it entirely, although we can be almost entirely certain that he would otherwise not have failed to do so. (Victor Segalen: théorie et pratique du voyage, *p.58)*

White later claims: 'I have questioned Segalen a little in the same way as Segalen questioned Rimbaud' (*Les Finisterres de l'esprit*, p.10), and it is as if his aim is accordingly to work through the enigmatic, unfinished elements of his predecessor's writings.[24] This is particularly clear in relation to Segalen's death, already mentioned above, on which White remains one of the most original commentators. In 'Season's End at Huelgoat', he states: 'This site in the forest of Huelgoat marks the end of a life devoted to a radical kind of poetic research' (p.198), but in a Whitean sense, this end or limit is to be read not so much as a conclusion as a potentially new beginning.[25] Refusing speculation on biography or nosology – 'I am not going to dwell on the 'mystery', still less attempt a diagnosis of Segalen's physical state at the end of his life' – he devotes himself instead to a reflection on 'the questions he was asking himself at that time, the projects he was contemplating', using the detail of the copy of *Hamlet* found by the author's corpse to tease out any such projects' ontological dimensions (*Les Finisterres de l'esprit*, pp.61-65). At times, prolongation even verges on correction, especially in the reading of Segalen's 'Le Double Rimbaud', in which White challenges Segalen's dismissal of the poet's (largely imagined) Abyssinian writings as evidence of his having 'gone off the track, lost his way', and sees them instead as the 'opening up of a new field of poetics, [...] a first outline of geopoetics' ('The Voice of the Desert', pp.155-56).

Segalen's initial impact is undeniably formal, although it will be demonstrated below that in both Segalen and White ideas and the forms in which they are articulated are intimately related. *Victor Segalen: théorie et pratique du voyage* is itself, for instance, a profoundly Segalenian text, with the fragmentation of its argument, both by quotation and more markedly by a proliferation of 307 footnotes, suggesting the baroque working practices of Segalen himself, seen in particular in the unfinished, unfinishable *Essai sur l'exotisme*. White compares his own text to the 'land of loess, covered with fissures and abysses' (p.7), suggesting that it is not for lovers of 'boulevards', but has been produced instead for those drawn to 'furrowed, uneven paths'.²⁶ These comments from the 1979 'avertissement' are echoed and developed in White's more recent reflection on the 'strangeness' of the French essay tradition in *The Wanderer and his Charts*:

> *It means in the first place leaving the harbour of fixed identity in order to plunge into the floating life, following the transformations of the self and the meanderings of thought. It implies also abandoning established genres. The essayist is out on his own, working in the open. Knowing very well that the last word will never be pronounced, maintaining a distance both from dogmatic totality and the detailed report, he makes attempts, essays, he tries out ways, he takes soundings.* ('Aquitanian Affinities', *p.58*)

The *essai*, as Montaigne developed it and as subsequent authors such as Segalen and White have adapted it to their own purposes, is not then a generic structure, but the reflection of an epistemological stance (or, in White's terms, of a 'topographie mentale' [mental topography]).²⁷

This abandonment of established genres is epitomized by *Equipée*, the generic instability (or rather its defiance of categorization) of which suggests that White's own distinction between 'waybook' and 'essay-book' is perhaps ultimately borne of taxonomic necessity rather than as a result of any prescriptive characteristics. *Equipée*, a text whose importance to White is reflected in the fact that it is the only one of Segalen's texts of which he has presented an edition, suggests that these two forms may co-exist interdependently.²⁸ That the first publications on Segalen coincide with initial experimentation with the form dubbed the 'waybook' or 'poetic roadbook' (in French, 'livre de voyance' or 'voyage-voyance') suggests nevertheless a tangible impact of texts such as *Equipée* on White's conception of the literary forms appropriate for the articulation of his travel and thought. Segalen's experimental Chinese journey narrative, a synthesis of at least two itineraries in which specific sites are absent and where chronology is reduced (like the text itself) to an accumulation of *étapes*, may be read as a precursory exemplum – a 'sino-topicologico-geopoetic journey' ('Aux limites de la littérature', p.20) – of the waybook, the form White develops increasingly as his own. Reflecting the description of the genre outlined in 'Writing the Road', *Equipée* combines 'inner and outer landscape, geography and intellectual space, topography and the imagination' (p.108). Philosophical reflection on the relationship of the imaginary and the real is not in the text juxtaposed with an experiential, sensory, at times almost phenomenological sensitivity to the rigours of travel; instead, these two aspects, defying any idealist or sensual separation, are forced to co-exist.[29]

It is this double aspect of Segalen – seen as an 'outgoer' or 'nomadic subject', i.e. not a social person but 'an intention and a trajectory' –,[30] encapsulated in the very poetics of *Equipée*, to which White is drawn. In White's terms, Segalen is both 'a lover of the most immediate reality' (an aspect highlighted in writings on the author's Polynesian cycle) and 'an enthusiast of the imaginary', in short 'a concrete being allied to an exacting mind' ('Voyage au pays du réel', pp.77, 79). In the tensions of this identification, *Equipée*'s point of departure and final destination – the 'room of porcelain' – plays an essential role. On the one hand, as White suggests in *Victor Segalen: théorie et pratique du voyage* (p.28), it represents the artist's brain; on the other, it belongs to a series of privileged 'workplaces' or sites of reflection – a Taoist hermitage in the mountains, Montaigne's tower near Bergerac, Thoreau's cabin at Walden, Nietzsche's inn at Sils-Maria, Spinoza's workshop at Rhynnsburg – that in White's work are complemented by the Pyrenean study in Pau and subsequently the Far-West 'cosmopoetic laboratory' at Gwenved in Trébeurden, the Breton 'House of Tides'.[31] Other similar interior spaces exist – Mallarmé's silent study, Villiers de L'Isle-Adam's 'palace of dreams', Huysmans's 'cabinet Des Esseintes' – but their Symbolist overtones and idealist enclosure divorce them from any exterior connection.[32] The 'room of porcelain', like White's own library-cum-scriptorium-cum-observatory, is hermitic but not hermetic, a place of withdrawal whose existence is justified by the sorties into the tangible, palpable outside world it permits. In *Equipée*, the obverse of the narrator's 'hard and glistening palace where the Imaginary thrives' (p.42) are the 'zones left blank' (p.45), those white spaces alluded to by White in the epigraph of 'La route transhumaine', where the traveller negotiates an encounter with the 'réel'.[33] This engagement with the 'physico-mental landscape' is seen in the early texts devoted to Segalen in erotic terms, with the dimensions of travel illustrated by the epiphanic meeting of Segalen's narrator with the 'indigenous girl' and the exchange of gazes in which this culminates.[34] What is presented initially as 'erotocosmology' comes to form the basis of a geopoetic understanding of the traveller's presence in the world, 'the search for a site (*topos*), words (*logos*), and a moment where these two coincide perfectly' (p.34).[35]

Although White pays attention throughout his writings to the two principal cultures by which much of Segalen's work was triggered – Polynesia and China – these are invariably related to Brittany, the site of birth and death, of departure and arrival. A brief consideration of what White dubs the 'latent Breton-ness' of Segalen's work (*Victor Segalen et la Bretagne*, p.22), a recurrent concern since the early texts such as 'Un Celte en Asie', will serve as a conclusion to the present reflection. According to White: 'It was by travelling elsewhere that Segalen reached the depths of his own self and a consciousness of the connections he had lost', and a similar point might be made about White's own reconnection with Scottish culture.[36] This focus on Brittany is not surprising, for White himself has now lived in the Côtes d'Armor, a place where for him *topos* would seem to have coincided with *logos*, for over two decades. The 'Breton' Segalen, popularized by cultural activists such as Xavier Grall, is not, however, one that interests White.[37] Indeed, when asked about Grall during a 1980s television interview, he stated – much to the chagrin of at least one Grall partisan – that 'if you want to cite a modern Breton oeuvre of considerable stature, you would have to mention Victor Segalen's itinerary'.[38] In *House of Tides*, White counters what he dubs 'localist couthiness' (p.5) and the mummification or folklorization of local cultures associated with 'the ethno-boys' (p.189); his engagement with Segalen's *celtitude* or *bretonnitude* reveals an alternative attitude to place, Glissantian in its emphasis on openness and interconnection – an attitude that reflects 'locality without localism' (*Aux Limites*, p.1). This formula, emerging in many ways from a close reading of Segalen's entirely unfinished and largely imaginary Breton cycle of works, encapsulates an approach to place central to any mature formulation of White's geopoetics. Segalen's relationship to his native Brittany reveals not a pancelticism but an intellectual nomadism. As such, it contributes to White's reflection on the local and the global, suggesting a model that transcends the entropic dimensions of customary exoticizing manoeuvres whilst at the same time presenting new configurations of place, language and self.

NOTES

1   Kenneth White, *Le Lieu et la Parole: entretiens 1987-1997* (Cléguer: Editions du Scorff, 1997), p.32. References to White's texts specifically devoted to Segalen are incorporated in the text. Full bibliographical details of these items are included at the end of this article.

2   *Pour une littérature voyageuse* (Brussels: Complexe, 1992). For a more detailed discussion of the movement, see my 'Pour une littérature qui dise le monde', *Association for the Study of Caribbean and African Literature in French Bulletin*, 19 (1999), 30-33, and '*Fin de Siècle, Fin des Voyages*: Michel Le Bris and contemporary travel writing in French', in Michael Bishop and Christopher Elson (eds), *French Prose in 2000* (Amsterdam: Rodopi, 2002), pp.47-55. The term 'movement' is potentially erroneous, for it suggests a coherence to which the authors linked to *Pour une littérature voyageuse* have never pretended. They are more accurately a heterogeneous grouping with cognate interests and some shared concerns. I retain 'movement', however, for ease of reference. White seems to signal an ironic awareness of the tendency of literary 'movements' to be anything but dynamic or mobile when, in 'Petit album nomade', he calls for 'a movement which would be like an initiation into stepping "outside"'. See *Pour une littérature voyageuse*, pp.167-96 (p.176).

3   'Petit album nomade', p.182. White's aim, however, is to '*redire le monde*' [*re*articulate the world] (*Le Lieu et la Parole*, p.62; my emphasis), the prefix here appearing to challenge the claims to primacy of Le Bris's 'littérature qui dise le monde' and accepting that travel is inevitably a process of connection with the past and with previous travellers, of echo and quotation. I would accordingly attenuate Jean-Didier Urbain's critical conflation of White and Le Bris in 'Les Catanautes des cryptocombes - des iconoclastes de l'ailleurs', *Nottingham French Studies*, 39.1 (2000), pp.7-16).

4   The bibliography includes: *Les Limbes incandescents, Dérives, Segalen: théorie et pratique du voyage, Lettres de Gourgounel, En toute candeur, Le Visage du Vent d'Est, La Figure du dehors, La Route bleue*, and

L'Esprit nomade. These compare to, for instance, three texts by Nicolas Bouvier, four by Jacques Lacarrière, five by Michel Le Bris, and three by Jacques Meunier. White also contributed to the movement's relatively short-lived journal, *Gulliver*. See 'Le clodo de Hokkaïdo', *Gulliver*, 2-3 (1990), pp.253-61.

5   In 'Petit album nomade', White warns for instance against a genre constituted of 'documentaries [...] written with flat feet' (pp.179-80).

6   For previous attention to the links between White and Segalen, see Pierre Jamet, *Le Local et le Global dans l'oeuvre de Kenneth White: Monachos et Cosmos* (Paris: L'Harmattan, 2002), p.240, and Olivier Delbard, *Les Lieux de Victor Segalen: paysage, pensée, poétique* (Paris: L'Harmattan, 1999), pp.191-93. The connections between Segalen and Bouvier have been explored by Jean-François Guennoc in 'Victor Segalen et Nicolas Bouvier: prolégomènes à une étude comparative', *ATALA*, 7 (2004), available at http://cru.chateau.free.fr/Guennoc.htm. When read in relation to the present study, Guennoc's article suggests the need for triangulation and the preparation of a third piece, on White and Bouvier. Bouvier, as well as borrowing the opening epigraph of *Le Poisson-scorpion* from White, includes a letter to him in *L'Echappée belle: éloge de quelques pérégrins* (Geneva: Metropolis, 2000), pp.141-47; and White contributed a text entitled 'Lettre de la montagne' (pp.25-28) to a posthumous collections of essays, *Le Vent des routes: hommages à Nicolas Bouvier* (Geneva: Zoé, 1998), in which he claims that the pair are linked by 'a love of the Earth, a delight in wandering' (p.26).

7   A selective list of conference papers, lectures and radio broadcasts is provided in *L'Itinéraire de Kenneth White* (Rennes: Bibliothèque municipale de Rennes, 1990), pp.52-55, including 'Celtisme et Orientalisme' (Paris, 1978), 'L'esprit marin: la mer, le voyage, l'exotisme, Segalen' (*Les Nuits magnétiques*, France-Culture, 1986), 'Stevenson, Segalen et autres voyageurs de l'esprit' (Vannes, 1987), and 'À la recherche d'un récit immémorial: sur Victor Segalen' (Brest, 1990).

8   The spectral imagery of Segalen's haunting presence recalls Rimbaud's status as a 'spectre' in Segalen's own work, discussed by White in the opening paragraphs of 'The Voice of the Desert' (pp.143-44). He refers in particular to a manuscript fragment drafted in Aden on 16 May 1909.

9   See 'Elements of a New Cartography', in *The Wanderer and his Charts* (Edinburgh: Polygon, 2004), pp.149-66 (pp.161-62).

10   See *Isolario: les îles de la grande solitude* (Paris: Alternatives, 2002), p.35. The 'exote' is Segalen's term for a 'voyageur-né' [born traveller], sensitive to the world's diversity despite its apparent decline. In calling him a 'wanderer-on-the-alert-at-the-heart-of-things', Nicolas Bouvier suggests that White has qualities associated with this Segalenian figure (*L'Echappée belle*, p.146).

11   On the unavailability in English translation of these key 'essay-books', see Norman Bissell's interview with White for *Open World* magazine,

reproduced as 'A new energy-field', in *Coast to Coast: Interviews and Conversations 1985-1995* (Glasgow: Open World in association with Mythic Horse Press, 1996), pp.103-16 (p.116). At least two of White's essayistic texts on Segalen are available in English: 'Segalen and Rimbaud' (2000), a translation of the final section of *Les Finisterres de l'esprit*, and 'Season's End at Huelgoat', in *House of Tides: Letters from Brittany and other lands of the West* (2000).

12   See, for instance, *The Great Statuary of China*, trans. Eleanor Levieux (Chicago and London: Chicago University Press, 1978), *Essay on Exoticism: An Aesthetics of Diversity*, trans. and ed. Yaël Rachel Schlick (Durham and London: Duke University Press, 2002), *A Lapse of Memory*, trans. Rosemary Arnoux (Brisbane: Boombana Publications, 1995), *Paintings*, trans. Andrew Harvey and Iain Watson (London: Quartet, 1991), *Stèles*, trans. by Andrew Harvey and Iain Watson (London: Jonathan Cape, 1990), and *René Leys*, trans. J. A. Underwood (London: Quartet, 1990). *Equipée*, one of White's key points of reference, has not yet appeared in English translation.

13   See Ron Shapiro, 'In Defence of Exoticism: Rescuing the Literary Imagination', in Isabel Santaolalla (ed.), *'New' Exoticisms: Changing Patterns in the Construction of Otherness* (Amsterdam: Rodopi, 2000), pp. 41-49 (p. 43). Segalen is notably included by Said in his catalogues of 'Orientalists'. On this subject, see my 'Edward Said, Victor Segalen and the implications of post-colonial theory', *Journal of the Institute of Romance Studies*, 5 (1997), 323-39. It is significant that White sees in Segalen's work not *orientalisme* but *orientation*, i.e. a break with Western exoticizing traditions and notions of an East-West binary ('Un Celte en Asie', p.189).

14   Although connections between White and the Martiniquan postcolonial essayist, poet, novelist and theorist Glissant are rarely cited, White was awarded in June 2004 the Prix Édouard Glissant for 'his openness to the cultures of the world'; White himself cites Morin's multi-volume work *La Méthode* in a number of essays, including *Une apocalypse tranquille*. It is significant that a text by Glissant, 'Naître au monde', is included in the geopoetic journal, *Carnets de route* (Editions de l'Atelier du Héron), 9 (1997).

15   See *Le Lieu et la Parole*, p.31.

16   See Olivier Delbard, *Les Lieux de Kenneth White*, p.193.

17   Michel Le Bris, 'Présentation', in *Victor Segalen, Voyages au pays du réel: oeuvres completes* (Brussels: Complexe, 1995), pp.7-27.

18   On Segalen's reception – both posthumous and 'post-posthumous' – see John Pilling, 'Meditations on the Exote: Victor Segalen', *PN Review*, 30.2 (2003), 54-56.

19   See Charles Forsdick, *Victor Segalen and the Aesthetics of Diversity: Journeys between Cultures* (Oxford: Oxford University Press, 2000), pp.2-8, André Lebois, 'Agonie et mort de Victor Segalen (d'après les carnets

inédits de Jeanne Perdriel-Vaissière)', *Le Thyrse*, 67 (1965), 551-62, and Dominique Mabin, 'La mort de Victor Segalen', *Victor Segalen, Cahiers de l'Herne* (Paris: L'Herne, 1998), pp.121-44.

20   In his preface to *Equipée*, 'Aux limites de la littérature', White writes: 'I am speaking of another type of writing, of another order of writers: that of intellectual travellers, pilgrims of the void. When I happened upon Segalen's work (thirty years ago now) for the first time, I saw instantly that I was dealing not only with a first-class writer, but also with a writer who belonged to that class' (p.18). The first version of 'Les portes bleues de janvier', published in 1970, suggests by its quotation from Pierre-Jean Jouve's preface to *Stèles, Peintures, Equipée* (a volume republished by Plon in 1970) that it is through this edition that White first engaged with Segalen's work.

21   Olivier Delbard, who recognizes in Segalen 'the most outstanding, the most comprehensive, the most private figure, constituting, what is more, one of the main strands of his research', outlines a number of these parallels: 'Celtic roots, a liking for travel, a fundamental 'attraction' to the Orient, great intellectual, spiritual and artistic rigour' (*Les Lieux de Kenneth White*, p.191).

22   In *Victor Segalen et la Bretagne*, White cautiously describes this tendency to 'lier un nom de famille à une tendance de l'esprit' [linking a surname to an intellectual tendency] (p.9).

23   See Jean-Yves Kerguelen, *Kenneth White et la Bretagne*: 'tout en cheminant avec son compagnon de route, White dessine son propre champ' [while walking alongside his travelling companion, White sketches out his own field] (p.34). White makes clear the evolution of his engagement with Segalen by presenting *Les Finisterres de l'esprit* as a supplement to 'Sur la route transhumaine' (*Les Finisterres de l'esprit*, p.10). This sense of two parallel, yet complementary trajectories emerges from White's very first text on Segalen, the 1970 prose sequence in *Les Lettres nouvelles*, where (in a passage subsequently edited in *Dérives*, the English translation of which has already been cited above) he describes: 'Segalen, travelling through the yellow lands, along the Blue River, into the Empire of himself... And K.W., seeking – but not seeking too much – the White World' (p.68; emphasis in the original).

24   White writes, for instance, in relation to Segalen's unfinished manuscript dossier *Les Hors-la-Loi*: 'Owing to lack of time, Segalen did not complete this book as, for the same reason, he did not complete so many others he had in mind or might, in due course, have conceived. If he had, I might not be writing this essay on mine' ('The Voice of the Desert', p.151). This heuristic engagement or cumulative approach, dependent on subtle distinction, careful challenge and the organic development of new ideas, attenuates James Kelman's comments on what he sees as White's systematic 'finding a like-mind in whomsoever he pleases'. See 'There is a

First-Order Radical Thinker of European Standing Such That He Exists: or, Tantalising Twinkles', in *'And the Judges Said...': Essays* (London: Vintage, 2003), pp.187-93.

25   See White's comments in *Les Finisterres de l'esprit*: "limit' doesn't only mean the place where something finishes, but also the place where something begins' (p.45).

26   The relationship between landscape and literary form resurfaces in White's comments on the geological formations near the place of Segalen's death: 'There are boulders scattered throughout the forest of Huelgoat, huge moss-covered lumps, and sometimes split, the way granite often splits [...]. [T]he ground term, the operative term is *chaos*. It's in that sense of chaos that the poetry lies, and it's geological poetry' ('Season's End at Huelgoat', p.196).

27   I use *essai* in contrast to the English-language 'essay', a form that (in White's terms) 'rarely go[es] beyond charming chit-chat and impressionistic rambling'. See 'Aquitanian Affinities', in *The Wanderer and his Charts*, pp.47-58 (p.58). On the competing French and British traditions of the essay, see Peter France, 'British and French Traditions of the Essay', in Charles Forsdick and Andrew Stafford (eds.), *The Modern Francophone Essay: sociology, genre, écriture* (Bern: Peter Lang Publishing) [forthcoming].

28   On this generic instability, see my article 'Les enjeux génériques chez Victor Segalen: le cas d'*Équipée*', *Cahiers de l'Association Victor Segalen*, 6 (2000), 117-28.

29   On the mutual dependency of the 'real' and the 'imaginary', see 'Sur la route des stèles: Victor Segalen dans les profondeurs de la Chine, 1909 et 1914': 'Without the charge of the real, the imaginary is weakened, becomes a hollow fantasy; without the force of the imaginary, the real becomes stodgy and loses its impact' (p.268). This co-existence is encapsulated in the title of Nicolas Bouvier's one poetry collection, *Le Dehors et le Dedans* (Geneva: Zoé, 1986).

30   Kenneth White, *Geopoetics: Place, Culture, World* (Glasgow: Alba Editions, 2003), p.13.

31   For a discussion of these sites, see *House of Tides*, p.45, and *The Wanderer and his Charts*, p.47.

32   See *Les Finisterres de l'esprit*, pp.15-16.

33   See *Équipée*, pp.42, 45. The epigraph of 'La route transhumaine' (p.182) is taken from the text's fourth étape: 'Every question and all uncertainty are carried to an extreme when, abandoning the mapped areas [...] we venture into the zones left blank'.

34   The relationship between the feminine figure and the 'pays du réel' is analysed by Olivier Delbard, *Les Lieux de Kenneth White*, p.67. The meeting with the 'fille aborigène' is cited and discussed in both *Victor Segalen: théorie et pratique du voyage*, pp.32-33, and *Les Finisterres de l'esprit*, pp.33-34.

35 The shift I am suggesting can be detected in the re-editing of the initial version of this text, published in 'À la recherche d'un récit immémorial': 'the search for a site (*topos*), words (*logos*), and a moment (*often presented in terms of sexual intercourse*) *where self and world* might coincide perfectly' (p.23; my emphasis).

36 *Le Poète cosmographe*, p.152; cited by Olivier Delbard, *Les Lieux de Kenneth White*, p.192.

37 The notion of a 'Breton' Segalen was perhaps first suggested by Yves Gestin in his *Finistériens de marque* (Quimper: Ménez, 1956), pp.159-63; it has been developed by other Breton cultural activists such as Per-Jakez Helias in 'Un grand aventurier breton: Victor Ségalen', *Midi à ma porte* (Ouest-France, 1988), pp.284-91, and has been given a more attentuated, 'postcolonial' emphasis by Marc Gontard, for whom Segalen is central to any understanding of a distinctively Breton 'Francophone literature'. See, for example, 'Passion de l'autre, mal de soi: Segalen et Robin', *Plurial* 8 (1999), 9-11.

38 See Jean-Yves Kerguelen, *Kenneth White et la Bretagne*, pp.7-8.

Kenneth White on Victor Segalen: Selected Writings

'Un Celte en Asie', in *La Figure du Dehors* (Paris: Livre de Poche, 1989), pp.187-98. [First published by Grasset, 1978.]

'Les portes bleues de janvier', in *Dérives* (Paris: Les Lettres Nouvelles; Maurice Nadeau, 1978), pp.91-106). [First published, in a slightly different version, in *Les Lettres Nouvelles*, May-June 1970, pp.57-70.]

'À la recherche du soleil', *Les Nouvelles littéraires*, n°2671, 25 January 1979, p.18.

'Celtisme et Orientalisme', in *Regard, Espaces, Signes* (Paris: L'Asiathèque, 1979), pp.211-21. [Republished version of 'Un Celte en Asie'.]

Victor Segalen: théorie et pratique du voyage (Lausanne: Alfred Eibel, 1979).

'La Chine intérieure de Segalen', *Le Monde*, 13 June 1980.

'Voyage au pays du réel', in *Une apocalypse tranquille* (Paris: Grasset, 1985), pp.77-79. [Republication of 'La Chine intérieure de Segalen'.]

'La route transhumaine', in *L'Esprit nomade* (Paris: Grasset, 1987), pp.182-228. [Republished version of *Victor Segalen: théorie et pratique du voyage*.]

'The blue gates of January', in *Travels in the Drifting Dawn* (Edinburgh: Mainstream, 1989), pp.68-79. [First published in *Dérives*, 1979.]

'À la recherche d'un récit immémorial', *Cahiers du Cerf*, 20.6 (1990), 7-26. [Special issue entitled *Légendaire et mythe dans le roman contemporain*.]

'Mon voisin, Segalen', in *Aux limites* (Paris: La TILV, 1993), pp.13-36. [Republication of 'À la recherche d'un récit immémorial'.]

'Les Finisterres de l'esprit', in Jean Balcou and Yves Leroy (eds.), *Victor Segalen: Actes du Colloque de Brest* (Brest: Centre de Recherche Bretonne et Celtique; Le Quartz, 1995), pp.203-13.

Les Finisterres de l'esprit (Cléguer: Editions du Scorff, 1998). [Contains three essays: 'L'itinéraire de Victor Segalen' was originally published as 'Mon voisin, Segalen'; 'Les Finisterres de l'esprit' is reproduced from *Victor Segalen: Actes du Colloque de Brest*; 'La voix du désert' was previously unpublished.]

'Season's End at Huelgoat', in *House of Tides: Letters from Brittany and other lands of the West* (Edinburgh: Polygon, 2000), pp.193-201.

'The Voice of the Desert: Segalen and Rimbaud', in Charles Forsdick and Susan Marson (eds.), *Reading Diversity* (Glasgow: Glasgow French and German Publications, 2000), pp.143-56. [Translation of 'La voix du désert', the final section of *Les Finisterres de l'esprit*.]

'Aux limites de la littérature', texte-préface in Victor Segalen, *Equipée* (Spézet: Coop Breizh, 2001).

Victor Segalen et la Bretagne (Kergoulouet: Blanc Silex, 2002).

'Sur la route des stèles: Victor Segalen dans les profondeurs de la Chine, 1909 et 1914', in Pierre Fournié and Sophie de Sivry (eds.), *Aventuriers du Monde: les grands explorateurs français au temps des premiers photographes, 1866-1914* (Paris: Iconoclaste, 2003), pp.268-77.

'The Road to Rangiroa', in *Across the Territories: Travels from Orkney to Rangiroa* (Edinburgh: Polygon, 2004), pp.197-234.

FROM WASTE LAND
TO WHITE WORLD
Michèle Duclos

T.S. Eliot can hardly be considered one of Kenneth White's close intellectual companions. Major differences manifest themselves in their existential careers. In a way it could be contended that Eliot's statement in 1927 when he became a British subject – 'I am classical in literature, a royalist in politics and an Anglo-Catholic in religion' – summarizes values that White consistently rejected from the start.

Yet the American heir to an aristocratic family and the son and grandson of Glasgow proletarians have in common more basic characteristics as poets and thinkers than would appear at first sight: and first and foremost, at half a century's distance and whatever the discrepancy in the remedy each would expound and apply in his poetry and his essays, a conviction that our Western civilisation has suffered from an increasingly psychical split between thinking and feeling, which ought to be made good, or at least improved, by means of a new aesthetics.

Both brilliant students in their respective universities (Harvard and Glasgow), they reacted against their narrow Protestant backgrounds and the philistine culture that went with it; both travelled to study at foreign universities in Germany and France, and gave up prospects of brilliant academic careers at home, electing for exile in what seemed – to them – more promising cultural territories, each finally taking up the nationality of his new country without denying his home one.

Concerning influences on their art and thought, they were attracted for similar reasons to certain French poets (Tristan Corbière) and German thinkers (Oswald Spengler and to a lesser extent Hermann Hesse). Eliot in his notes to *The Waste Land* acknowledged a debt to Celtic lore (referring to the Grail legend and to James Frazer) whereas White has regularly insisted on the powerful originality of Gaelic medieval poetry and on ancient Celtic naturalism in general as a potential asset for a revival of Western culture. Both poets refer to pre-Socratic non-Aristotelian logics, particularly as embodied by Heraclitus. (Quoted by Eliot in an epigraph to *Four Quartets*, while in his last but one stanza of his *Walking the Coast* White appeals to the heraclitean 'armonia'.) Of even greater moment is their attraction, at the start, to Eastern thought and practice for a solution to the Western estrangement between life and thought, philosophy and poetry (Eliot more like an Indian Brahmin, to the Upanishads, White, more of a 'bodhisattva', to the Taoist and Buddhist monks and poets), even though each emerged from his oriental period with a diverging solution for our ailing culture: Eliot firmly advising a return to a Christian form of community, White proposing a new cultural space based on geopoetics.

As Professor of Twentieth-Century Poetics at the Sorbonne, White lectured on Eliot among other – mainly American – poets, in whom he detected an often underground trend to move away from the prevailing dualistic metaphysics, White's approach to the art of creative, 'projective' criticism being a dynamic of subjective and objective. Here as for the other poets, White went diachronically through Eliot's major poems and essays, bringing out the main features of his art and thought. Starting with Eliot's self-irony in 'Prufrock' (noted by Laforgue and Corbière), White proceeded to *The Waste Land* which was seen and analysed as the indictment of a European civilisation deprived of spiritual values. But White's 'culturanalysis' reveals its keen originality when he detects a final period in Eliot's last poems and a few short, little-known prose texts that reveal the impact of the American landscape upon his mind. White considered that in 'Marina', 'Eliot's navigation ends in an unknown space.' In *Four Quartets*, White went on, 'Grace is dissolved in space, with no intervening ideology'. In these poems, White contended, Eliot 'rediscovers the earth' and approaches a 'rewording of the world'. White himself, in one of his major poems, 'The House at the Head of the Tide', contemplates writing a fifth quartet to prolong and project Eliot into that other space.

The attempt to repair the split in the modern Western psyche (Eliot's famous dissociation of sensibility) – the ontological estrangement between man and the surrounding world – implied for both poets interrogations concerning the function, form and technique of poetry. In such fields also they followed the same path at the start.

First and foremost both advocated that poetry should return to prose for its content and language, taking from the totality of the linguistic gamut and human experience materials and elements to enlarge its vistas and impact.

To both poets modern poetry, in the expression of the maimed psyche, either gave vent to merely personal emotions or got lost in abstraction. Henceforth a new technique was required to take into account simultaneously both the emotional and the intellectual sides of the psyche of the poet, and of his readers. So the poet should refrain from stating plainly and openly his individual feelings or thoughts. This indirect way of taking into account the psyche in its fullness Eliot presented as the 'objective correlative', ranging from simple sequences such as those of *Gerontion* to the complex multiplicity of *The Waste Land*.

Although he mostly wrote to begin with in the first person singular out of his own life experience and background, White too firmly rejected the expression of an individual, sentimental 'I'. The various individual figures whom he later turned into subject matter for his poems, from Brandan to Melville or Hölderlin, can be considered as embodiments of precise views of his world. He even outEliots Eliot in the technique of indirect, imaged, statement. Indeed where the author of *Tradition and the Individual Talent* made it clear that the poet is to be viewed and must view himself as a mere link in the field of the history of culture, White went further: to him culture and nature alike are to be considered as fields of (physical or mental) energy and the poet is a temporary 'psychic energy' in that great field. He even goes to the extent of, technically, idiosyncratically, expressing his own concepts indirectly through quotations from poets and thinkers of 'nomadic' views similar to his own. Finally, Eliot argued that a complex, chaotic civilisation demanded a rejection of the usual plain, linear narrative.

Mainly in their long poems, both poets have evolved techniques and organic forms that they considered suitable to their thematic intentions and to the cultural background of their period. Eliot, reviewing Joyce's *Ulysses* in *The Dial* in November 1923, insisted on the practice of the 'mythical method' as 'a simple way of controlling, of giving a shape and a significance to the immense panorama of futility and anarchy which is contemporary history'. (Later he resorted to traditional imagery when he had recovered a spiritual balance.) As for White, if it is possible to see a mythic force at work in some of his earlier poetry, as in the 'white world' concept, and if early on he was interested in Yeats's attempt to work out a modern equivalent of the old myths that had 'married people to rock and hill', there is in White's work no direct employment of myth (no 'myth-malarkey' as he says in the poem 'Ovid's Report') and his poetic method is not mythological. He begins in fact with Yeats's late rejection of his myth-making and his resolution to 'walk naked' (as in the poem 'A Coat').

At the end of the First World War, Eliot in his *Waste Land* offered an exposure and symbolic epitome of what might appear as the final downfall of Western civilisation, making his point dramatically via 'a heap of broken images', a series of scenes totally heterogeneous in their origins and semantic qualities. At the core of *The Waste Land,* the psyche of the major witness of this centreless poem assumes a number of fleeting heterogeneous identities through time and space, as in the Grail legend the King Poet, sexually maimed, who is also Tiresias the Greek seer, observes a land whose natural elements are either polluted or scorched. We also witness a disruption of the certainties of time, space, and the unitary principle of non-contradiction that up until recently prevailed in the scientific vision of the world. The text is made up of a 'cubist' assemblage of heterogeneous elements of varied, sometimes worthless or meaningless qualities. Eventually the poet looks to the East's unitary vision of the world to rescue the inhabitants from their psychical and spiritual death.

My contention is that White's long poem, *Walking the Coast,* while containing, explicitly or implicitly, all the references of Eliot (and perhaps more), goes beyond the tormented psychology and the metaphysical questioning of Eliot into more original territory. At the beginning, the central, dynamic figure of the Poet's 'I' puts an epistemological query:

how
out of all the chances and changes
to select
the features of real significance
so as to make
of the welter
a world that will last
[...]
developing into
new harmonic wholes
so to keep life alive
in complexity
and complicity
with all of being -

An apparently abstract philosophical poem seems to be lurking ahead. But after moving along the Atlantic coast from Ayrshire to the Hebrides, with evocations along the way of local intellectual figures, as well as of local phenomena, the poem enters, in abstraction and concretion, and their dynamic conjunction, in a Heraclitean harmony, a territory that it is difficult to define, being neither mythological, religious, metaphysical nor mystic, but nevertheless powerful. This is where 'white world' (an uncoded area) is ultimately worded.

Finally, two shorter poems epitomise the differing world-views of the two poets. Eliot's 'Gerontion', as a companion piece to *The Waste Land*, stages as its 'objective correlative' a pre-Beckettian old man, blind and paralysed, whose only present scenery is 'Rocks, moss, stonecrop, iron, merds', pondering over the contrast between a glorious past and a mediocre present all connected with human history. White's 'Labrador' also presents us with a figure at the end of a life-long voyage away from a too noisy and confused civilisation. He has preferred 'the lonely ways of the sky of sands / the gull path', he has 'thought of the earth / in its beginnings', 'aware of a new land / a new world [...] a whole new field / in which to labour and to think'. The image of the poet evoked here answers neither to the classical nor the romantic type of modern Western poetry, rather to one who has gone right back to first principles, worked out an original practice, and made a new beginning.

At the end of *The Waste Land*, Eliot quotes the Brihadaranyaka Upanishad: 'Da, datta, dayadwam' ('giving, sympathizing, organizing'). While he would probably prefer a different formula, White could perhaps accept such a programme.

In conclusion, we might say that White and Eliot agree more or less on the need for a programme. Where they differ, especially in the ultimate reaches, is when they get down to the 'gramming'; the grammar (of living, thinking, writing).

IN ARAB LANDS:
A GEOPOETIC SKETCH
Omar Bsaïthi

European travellers to the Orient often highlighted the 'Biblical feeling' of the land, and most of them have had the impression of going back to the origins of humanity in general and of European civilization in particular. Kenneth White touches on similar ground in 'The Book of the Golden Root', a text which recounts his trip to Tunisia:

> *I'm back in biblical country. I'm moving with my feet through the pages of a book, and it's the illustrated Bible I possessed as a child. [...]*
> *That old shepherd, and his flock of sheep and goats spreading slowly over the sunburned landscape...That young veiled girl passing:*
> 'Thine eyes are like the fish pools of Heshbon, by the gate of Bath-Rabbim.'
> *The feeling that I'm starting from the beginning again.*[1]

The image of the desert as a living book through which the traveller moves is frequent in Orientalist writing but it is essential to point out that, with White, it is the landscape that comes first. Landscape forms the foundation of White's approach and is a necessary step towards his exploration of *mindscapes* in different cultural and geographical contexts.

White's geopoetic peregrinations take place most often in European, Asian or American settings, with beaches, valleys and mountains as a background. In the North African context, however, the landscape is different. Travelling in Southern Tunisia, White meets scrubland and desert which prove rich with possibilities of geopoetic contemplation. Indeed, 'The Book of the Golden Root' illustrates basic elements of White's geopoetics, namely by highlighting mental as well as geographical exploration. Besides, in a typically Whitian manner, the text mixes prose and verse: a sight, a landscape, an experience gives birth to a poem; there is also a play of intertextuality when White refers to a dialogue between a Taoist master and his disciple, an occasion for reflections on travel and self-knowledge. The general pattern is archipelago-like, as the text is made up of a series of numbered, apparently unrelated fragments, sometimes including just one or two sentences.

What comes across most powerfully is the reflection and the sense of movement through a landscape. Sitting in his cabin on board the ship that has just left Marseilles, White recalls Hu-ch'iu Tzu correcting his disciple's conception of travel:

He whose sight-seeing is inward, can find all he needs in himself. Such is the highest form of travelling, while it is a poor sort of journey that is dependent upon outside thing.[2]

White humorously comments that maybe he is still at the stage of 'going places', but that, sooner or later, this going always leads him to the no-place. The journey in the Whitian context is not merely physical; it is also mental and it aims at a closer contact with the world and a better knowledge of the self. When White travels, he does not visit only places, he also, and maybe more eminently, explores hitherto unknown or little known mental grounds, looking for signs of human emancipation, including his own. The notion of emancipation comes up in a rather surprising manner in the text. White having had some Barbary figs for lunch, his hands are filled with prickles; a Frenchwoman, a tourist, starts extracting them with her tweezers. Soon a dozen Tunisians who all want to help extract the prickles surround him. There follows a fragment with just one reflection: 'I have extracted by means of the pincers of self-knowledge the thorns of divers opinions from the deep recesses of my mind',[3] which is a metaphorical formulation of one of White's fundamental principles, namely the necessity of a radical revision of conventional categories, if one is to reach an adequate knowledge of one's self. There are other moments of illumination where a concrete physical experience generates a flash of mental exaltation: sitting in a corner of the mosque, with the murmur of prayers from the hall, White meditates: 'The truth flashes by like lightning in between the gaps created by the absence of thought'.[4] Or again, watching an old fisherman on the shore, he composes a poem (dare we call it a long haiku?):

The old black man
in tattered shirt and faded blue shorts
walks up and down the beach
up and down the beach
slowly
all morning
on the lookout -
then suddenly he crouches
eyes fixed
and stalks into the sea
his net at the ready
casts it
and carefully
hauls it in:

ten silver fish
flapping in its meshes[5]

White's sharp awareness of all levels of experience is eminently present throughout the text and records such things as eating a pomegranate in a palm grove near Gabès, sharing biscuits with some children, watching a girl performing a belly dance. The most significant episodes, however, are the ones related to moving over the ground. At one point, White goes south to the oases. Travelling towards one particular oasis, he perceptively catches moments in the movement:

Out of Gabès, moving west. Wind blowing. Little sand columns whirling and whisking out in the scrubland. A herd of black goats. Long line of telegraph poles leading into nothingness. My dusty feet. A woman goes by, water jar on her back, dark red robes, heavy silver jewelry. Sidi Mannsour. Then the scrubland again. Tents stretched over walls of earth and brushwood. El Guetar. Soon after, the palm trees begin, and it's the oasis of Gafsa.[6]

The 'haiku feeling', if I may call it so, is present in the succession of evocative snapshots which are as many moments of intense perception, containing the total experience, from the blowing wind to the woman with the jar and, of course, the landscape. The physical, geographic element is obviously present, together with the mental element - following the telegraph poles into nothingness - but there is also the cultural element: attention is paid to the woman's dress; later in the essay, White will write a poem on a Berber brooch. Sounds from a local marriage ceremony evoke in him a particular sensation:

Rocky, desertic landscape. Down in the village, a gathering of red-robed women - it's a marriage, the boys say. And then a chanting rises in the clear air, a chanting interspersed with calls: red cries in the clear air.[7]

Having noted the nature of the landscape, White, haiku-wise, transposes the colour of the women's dress on to their chanting, thus blending the material and the immaterial. Obviously, there are moments in White's journey he considers highly because of their evocative power. Such moments of high intensity are sometimes embodied in arresting statements that turn up by chance, like the one which forms fragment 31: '"With a little earth, one makes many forms", says the potter at Guellala.'[8] The saying is left undeveloped, but with White's insistence on a new contact with the earth in mind, one may guess the real import he sees in the potter's sentence.

I had the chance of witnessing one of these evocative moments which later was turned into a poem. In March 1998 White took part in a conference that was held at the University of Oujda. As an aside, together with some friends, we made short trips to the surrounding regions, as White was keen on seeing the landscapes. Once we went south towards Tendrara, which is the beginning of the desert. All along the way, White's travel logbook was open on his knees and he constantly jotted down sayings and pieces of information. That was a droughty year and, mid-way between Oujda and Tendrara, we saw a tent beside a lorry and we got out of the car to have a look. It turned out that these people were shepherds moving north in search of fresher pastures and that the lorry they had rented for the purpose had broken down. The men had gone to look for help and the only person present was an old woman who, seeing us wandering about, came to enquire about our needs. She apologized for not being able to invite us to the tent, as the men were absent. To her question, we answered that we were simply having a look at the landscape. She urged us to look because, once one is under the earth, one will not be able to see anything. Back in France, White composed a poem, recording the experience. It is called *'Bedouin'*:

They'd come up from the Tendrara country
because of the drought and no grass

then the rented truck had broken down

so they'd pitched their tents there
in that area of wind and scrub

'Is there anything you need?' –
it was an old woman, small and spare
blue tatooings on a wizened face
hands and feet caked in dust
who'd hirpled over to speak with us

'Thank you, no, we're just moving around
from place to place in the Oriental
stopping here and there to look at the land'
'It is good to walk and look
while you're on earth, see the world
under the earth, you see nothing'

rosy light on darkblue rock
white snailshells dotting hard parched soil
a black-winged hawk

'*May Allah keep you and open the way, amen.*'

(Morocco, the Oriental region)[9]

As with the Tunisian experience, White's awareness of the environment includes various levels. In one glimpse, there are the woman's tattoos, the scrubland, the rosy light on the darkblue rock, the white snailshells and the black-winged hawk, not to forget the woman's invitation to see the world while one is alive. Like the Tunisian potter's, the woman's saying captured White's attention as one of those formulations which convey more than they show. The trip was short, the moment brief but it was geopoetics in the desert, in Arab land; it was part of a movement that explored geographic and cultural contexts across the world. It was part of a drifting that had high ambitions:

Drifting, drifting…that's the way it looks on the edges of our civilisation. A drifting, a searching, beyond all the known grounds, for an other *ground.*[10]

NOTES

1   Kenneth White, *Travels in the Drifting Dawn* (London: Penguin, 1989), p.149.
2   *Ibid*, p.146.
3   *Ibid*, p.153.
4   *Ibid*, p.153.
5   *Ibid*, p.153-154.
6   *Ibid*, p.154.
7   *Ibid*, p.156.
8   *Ibid*, p.159.
9   Kenneth White, *Open World: Collected Poems 1960-2000* (Edinburgh: Polygon, 2003), p.374.
10   *Travels in the Drifting Dawn*, p.7.

ON EXACTNESS:
READING KENNETH WHITE
IN THE TWENTY-FIRST CENTURY
Anne Scott

The earliest concept of finding oneself came from the sky. From the star patterns of the heavens, the first traveller on the sea established a first truth, with an X on his terrestrial chart. By this lodemenage he had his bearings, and the idea I wish to present in this paper is that the place he marked was 'ex-act'. That is, its source was 'ex-agon' – beyond the 'agon', the Action, which is Earth. His world received its leading grace from the stars and a trusted contract was made between the agon and the ex-act place beyond it. Anything that is shaped by the wind of the sea takes on a grace, like sails or sand-dunes, or a man in need of a Way. When he set down his place on his chart, he called it 'a reading'.

But if poetry is to give the world the words that must be said – give it 'a reading' for a Way – it must lead forward from this stage of our belittled existence, and at present I think Kenneth White's work may be the poetry most ready to carry what we need: that is, to step clear of the thinking of the agon and its terrible enactments, and retrieve the true and good 'architectures of ourselves' as habitants of a greater universe, the ex-act and open world:

a man needs to fix his knowledge
but he also needs an emptiness
in which to move.

When Kenneth White wrote that in *The Blue Road*, he could not know in just what emptiness a man would move in the early twenty-first century, or that 'the unlettered light' he saw in 'A High Blue Day On Scalpay' would be a darkness where words have failed. How is poetry to live now in such a light? What can it make, for a world grown little with fear and lies, that will restore us to a sense of our greatness as spiritual beings and an absolute part of Open Creation? We are watched incessantly, our positions tracked in the very terms of the ancient mapmakers, in minutes and seconds, literally 'to the last syllable of recorded time'. We need to shape our minds in a new space and a new emptiness, not here, in the clutter of the 'agon', but there, in the ex-act beyond ourselves as we have become.

So let me speak of a New Humanism, a corrected vision, a subtle touch on the kaleidoscope that alters patterns to bring us to an exactness of ourselves in the open world. We shall hear and know the Way best in White's call to 'uncover yourself to the bone' in 'Dreamground', and understand its essence in these verses, from 'Inconspicuous lodgings':

I've emptied this room
of all but a very few images

what remains is next to nothing[1]

That is where we are when there are no words to say where we are: next to nothing. And for healing we may come, first, nearer to Leonardo's drawing of Vitruvian man, ourselves located in the Circle universe, and proven its kin by the vertical of our spines and the straight horizontal of the earth.

We may learn to live with images of this partnership, to see what 'transparent figures' McTaggart was finding 'there at Machrihanish'. Our knowledge, and his, and White's, is in the 'correction' of the eye, and the changing of a word or a rhythm in a line. In the measuring of what has happened in our time, and to our time, we need to begin again from the ground, not to grieve further, but to find again the grace and rightness of ourselves, a lodemenage to bind us to universal partnership. Let me quote the whole of 'Dreamground':

I came in a stranger's guise
over the white pathway, the moon
glared: a glass eye, cold
rain pitted the snow, the firs
on my thought's ragged edge
threw their shadows over mine

a light upshone in a window
see: a robin perched on a twig
amid humps of snow. The bolt
had the touch of a friendly hand
easy and strong, the door watched
between the stove and the elements

I have the warm cup in my hands
and the poker is tuning up the fire
and the dead man I live with
looks at me, questioning
and I search for a word of greeting
in the grammar of moon, rain, snow, and fir
but there is no landscape, and no
language, only a ragged silence
and we sit there face to face
and listen to the falling rain -
blow out the lamp now, let
the stove burn deep in the darkness

uncover yourself to the bone.[2]

This is our state, confronting a civilization all but lost, in a 'ragged silence'. Uncovering ourselves to the bone is our zero, our North, where we begin to understand how we share the symmetry and exactness of the universe: and it is also our Way-school where we learn.

Kenneth White's poetic work realizes the *logos*, the path of learning to the ex-act. In dis-covering truth, he has had to search for and discourse the laws of the ex-act that govern the tides, the sun, time, way beyond the levels of our Drama, the Acts and the Action.

Sometimes he almost 'sees' his and our place in this greatness. Here is 'The Nameless Archipelago':

> *Out there*
> *nameless*
> *sometimes in certain lights*
> *I think I have it*
> *(that last glance over the coast rocks*
> *in the gathering evening…*
> *or in the white mist of early morning)*
> *but there's no exactitude*
> *(I'm not content to be a mystic)*
> *at other times I get exactness*
> *but I feel it as fragment*
> *(like picking up a stone*
> *with no sense of geology)*
> *I can sometimes even feel part of it myself*
> *when I'm swimming in the sea*
> *(marine yoga, kind of)*
> *but that's not knowing it*
> *and there's no expression*
> *(I'm not even sure any more what 'knowing' means*
> *and as to expression*
> *I don't just mean poetry*
> *I suppose what I'm after is closer*
> *to a kind of cartography)*[3]

With the chartmakers in the early seas, seeking the ex-act place and marking it. From these searches comes his philosophy, made now more vital and prophetic by events and our cultures than when the poems were written: and with the thinking, a vision of empty places where the ex-act – what he calls in this poem, 'the essential' – may 'happen'.

THE STUDY AT CULROSS

> *The lower room is full of objects*
> *history's ordered bric-a-brac*
> *in which visitors inherently bored*
> *show intelligent interest*

The upper room is still empty
there (in that small cartesian cell)
remains the merest chance
for the essential to happen[4]

This empty room I take to be a domain of otherness whose symbols are visible everywhere in the natural world, but where intellect and imagination are not enough to read them – symbols like the 'bubbles of thin bone' in Hugh MacDiarmid's poem 'Perfect', those 'twin domes / almost transparent, where the brain had been / that fixed the tilt of the wings', or like the coastline that made Kenneth White ask:

Write poems?

rather follow the coast
line after line

going forward

breathing

spacing it out[5]

In MacDiarmid's poem, the power 'that fixed the tilt of the wings' is a correcting one. Something we know, then, of the natural world – it has laws of exactness. It is a *'lighted* chaos'.

CRAB NEBULA

In this lighted chaos I
live and move and have my being
in this mass of incandescence
the birthplace of a world perhaps
at least of a dancing star

in this lighted chaos I
no longer think or feel but am
involved in this swirling matter
the form I was no longer holding me
the form I will be not even imagined[6]

In each verse, the 'I' stands beside 'chaos', alone on the edge of the line; but the second 'I' has moved from the early new world into a place of indecipherable change, which may be also a tiring house where a form emerges into exactness. Such light on the chaos is from the ex-agon, the ex-act, from the sun and the stars. The light of man's imagination and mind has the same source and together they become a shaping spirit.

It is hard to catch this defined form. Here is what Kenneth says in 'Winter Letter from the Mountain':

In this world
always harder and more acrid
more and more white

you ask me for news?

the ice breaks in blue characters
who can read them?

I talk grotesquely to myself
and the silence answers.[7]

But this is not a dead silence: it offers the only 'answer' to the questions asked, and by placing it at the end, White leaves a sound, the sustained sound of a touched violin string, a continuum of waiting to be heard only by the imagination, or the emptiness: but an answer and present. In Kenneth's 'Winter Letter', there can be no intellectual answer to the questions: only the sound of the silence that replies. The intellect begins a search, the imagination offers images for abstractions, and the process can end there in a poem, a song, a dance. But there are some who see onwards to another Way, where words, unreadable 'blue characters' in ice, have a sound beyond intellect – or are transfigured into snow:

THE END OF PHILOSOPHY

Snow drifting
across a window in Otterthal

snow
drifting
across a window
in Otterthal

> *in Otterthal*
> *across a window*
> *drifting*
> *snow*[8]

The words drift too, across the page, but what they say is not what the snowdrifts say. The poet can follow their motion but not hear the drifts – he is still the Dance and not the Dancer of the ex-act which speaks beyond philosophy in that Otterthal agon-world of small towns and windows.

But Kenneth White's poetry is where these borders are most observed: it is closest to the otherness, the silences, the ex-act where 'the essential happens'. He senses it most in the emptiness that has no real silence for him, where he may become one of the *sunyavada* travellers – those who walk the path of emptiness, where a poet must take his mind if he is to survive the 'agon'. His poetry is now a source where we may understand more about the emptiness we have made and the emptiness which will heal; and we will learn more by the shaping of his images than by argument, for they carry the patterns of the ex-act. They reveal the 'unknown architectures' of our selves, an idea to ennoble disillusioned minds. Here is what he says in the essay 'Rimbaud, Glasgow, and Ways West':

> *The real work consists in ... grounding a new anthropology, moving towards a new experience of the earth and of life. The Book of Chao puts it this way: 'Rising above symbols and entering the naked region'.*
> *One single beam of light annihilates the culture-comedy.*[9]

'An author is an augmenter', he says. One who adds to and gives shape to the undefined. That is, he is a chart-maker, and so are we all, between the stars and the sea.

We have need of new readings.

NOTES

1   Kenneth White, *Handbook for the Diamond Country, Collected Shorter Poems 1960-1990* (Edinburgh: Mainstream Publishing, 1990), p.161.
2   Kenneth White, *Open World, The Collected Poems 1960-2000* (Edinburgh: Polygon, 2003), p.50.
3   From 'Late August on the Coast' in *ibid.*, p.592.
4   *Ibid.*, p.77.
5   From 'Broken Ode to White Brittany' in *ibid.*, p.503.
6   *Handbook for the Diamond Country*, p.39.
7   *Open World*, p.110.
8   *Handbook for the Diamond Country*, p.117.
9   Kenneth White, *The Wanderer and his Charts: Essays on Cultural Renewal* (Edinburgh: Polygon, 2004), p.22.

GEOPOETICS AND ARCHITECTURE
Jean-Paul Loubes

> *There are many in this world whose minds dwell in brick-built houses: they can afford to ignore the thing called the outside. But my mind lives under the trees in the open... directly receives upon itself the messages borne by the free winds, and responds from the bottom of its heart to all the musical cadences of light and darkness.*
>
> *Rabindranath Tagore*, The House and the World.

In *Le Plateau de l'Albatros*, Kenneth White defines geopoetics as a field, that of a 'situated poetics'. If there is one expression of human culture that is situated by nature it is architecture. The question raised here is the following: is it possible to transfer from the field of poetics to that of architecture? Even more precisely, is it possible to identify a project, a process leading towards a 'situated architecture'?

Examples of transitions from thoughts formulated in another field (for example in literature, philosophy, social sciences, and geography) into that of architecture are not exceptional. One thinks of deconstruction, structuralism, expressionism, etc.

The worksite is in fact already being set out. In schools of architecture, students are getting more and more curious and interested in the openness to the world which they discover in the writings of Kenneth White. They take from them 'an impulse', 'a desire to live and experience the world', 'the search for a language capable of expressing a different way of being in the world'. At a time when an anonymous, all-purpose, repetitive architectural vocabulary is being rejected (or, at the most, tolerated with indifference), such terms have a particular resonance for them. Ordinary modern architecture appeals to no one anymore. Between an architecture that was narrative, eclectic, overloaded with idiosyncracies, but living and meaningful, and the beautiful white but mute objects that filled the dreams of the purists, there has developed the grey, everyday architecture of our cities. The search for an architectural language capable of expressing differently our presence in the world appears then as a feasible and exciting programme. The time has come to indicate a direction which could finally place architectural research outside the never-ending, circular 'problematics' in which it is confined, the whole subsumed under that grey, time-worn slogan: 'change and continuity'. 'Today, it is no longer a question of "continuity" or of "change", but above all of "finding new stimulation".'[1]

Beyond the drab context of reality as it is, there are in the professional magazines accounts of new projects and constructions. Consulting them allows one to see how things are changing and shifting, and I would like to present here some of these new projects since it seems to me that they present new connections with the *outside*. I consider them capable of feeding the debate which I presented in my introduction: the question of a situated architecture, the nature of a geopoetic approach to architecture.

But before discussing some of these architectural 'objects' which seem to me to hold promise, I would like to outline a few points which are conducive to a better reading of them in context.

1. Modern or Post-Modern

In 1974 a book appeared in Boston entitled *Form Follows Fiasco*. The title parodies the famous functionalist slogan, *form follows function*. The work was translated into French in 1980 with the following title: *L'architecture moderne est morte à Saint-Louis, Missouri, le 15 Juillet 1972 à 15 heures 32 (ou à peu prés)* (Modern architecture died in Saint-Louis, Missouri, on July 15th 1972, at 3.32 pm or thereabouts). This French title was inspired by a sentence taken from the book by Charles Jenks, *Post Modern Architecture*,[2] referring to the first voluntary demolition by explosives of a residential estate in Saint Louis in Missouri, symbolic of what one might call 'the crazy turn of the Modern Movement' in architecture.

That was thirty years ago. But some monsters take a long time to die.

The author, Peter Blake, declared in his foreword, at the end of a period of soul-searching of which the Americans are perhaps more capable than us Europeans: 'This book is first and foremost an indictment of the brilliant sophisms advanced by the Modern Movement and of those who, like myself, followed and promoted it wholeheartedly.' [3]

The Modern Movement was a sort of globalisation of human habitation. It preceded by about seventy years the globalisation of the economy. It was universalist and worked on the construction of a new mankind which would transcend particular cultures. Since it was based on the adage that 'people everywhere have identical needs', there was no awareness of what could be done with the 'local' in modern architecture and urban planning. So, in 1970, Tashkent was rebuilt for the Uzbeks, with the same theoretical equipment that was employed at Brasilia in the Amazonian forest, at Chandigar in the Punjab, or at Saint-Louis in Missouri.

The 'machine for living' spread everywhere, taking forms that the founders, Le Corbusier, Oscar Niemeyer, Mies van der Rohe, Walter Gropius, to quote only the best known, could never have imagined. Most founders rarely anticipate the deviations of their followers. A 'groundless' architecture was born. It did not lack beauty, and gave great satisfaction to several generations of architects (among them Peter Blake and the author of this essay).

Many of these people were intelligent and had their doubts. For example, Philip Johnson, who, in the words of Peter Blake, was 'probably the most intelligent architect of his generation',[4] declared in 1968 that 'modern architecture is a fiasco [...]. It is undeniable that our cities are uglier than they were fifty years ago'. Another, and not the least, James Stirling, one of the best contemporary British architects, said at the University of Yale in 1974 that '99 percent of modern architecture is boring, banal, arid and incongruous'. Sadly, as we know only too well, these reservations were not sufficient and the cancer gradually spread. The most recent site for its application is China, which took only ten years to eradicate its architectural culture and replace it with 'degree zero' architecture and urban planning. That was the caricaturish and degenerate finale of the Modern Movement.

Reduced to mere biological functions, like eating, sleeping, circulating, breathing, the phenomenon of living was emptied of two fundamentally important aspects: the *cultural heritage* of populations for whom 'machines for living' were built and the specificity of place, i.e. the site, its geography and its poetics. There is no 'co-presence' in the world any more.

Architects and the 'local'

Absorbed as they were in the universalist vision propagated since the twenties by the Modern Movement, it seems that it was difficult for architects to understand by 'local' anything other than localism, or more precisely, folklore, taking this word in its most debased and reductive sense. The term 'local' was understood in the most narrow way, as 'rootedness', with 'tradition' as the one and only reference.

Eager for the most simplifying, not to say the most simplistic theories, full of the sophisms evoked above, the dominant architectural culture finds it hard to get beyond a dualistic way of thinking that ranges 'modernists' against 'reactionaries'. In one corner, you have the heirs of the Modern Movement, convinced that they are in the vanguard of history, and in the other, those whose watchword is 'neo': such as neo-Basque, neo-Breton, etc.

Yet there are some signs in recent architectural production which show that we may be getting out of this schema. Some creators seem willing to develop ways of addressing 'the local' in an original manner. They try to go beyond the folkloristic vision of tradition, in order to ask themselves whether it can be given new life and nourish contemporary research. Here we are broaching the whole question of cultural heritage. What can contemporary creators do with this heritage? What we need in the production process that we call architecture is a reinterpretation of tradition, not a mere remake of outdated forms, as if time had stopped. This question involves of course a certain idea of mankind, and of living on and with the Earth. This kind of questioning had no place in the Modern Movement.

To give some idea of these first signs, let us look to Renzo Piano. With the Centre Pompidou in Paris he created what some describe as 'the last monument of High-Tech architecture'. Delocalised architectural vocabulary, a complete break with the context and the whole urban and architectural culture that it contained, a universe created *ex nihilo* by an architectural theory convinced that modernity could only be conceived as a denial of the local, it was a perfect example of groundless architecture. But, thirty years later, the same Renzo Piano is invited to propose a project for the Jean-Marie Djibao Cultural Centre in Noumea. Here the approach is completely different. The architect looks conscientiously into the local cultural heritage, into the architectural forms of Kanak culture, into the way in which this society lives and uses its space. He asks himself the fundamental question: what local information concerning the inhabitants and the site could be important for the architectural project?

This meant a radical change, a fundamental break with the Modern Movement. The problematics of the site become part of the project. The project is out, once more, to inhabit the site.

The following reflections are to be considered as a contribution to the general question of the way geopoetics looks at the city, at the urban phenomenon in which we are immersed. We tackle a complex question by way of a more limited fragment, at a more reduced scale, that of architecture. We are not saying that the shift from architecture to the city is made by a simple widening of perspective. Each level has its specificities, the two disciplines called architecture and urban planning enjoy a degree of autonomy, but both can be enlightened by geopoetics.

Let us concentrate on architectural thought and its relation to the world, trying to work out a kind of inventory in which geopoetics has a central role to play. There is nothing strange about such an exercise. Students in schools of architecture refer more and more to the work of Kenneth White, because they find in it not only a conceptual renewal, but a new way of going about things. The idea behind this approach is that architecture should break with its claims to autonomy, amounting to a kind of autism, and should get back in touch with the context, 'inhabit' the site again. Definition, form, materials, spatiality, inspiration, would derive from a relationship with the outside. Architecture would no longer be an autonomous sphere, it would be a dialogue with the Earth.

How can an architectural project be a dialogue with the Earth and in relationship to it? By means of a new *attitude*, where the culture or genius of the architect would not be the prime motivation of the project, but information emanating from contact with the outside. This is where the work and thought of Kenneth White comes in. What we are concerned with is, as aforesaid, 'a language capable of expressing another way of being in the world'.[5]

Geopoetic thought is central to this whole process. It means bringing into architectural space thought that was first expressed in the field of poetry, though by the time he wrote *Le Plateau de l'Albatros*, Kenneth White was already putting forward geopoetics as a general field.

What I want to present now, after the 'first signs' evoked above, are some architectural projects, which, while not referring (yet) to the work and thought of Kenneth White, seem to be going in the direction of geopoetics. As yet, they may be modest, but they do approach a new way of inhabiting the world.

2. Towards architecture as an 'experience of place'

The idea is to apply the theory of geopoetics to architecture. By doing so, we hope to succeed in changing the orientation of architectural practice towards one of a greater sensitivity to the world. Even more than a change of orientation, it seems that what is needed is a decentring. The training of the architect has to be more engaged in the development of sensitivity to the real world, than in overstressing the importance of the 'creative self'. Sensitivity to the Earth-world means, in geopoetic language, a substantial, grounded thought, a deep apprehension of locality. There we have a possible programme by which to leave behind the last gesticulations of the Modern Movement: to make architecture 'an experience of place'.[6]

I find in the work of Kenneth White this note which illustrates the question of the inside and the outside: 'Newton was only interested in the outside world, excluding the world of man. Later, Freud was to be interested only in the internal world of man, to the exclusion of the cosmos'.[7] Although it does not focus on the individual person, geopoetics is still interested in the human being. It tries to attain to and express the relationship between man and cosmos in all its complexity.

Geopoetics is concerned with *topos* (region, place) concerning 'poor and changing social situations'. Already Gaston Bachelard (in *Poétique de la rêverie*, quoted by White) was saying that 'site' was more important than 'fluctuating social situation'. But White clarifies further and expands more: 'This is no theme for parish pietists, or for people nostalgic for localism and identity, nor is it about some flat 'poetry' (the only one extant in a civilisation without culture), it is about the development of a thought and a knowledge that our civilisation has neglected and which remains to be developed.'

The poetics involved comprises 'a sense of the magnitude of the world and a fine perception of things',[8] it tries to fathom the relationship between the Void and the perceptible world, as White defines it in his *Letter to Milarepa*.[9] There we have a real programme for possible renewal.

In the meantime, as I say, there are signs, and tentative attempts.

Some architects have been able to move away from the consensus theory of the Modern Movement. They follow empirical paths, all of them rehabilitating a sensitivity to the local context. Of course these attempts can be situated in the general current of environmental and ecological thinking. Although disappointing in other respects, such thinking has in this particular case at least the merit of encouraging architects to look in directions their elders turned away from. They turn their attention to the site, the landscape in which the project is placed, to pre-existent forms, to climatic data, micro-reliefs and landscapes. All this forms a potential of information that will be decisive for the project. It must be emphasised that these approaches are contemporary and they are nourished by research in the field of the fine arts and anthropology.

Here are some examples of practices that at least in some respects seem to me to be moving in the direction of geopoetics.

Land Art

Its relevance to architecture is two-fold. On the one hand, it renews the method of placing an object in a site, and, by its very nature, this condition has to be an absolute must for any architectural object. Being an intervention *in situ*, the object of Land

Art is inspired and defined by stimulations from the site itself. Land artists do not see a sculpture as an autonomous object but rather look at the totality 'form-sculpture-place', and integrate into the creation the space where it is situated. Consider for example the installation of the sculptures of Carl André in a natural setting (for example, *Secant*, 1977, Nassau County Museum of Fine Arts, Roslyn). These sculptures, often minimalist, take on an increased dimension, an expansion, a respiration, thanks to the surrounding space. On the other hand, Land Art has a scale which brings it close to architecture. The parallel is fruitful. The paths taken by Land Art can very well accompany those of an architectural project.

That said, such transposition demands vigilance as we must not lose sight of the fact that the object of architecture is not only to occupy a space and to be seen, it is also a space for practices, customs and utility. Also, there are Land Art interventions which, with regard to nature, are closer to a relationship of domination and power rather than one of alliance and partnership. Too often we see a trial of strength with the site that the ego of the artist wants to subjugate. Obviously, this is not the sort of intervention we favour. Likewise, in the large scale artworks called Earthwork or Earth Art, if the earth is invoked as background and material, the huge scale required by the artist's megalomania excludes these interventions from our discussion.

Cabin architecture

As we have seen, one of the principle axioms of geopoetics is 'a relationship with the earth'.[10] It is possible to see cabin architecture in this light, as an interface between man and the world. More than the house, the cabin or hut allows us to *inhabit* the world and to be a part of it.[11] It reduces the distance between human inhabitant and cosmos. A practical form of our relationship with the world, one of the most simple and original ones, it forms a privileged object through which to explore the relationship between *inside* and *outside*, which is at the heart of geopoetics.

Inside-outside, ego and world: the hut has to be considered not only as an expression of *making* but also of *being*. Hence its attraction for a lot of people, and for architects. As to the general public, the theme is to be found in all kinds of reviews and newspapers, especially when some actor, media personality or photographer builds a luxurious hut in the trees.

With architects, the matter is more serious and more profound. Many of them are updating the cabin in contemporary projects. Some simply see it as trendy, related to a pseudo-return to nature, a consequence of the *soft* fashion in design, or as a simple temporary renewal of the aesthetics of the house, a search for new ideas. All this is not untrue, but beyond these shifts of fashion, there is in this renewal a radical break with the way we look at the house. The days of the 'machine for living' are over. Now, it is a question of inhabiting the world, of finding a better well-*being*.

Scandinavian architecture

If concrete examples, beyond the cabin, are needed to illustrate these new perspectives, we can look to Scandinavian architecture. Even the Modern Movement in Scandinavia avoided the megalomaniacal or simplifying excesses which elsewhere characterised this trend. The modesty of Finnish or Norwegian architects expresses a sensitivity to place and the people living there. Rather than being an expression of personal genius, the project strives to be a sensor of the cosmos, to become an echo of an oceanic sky, the horizon of a glacier, a field of heather or a rocky environment.

These three examples are what I see as intermediate stages on the way to a complete geopoetic conception of things. It remains to establish in architecture what Kenneth White calls 'the great work-field'.[12]

NOTES

1   Christian Norberg-Schulz, *L'Art du lieu* (Paris: Editions du Moniteur, 1997). Requiring architecture students to read this work is an exercise in cleanliness, a sort of *kriya*. To leave it at that and to nourish them by recommending notably the reading of Norberg-Schulz, could constitute the rest of the syllabus.

2   Charles Jenks, *Post Modern Architecture* (Academy Editions, 1997).

3   Peter Blake, *L'Architecture moderne est morte à Saint-Louis, Missouri, le 15 Juillet 1972 à 15h32 (ou à peu près)* (Paris: Editions du Moniteur, 1980).

4   *Ibid*, p.12.

5   Kenneth White, *Le Plateau de l'Albatros, introduction à la géopoétique* (Paris: Grasset, 1994).

6   Kenneth White, *Une stratégie paradoxale* (Bordeaux: Presses Universitaires de Bordeaux, 1998), p.146.

7   *Ibid*, p.109.

8   *Ibid*, p.151.

9   *Ibid*, p.157.

10   *Ibid*, p.201.

11   Jean-Paul Loubes, 'La cabane, figure géopoétique de l'architecture', in *Cabane, cabanons et campements* (Université de Provence-CNRS; Editions de Bergier, 2001).

12   See the book with that title: *Le champ du grand travail* (Brussels: Didier Devillez, 2002).

CANONS TO THE LEFT OF HIM, CANONS TO THE RIGHT OF HIM: KENNETH WHITE AND THE CONSTRUCTIONS OF SCOTTISH LITERARY HISTORY
Stuart Kelly

One yearns, in a strange way, for the neatness and sense of closure provided by the Aristotelian syllogism. Applying the old methodology of 'All men are mortal: Socrates is a man: therefore Socrates is mortal' to Kenneth White and his place within the idea of Scottish literary history would, if nothing else, reduce the length of this paper. But if we run the mediaeval logic, it just doesn't work: 'Kenneth White is a poet; Kenneth White is Scottish' does not lead, unfortunately, to 'Kenneth White is a Scottish poet'.

The purpose of this study is to clarify the relationship between White and the emergent canons of twentieth and twenty-first century Scottish poetry, and in doing so, not just provide a summary of the critical reception of White's varied oeuvre, but unveil some of the ideological stresses and fractures that operate on the establishment of literary reputation and the construction of the 'canonical', particularly in Scotland, and particularly in poetry.

*

Before embarking on the literary world outside of White, it would be apposite to begin by asking how White responds to the question. On the one hand, White has studiously avoided the question of his place within the ecosystem of Scottish literature. 'I prefer to work outside of all milieux', he said to David Kinloch, in an interview in *Verse*. 'I have no respect for tradition as such', he maintains in the same piece. In an interview with Elizabeth Lyon in *ArtWork*, May 1983, White formulated his distance from the idea of a literary history constructed by geographical and historical roots in a style which one might label as typically, one might even say Scottishly, thrawn manner: 'In any case, a writer isn't a leek'.

On the other hand, it would be naïve to ignore the importance White places on his own Scottishness, even if it is bounded by caveats against nationalism and parochialism. In an early letter to Hugh MacDiarmid, White describes himself as 'a transcendalist Scot – how's that for a GROTESQUE appellation', elegantly implying both a connection to the country of his birth and a soaring away from it, before scotching the whole phrase with a sly self-deprecation. Moreover, in White's non-fiction writing, there has been a consistent fashioning of a Scottish canon which he considers as formative. Just as MacDiarmid rewrote the canon with his clarion call of 'Back to Dunbar!', and just as many contemporary Scottish novelists, from Irvine Welsh to Allan Massie, navigate the swathes of literary history by invoking either Sir Walter Scott or Alexander Trocchi, so too White engages in the process of electing his ancestors.

The early mystic and heretic Pelagius; the polymathic and demonic Michael Scott; Thomas Urquhart, the translator of Rabelais; the sceptical David Hume and the visionary Patrick Geddes are all advanced as precursors, fellow-travellers and kindred spirits. In *On Scottish Ground*, White also reaches an uneasy alliance with Burns, reclaiming the roister-doister of fable as a degenerated shaman. Of course White, like Edwin Morgan, is equally open about the non-Scottish elements of his personal pantheon; nonetheless, the staking out of a distinctively Whitean version of Scottish literary history is clear evidence that, even if his detractors insist otherwise, Kenneth White thinks that Kenneth White is a Scottish poet, and, like the Shetlander to the incomer, can point to sufficient graves in the graveyard to justify his genealogical presumption.

*

In his own, Scottish, Temple of Worthies, White gives clear prominence to Hugh MacDiarmid and his relationship with MacDiarmid is central not only to his own public self-image, but to the whole problematic quagmire of how the history of twentieth-century Scottish literature is constructed. In order to begin to understand the context in which White is discussed, we have to look at the non-existent Club from which he was excluded.

It was, apparently, Peter de Francia who suggested to Sandy Moffat that he should 'paint that generation of Scottish poets...'. I think his words were 'before it's too late'. That painting, entitled *Poets' Pub*, is not, in fact, any attempt at commemoration, let alone reportage or documentary. No such meeting ever took place. Completed in 1980, two of the figures, Sydney Goodsir Smith and Hugh MacDiarmid, were already, by then, dead. Of the poets in the picture, only one, Edwin Morgan, is still alive. It is fundamentally a fiction, a response to some yearning for a 'group' or 'movement' that Scotland could hold up against Bloomsbury Square, the Cabaret Voltaire or the Algonquin Hotel.

It is a painting that ignores many aspects of the group. Presented as if homogenous, it fuses the cut-glass tones of Norman MacCaig with the linguistic anarchy of MacDiarmid. It elides Iain Crichton Smith's wary, testy attitude towards technology with Morgan's wholehearted embracing of it. Personal grievances are airbrushed out in favour of affable, boozy, bonhomie. Orcadian and Borderer, homosexual and homophobe, traditional and avant-garde are all subsumed under the glorious banner of the supposed 'Scottish Renaissance'.

And yet, despite, or because of, its manifest agenda, the picture has become synonymous with the 'Greats' of twentieth-century Scottish poetry. It is on the homepage of the Scottish Poetry Library's website. It is on the cover of Edinburgh University Press's Norton style anthology of twentieth-century Scottish literature. MacDiarmid, Mackay Brown, MacCaig, Morgan and Crichton Smith have been on the curriculum for 'English' in Scottish schools for nearly twenty five years now. *Twelve Modern Scottish Poets*, edited by Charles King and published by Hodder and Stoughton, and for many years the standard school textbook – indeed, the school-book I used – featured all of the subjects except MacDiarmid's biographer, Alan Bold, and the Gaelic poet Sorley MacLean. Every anthology of Scottish poetry, twentieth century or otherwise, uses this grouping as the selective spine: more of this anon. I am not saying that these poets do not deserve to be appreciated, taught and studied: I am saying that it is only one, and at that, an interim judgement, and that needs redressing. *Poets' Pub*, fundamentally, is a desire for the canon that became its realisation.

*

So who's not in the pub? Who's in the Avant-Garde Arms, or the Neglected Genius's Head, next door? And can they be lumped together any more satisfactorily than the denizens of the Milne's Bar Big-Guns?

Well, to begin with, there's George Bruce, another poet of cliffs and open-ness, and 'rocky sea-girt landscapes', as Charles King said, and Tom Scott, the apprentice builder, euphemistically described as a stonemason by Francis Scarfe when including him amongst the 'Apocalyptic' school along with McCaig. But both achieved a modicum of recognition (not least from our old friend Charles King, though both have found less favour with the editors of the *New Penguin Book of Scottish Poetry*). Casting further afield, Hamish Henderson, the collector of folk ballads and author of *Elegies for the Dead in Cyrenia*, and Derick Thomson, the editor of the Gaelic magazine *Gairm*, were both barred from the Poets' Pub because of regular brawling with the Old Regular, MacDiarmid.

Veronica Forrest-Thomson, the least confessional, most exquisitely stammering poet of her generation is probably out because she went to Cambridge and started hanging out with the French (incidentally, there are no women in the Poets' Pub: it is almost archetypally canonical in being all white, mostly straight, mostly dead, and all male: the only women in the picture are a prostitute and a symbol of Liberty). Burns Singer, a brilliantly tortured master of poetic syntax, is also out; possibly because of working in England for the *Times Literary Supplement*; possibly because of being originally the Jewish American Hyman Singer. W. S. Graham fled to the Cornwall Coast, and, despite occasional, enthusiastic notices, has received relatively little serious critical attention.

There are, as you see, Scottish poets and Scottish poets; and Kenneth White is certainly a Scottish poet of one kind. There is a fascinating letter from Edwin Morgan to Alec Finlay, the son of Ian Hamilton Finlay (another figure sipping his strong tea in the Avant-

Garde Arms rather than the Poets' Pub) where he recollects to whom in Scotland Alexander Trocchi chose to send his first Sigma pamphlet: MacDiarmid, Morgan, Tom McGrath, Ian Hamilton Finlay and Kenneth White. Before the Poets' Pub was immortalised, it looks as if some of the clientele were having a swift half next door as well. Unfortunately, there is not time here to consider another nexus which might feasibly enlighten: the shamanic magnetism between Kenneth White and Joseph Beuys.

*

Trocchi certainly had the knack of identifying the writers whom one would readily associate with a Scottish avant-garde. However, as he himself found out at the Writers' Conference organised by John Calder in 1962, MacDiarmid especially was both the leader of the avant-garde and the acknowledged elder statesman of poetry at one and the same time, and brooked little challenge to either position. White, again in a correspondence with MacDiarmid, is aware of the double role the poet played; thanking him for the sponsorship that facilitated him being awarded a Scottish Arts Council bursary in 1975, and declaring that 'for me, [the] avant-garde is represented by yourself' two years later.

MacDiarmid's legacy to the next generation of Scottish poets was, in MacNeice's phrase, incorrigibly plural. Different aspects of his oeuvre have been deployed by different factions as the 'true' MacDiarmid. For some, this is the early, lyrical work in synthetic (or actual) Lallans, for others, especially the Informationists, of whom more presently, the radical, dictionary-exhausting melange of 'To Circumjack Cencrastus'. White gravitates towards the late MacDiarmid most frequently, the poet who attempted to unify science and poetry in an attempt to understand the intrinsic otherness of the material world. White's MacDiarmid is represented, par excellence, by 'On a Raised Beach', the homage to 'the stones that are at one with the stars'.

*

So much for the broad overview: let us turn to the specifics of White's critical reception in Scotland. Anthologies are the most blatant statements of canon formation, and, judged by his representation in these alone, it would appear that the 'neglected' label fits White well.

David McCordick's 1000 page anthology *Scottish Literature in the Twentieth Century* omits mention of White altogether. So too does the *Penguin Anthology of Scottish Poetry*, edited by Mick Imlah and Robert Crawford (the noted professor at St Andrews University and a one-time member of the so-called Informationist school of poetry). He was also unrepresented in the volume's predecessor, edited by Tom Scott, or the Oxford anthology edited by Scott. White does not appear in the Penguin book of poetry written after 1945, edited by Simon Armitage and Robert Crawford; but he does manage to be included in the anthology *Scottish Religious Poetry*, edited by James McGonigall, Meg Bateman and Robert Crawford. Similarly, White is not represented in Roderick Watson's Edinburgh University Press collection *The Poetry of Scotland*. Douglas Dunn's Faber anthology of twentieth-century Scottish poetry includes three pages of White's poetry: in context, though, this is less than that afforded to the founder of the Glaswegian 'hard man' school of novels, William McIlvanney. Maurice Lindsay's anthology of twentieth-century Scottish poetry, published by Robert Hale and which went through four editions, also includes a solitary poem by White. There is nothing of White's in Sean O'Brien's anthology of contemporary poetry, *The Firebox*, and nothing in George Bruce's anthology of poetic landscapes *The Land Out There*, nor in Ivo Mosely's book of 'Green' poetry, nor even in the *Oxford Book of Bird Poetry*.

The thirteen volume series 'Penguin Modern Poets', which presented three poets in each book and did have a leaning towards the avant-garde, as displayed by the volume offering a collection of Iain Sinclair, Douglas Oliver and Denise Riley, did not, however offer a place to White, despite Penguin's publication of his non-fiction. Nor do the Etruscan Readers series make any mention of White's poetry. The most influential recent anthology, *The Dream State*, edited by Donny O'Rourke and re-issued in 2002, excluded White on the grounds of age.

Can any defence be mounted of this almost absolute neglect? In terms of the Penguin Modern Poets series, it is admittedly difficult, though not impossible, to think of two other writers whose work would complement and parry with White's poetry. As for the numerous editors who chose not to reproduce White's work in anthologies, it is not special pleading to suggest that White's work is difficult to anthologise. White's triple production of poetry, theory and way-book, is a unified whole. He himself has compared it to a single arrow, comprising shaft, point and body. It is diminished if read in isolation; and isolation is the principal organisational strategy of the anthology.

In this respect, White's fate is paralleled in the similar, relative neglect given to Iain Hamilton Finlay and Gael Turnbull. All three produce work which cannot easily be represented in anthology form: one cannot 'lift' a section of the garden at Little Sparta, or include Turnbull's magnificent poem on a Mobius Strip or his haptic poetry machines, any more than one can select a work by White which is not bolstered and contextualised by his other, non-poetic, writings. Nonetheless, imaginative editors, especially Alec Finlay and Ken Cockburn, have gone some way in redressing this imbalance with their admirable 'Pocket Book' series.

Anthologies are the most prominent incarnation of the canon, yet they are not the sole indication of cultural status. The large, critical primer edited primarily by Douglas Gifford – *Scottish Literature* (Edinburgh University Press, 2002) – includes White at the peril of a deep rooted uncertainty – one might even say an anxiety – about how actually to present his work. We are informed that, he is 'essentially aiming to avoid the Western tradition', a point then contradicted by the assertion that he 'owes something to Whitman and MacDiarmid', finally resolved in the startlingly bogus synthesis that White's work is 'a blend of Celtic and Zen mysticism'. James McGonigall reads White as a counterpoint to the Informationists: whereas their poetic practise is quintessentially in the fabric and textures of the written form; White's is located in a transcendental experience outside of the text. This point was also articulated by Robin Fulton in his essay on White in *Contemporary Scottish Poetry* (1975), and the lineaments of the argument can be detected in Edwin Morgan's uncharacteristically churlish review of White's Collected Longer Poems in *Books in Scotland*, where he girned that 'the lines [...] do not seem to have been thought about at all' – by which I take it he intends the criticism purely on the level of the phonetic structure rather than semantic intent of the lines.

White responded to Fulton's criticisms in 'The High Field', reproduced in *On Scottish Ground*. Although I have no wish to reopen that particular debate, it is curious to notice that Fulton's objections rest on the idea that the poem is an abandoned chrysalis of the experience, a signifier to an absent, transcendental signified. Yet this very aesthetic underpins the work of the English Romantics, Wordsworth and Coleridge in particular, and goes unmentioned in discussions of T. S. Eliot: 'we had the experience / But missed the meaning, or the approach to the meaning', says Eliot, articulating the impasse Kenneth White seeks to circumvent.

Incidentally, White reviewed the Gifford critical primer for the Scotsman (3 August 2002), and his trenchant engagement reveals another aspect of his on-going commitment to and concern with aesthetic debate in Scotland. I can't resist quoting one section, especially as it shows just how witty White can be (pace, the comments of Richard Price – another erstwhile Informationist - on the lack of humour in White's work in *Scotland on Sunday* in September 2003):

> *What sharp Scoticity there is in these pages gets lost in a huge overdose of secondary Scottishness. I imagine a student of ScotLit, fresh, say, from Inverness or Reykjavik, taking the train from Waverley to Glasgow, making her way to that delectable grey place where the Kelvin vomits into the Clyde, and there, after watching for a while the last lone swan, probably dying of cancer, drift away into the gathering dusk, quietly committing suicide. The obituary would read: 'She died, with Eddie Lamont's latest novel* Blank Dank Blonk *on her lap and Scottish literature coming out of her ears.'*

White has not received as much academic attention as he deserves. With the exceptions of this volume's editor, Gavin Bowd, and the late, deeply-missed Tony McManus, there has been little in the way of sensitive critique. Tellingly, there are no monographs on White's work in English, whilst Morgan and MacDiarmid support a burgeoning academic-critical industry.

There is ample evidence to support the claim that White has been ignored. There is also evidence to the contrary, not the least being the existence of this volume in itself. As well as celebrating the fortieth anniversary of White's work, it follows the publication of the *Collected Poems*. This in itself is no small achievement: apart from Morgan, the only other living poet who has such a monument is Liz Lochhead.

White's outsider image confers on him a certain celebrity. For example, *Chapman*, the long-running literary magazine, devoted an issue to White in 1990, long before it gave similar attention to Ian Hamilton Finlay, Edwin Morgan and Hamish Henderson. The issue itself is, unfortunately, deeply flawed. Supposedly in the interests of balance, a piece was published by Graham Dunstan Martin which positively reeks of xenophobia and philistinism. It has, perhaps, been to White's disadvantage that he has been described as the premier poet of postmodernism. The term tends to act as a red rag to a bull for certain reviewers: it guarantees a thunderous chorus of disapproval, and a rabid denunciation of Derrida, Foucault, Kristeva and any other theoretician the critic in question can remember having heard of, but never taken the trouble actually to read. Martin's essay, as well as Adam Thorpe's review in *The Observer*, are models of this.

White has also enjoyed the influential support of Catherine Lockerbie, firstly as literary editor of *The Scotsman*, where she championed White as the 'best known unknown author', and subsequently as director of the Edinburgh International Book Festival. In these first three years of her directorship, White has been accorded a great deal of prominence. In contrast to most other Scottish poets at the Festival, he is given sole occupancy of his stage. White is to be commended for having used such a platform to attempt to stimulate debate; and it is to the shame of the Fourth Estate that we have responded, not with continuing and expanding the debate, but by reporting it as a regulation spat.

There is, however, a danger for White in being typecast as the totem of avant-gardism in Scotland. His elevation is also an isolation; and in separating him from interaction with other avant-garde figures, there is a faintly discernible whiff of tokenism. Since marketing and advertising have adopted wholesale the language of avant-garde acclaim, a 'radical' has become a necessary element of any self-respecting literary event. It would be regrettable indeed if White's position as honoured outsider served to occlude other forms of avant-garde literary activity. Like MacDiarmid before him, White is precariously poised between veneration and suspicion.

*

White, like MacDiarmid, is and is more than a Scottish poet. Will he have a similar influence? With the passing of Tony McManus, and despite the work currently being done by Norman Bissell, it seems increasingly unlikely that the future of geopoetics in Scotland is a certainty, especially considering the extent to which all verse is marginalised on such programmes as Creative Writing courses. This should not blind us to the fact that there exists a constellation of writers whose work bears comparison with White's, and whose informing context might secure his cultural position. I'm thinking primarily of Bill Duncan, the author of *The Smiling School for Calvinists*, and in particular his haunting sequence of poems on Hirta, and his internet project *The Haar*, a synthesis of geopoetic and psychogeographical works. Gavin Bowd's own poetry shows the influence of White, transposed on to different, more politicised landscapes. Valerie Gillies's site-specific works may owe more to Hamilton Finlay on the surface, but the terse, chiselled verse forms could easily be compared with White's own. And when Norman Bissell referred to White's aesthetics as 'Buddhism without the Buddha or the ism', he could as well have been discussing Alan Spence's mordant works, *Glasgow Zen* and *Seasons of the Heart*. John Burnside's 'Poet's Polemic', printed in part in *The Scotsman* in September 2003, reads like a geopoetic manifesto with added wool, with 'spirituality' in place of Heidegger. That it is even possible to find these parallels, suggests that White is more hard-wired into contemporary Scottish culture than one might otherwise imagine.

Why, though, was my opening syllogism so contradictory in the first place? Why, other than his choice of domicile, has White been regarded with such uneasiness in Scotland?

I would suggest that White's aesthetic still presents a challenge which most Scottish poets refuse to face. In Burnside's polemic, he maintains that 'poetry does not seek to change the world – on the contrary, it aims in every possible way to reaffirm that world'. This seems antithetical to White's view of the function of poetry. His work asserts that poetry does change the world, and changes the poet with it. Although White has always been slightly retiring about the events of May '68 in France, a quotation from the arch-situationist Guy Debord seems to encapsulate White's aesthetic: 'that which changes our way of seeing the streets is more important than that which changes our way of seeing painting.' For *les pavés,* substitute *la plage.*

This approach – let's call it the Interventional Model of Poetry – is shared by a number of the authors previously mentioned: Hamilton Finlay, Gael Turnbull, Veronica Forrest-Thomson, Iain Sinclair, Douglas Oliver, Tom McGrath, and especially MacDiarmid himself, and the shade of André Breton. Conversely, many of the more lauded figures adhere to the idea that the poem's function is to be, and be beautiful in and of itself – let's call it the 'All Dressed Up And Nowhere To Go' Model. White has consistently maintained that poetry requires work on the self itself. This is what unnerves the majority of critical commentators. His aesthetics are not detachable from a vision of vitality, an attitude towards the world itself: anti-Ivory Tower poetics.

Let us not forget that landscape is itself a verb as well as a noun. White's poetry is about happening and changing, not being, and being regarded. As such it offers a provocative challenge to those who would prefer poetry to languish in the domestic boudoir, cooing over the incidental. We live in an age where the poem as therapeutic out-pouring is all too frequent: White's importance lies in his commitment to the idea of the poetic act as work, rather than leisure, diversion or hobby.

GROUNDING A WORLD
Kenneth White

With the title for this symposium in mind, and referring to a
book that used to be read a lot here in St Andrews, I might have
entitled my own communication: 'Forty years in the Wilderness',
using a Latin epigraph: *Vox clamantis in deserto*. While not
discarding totally the time factor (I'm thinking there of Dogen
Zenji's 'Forty years have gone by/as fast as a running rabbit/or a
crow across the sky'), I prefer to set aside any *tempus fugit* pathos
and follow a poetic-intellectual path, a path into a large space, under
the title: 'Grounding a World'.

When John Knox, up here in St Andrews, still a monk and
about to become a galley-slave on the Loire, was asked to talk out in
public for the first time, he was unable to utter a word and burst
into tears. I hope and intend to be more articulate, but I do want,
not without emotion, to thank all those involved, including of course
the speakers who have preceded me in this colloquium. Not that I
think they're all right! It will be up to the reader to decide what is
truly pertinent to the work in question and what belongs rather to
the context of the interpreter.

A colloquium is a 'speaking together' (*colloquere*), but in
addition to *colloquere*, I like to think of the word *collocare* (bringing
places, *loci, topoi*, together), and see in a colloquium a relocation of
perspectives. That's what a work does, an *opus*, an operative
creation – it's something like a new tectonic mass, a Drumalban, a
Cairngorm, an Alp, a Pyrenee on the conventional cultural crust. A
work carries potentially a transformation of model and canon. It
bears within it the emergence of a new paradigm. I'm using the word
'work' in a very strong sense. There is always, at any period, a great
amount of 'cultural production'. There is very little epochal art.

To the work, over time, through thick and thin, in the midst of oppositions, blockages and confusions, accrues a crystallisation of interpretation and evaluation, in that order: no evaluation without interpretation. And sometimes the *means* of interpretation are simply not to hand. What passes for criticism is often no more than superficial impressionism or expressionistic belly-rumbling. As to evaluation, that implies a defined context, a horizon of intention, and this too is so often lacking. When I started writing as a student of language, literature and philosophy in Glasgow, I wrote a rambling screed of a thing called *Logan* (the man looking for *logos*) which bore as its epigraph this phrase of Wittgenstein's: 'Consider the geography of a country for which there is no map, or only a fragmentary one.'

My fellow-speakers have all had, each in his or her own way, this kind of situation in mind. Which makes this colloquium a significant increment of forces – like the wild white waters of the Corrievreckan.

It remains for me to try to sum up (a summing-up which will also be an outline of ongoing project) how I myself see those 'forty years of the White World'.

*

To get at that notion of 'white world', I have in fact to go back beyond the publication of my first book, *Wild Coal*, at a small printer's in the Rue Denfert-Rochereau in Paris. I have to go back to a shore on the west coast of Scotland.

Speaking of his own research and itinerary Isaac Newton has this: 'I do not know what I may appear to the world, but to myself I seem to have been like a boy on a seashore, diverting myself in now and then finding a smoother pebble or a more attractive shell than ordinary, while the great ocean of truth lay all undiscovered before me.' That's pretty well how I acted and felt on the shore at Fairlie. The 'white world' meant, in the first place, an abundance of white phenomena: fragments of quartz, shells, bird's wings, the foam of breaking waves, with a kind of overall sense of 'white noise' (an alban tumult), and rhythm, pattern.

That reminds me, still on the geophysical plane, of a remark by Einstein on James Clerk Maxwell, saying that Maxwell's equations were the most important event in physics since Newton's time, not only because of their wealth of content, but because they *formed a pattern* for a new type of law (my emphasis). What I was out for, obscurely, intuitively, was a new event in poetics: a space of being, allied to a transpersonal language. It was like those white spaces intelligent mapmakers left on their charts from the fourteenth century onwards, instead of filling them up, as so many others did, with fantasy and legend: mind-cinema, 'literature'.

Later, I gave more and more content to the original vague but moving intuition. There was the original name of Scotland: Alba (the white country). There was the name given to the area of greatest concentration in ancient Celtic culture: white field (in Gaelic, *finn mag*), white ground in Brythonic (*gwen ved*). When I began delving into Far Eastern thought, it was to discover that, in Buddhism, the most far-out identity is described, analogically, as 'a white heron in the mist'. The fact of my own name was a coincidental bonus, but it gave me the sensation of being almost anonymous. It was me, and yet away out beyond 'me'.

Later on, again, I was able to see the white world element as a live current in world culture and as a distinct movement in late modern poetics. I've gone into this elsewhere in essays and in interviews (in *Coast to Coast*, in *On Scottish Ground*), so I won't expatiate more on this theme here. Suffice it to say that there were enough congruent elements around, in fact an incredible amount to make the concept both attractive and cogent.

It was the first synthesizing concept I used. But I pretty soon set it aside, because I saw it misinterpreted in two different ways. Some rejected it, choosing to see it (looking through the wrong end of the telescope), only as some kind of narcissistic ego-trip. Others again were attracted to it, but for the wrong reasons, seeing in it some kind of hyperidealist, spiritual otherworld.

That's why for years, I talked rather of blue roads, red canyons, grey fjords, yellow sands, letting the whiteness shine through from the background in its own. Which reminds me of a passage in the *Conversations* of Confucius where somebody quotes a line from *The Book of Odes* about 'white silk overspread with colours', asking Confucius what it meant. 'Colour comes *only after the preparation of the ground*', said Confucius (my emphasis).

That's why also, when, forty years after *Wild Coal*, I brought out my collected poems, I didn't call the book 'White World', but *Open World*.

*

The constant is *world*.

What we commonly call 'the world' is a hotchpotch of half-concepts, a rush of needling preoccupations and anxieties, and a mass of details devoid of synthesis. It's a world in this sense that Wordsworth had in mind when he said 'the world is too much with us'.

Mankind has invented all kinds of ways to get out of the world in this sense and into something more satisfying: drugs, religions, revolutionism. Most people conceive of art in analogous terms: as fantasy, dream, imagination – anything to distract attention from 'the world' for a while. I've used myself, at one moment or another, all of these methods, in passing, but what I'm out for fundamentally is something else.

What I called from early on world-poetics (later, geopoetics) was based on a subtly sensitive and intelligent relationship between the human mind (body-mind) and 'what's out there'. If we use 'world' for the ordinary context, World, with a capital, for all the otherworlds, the world I'm implicated in might be written with italics, *world*, to indicate that it is in process, as also that it contains the trembling of existence and is not fixed and coded.

In order to approach it now in more immediately historical terms, let me first of all present its opposite.

In the 1830s, William Buckland, professor of geology at Oxford, England, announcing his course for the year, promised that 'the indications of the power, wisdom and goodness of the Divinity will be demonstrated from the evidence of design in His works, and, particularly from the happy dispensation of coal, iron and limestone, by which the Omnipotent Architect or Divine Engineer has assured manufacturing primacy to his British creations'.

There you have somebody professing with imperturbable aplomb the total solidity of a perfect World: Britain as heaven on earth. The deadweight complacency of this statement, its heavybooted localist ideology, its industrial optimism, the hollow ring of its rhetoric, its sheer pompous inanity, can only make us smile today, and turn away.

To what?

Mostly, to the hotchpotch I evoked earlier. To a literature and an intellectual problematics that, when not merely formalistic or fantastical, is never more than sociologistic.

We live in a civilisation that, from a belief in futurity on all levels, has come to a sense of futility, only superficially covered-over with all kinds of 'culture' (in the hotchpotch sense of that word).

It has long been high time to attempt something at once more radical and consequential.

I've written essay upon essay, poem upon poem, text upon text, along these lines. It's the whole process of geopoetics, going from the historico-cultural to the philosophico-poetical.

Here I'll just present the merest sketch, bringing in some new references.

*

For a start, let me make it clear that by 'grounding', I don't mean a mythological base, nor a religious one, nor a metaphysical-ontological one (the *ontos on* of Plato). I mean a relationship to the earth, an original relation to the universe.

As to the notion of world, 'world-forming' (*weltbildend*) is how Fink and Heidegger characterize the human being in their book on Heraclitus.

Heraclitus presents an original field quite different from the 'bases' of myth, religion or metaphysics. Of Heraclitus, Socrates said that to understand him, you had to be a good swimmer. As for Plato the idealist, he was exasperated by what he called 'the screeching birds of Ionia'.

Rough waves and screeching birds – that was a landscape familiar to me...

Hume the Scottish sceptic loathed any talk of 'perfect worlds', conceiving 'world-making' in close connection with Nature seen as containing 'an infinite number of springs and principles'.

'The field is the world', said Hume. Reversing the proposition, we might with just as much pertinence say: the world is a field.

That's what's been happening in science over the past century or so: the move from a mechanical view of the universe to a field view. In physics, we've gone from a theory closed in on itself to an open theory which will probably never be complete because with every advance it makes, it creates a further opening: wave mechanics, qualitative dynamics...

Probably every great artist has this sense of things (it's the 'anarchy' of art). In an essay on Michelangelo, the poet Ungaretti has this arresting phrase about his work: 'The world no longer knew what it was.'

With Michelangelo, all the frameworks had broken, all the canons of sculpture, painting, architecture had exploded. He felt that classical art had nothing more to teach him. As to Christianity, he went through the ritual motions, used the models, but his mind was obviously moving elsewhere. Look at his *Pieta* in Milan. The model's there, the common image, the icon, but what you're most aware of is a tremendous energy that, while sculpting forms, leaves a lot of the rock raw.

In a similar way, Saint-John Perse (who had no time to waste on Paul Claudel's religious beliefs) writes to Claudel in these terms: '*Je ne cesse d'aimer chez vous ce transport du réel qui vous laisse toujours si fort de base*' ('What I continually admire in you is that *transport of the real* that always leaves you on *such powerful ground*' – my emphasis).

From early on, I had that idea of ground in mind, with a notion of the inaugural and founding capacity of poetics. 'What abides is founded by the poets', said Hölderlin ('*Was bleibet aber/stiften die Dichter*'), and in his *Hyperion* (the man with hyper demands), we have this: 'What you are looking for is a world.' It was with such a general conception of things that I left on long years of intellectual nomadism.

*

Since the Renaissance (I refer to the image of Michelangelo evoked above), all the great artists, all the *real* artists, were going to be trying, with an alliance of resistance (Fenollosa, in his *Epochs of Chinese and Japanese Art*, describes Michelangelo as resisting, like some promontory in a storm, an increasing mass of triviality), radical research, essaying and travelling (I'm thinking there of Goethe's *Wilhelm Meisters Wanderjahre*, Moritz's *Anton Reiser*, Tieck's *The Wanderings of Franz Sternbald*) to work out the lines of a new world – not that caricature of the Old World that is the New World with capital letters, but a grounded existence, a live context, with a radiance.

In his *Journal*, Paul Klee has this: 'My head is incandescent, on the point of bursting. A world it conceals is asking to be born.'

I've just evoked 'long years of intellectual nomadism'. That term 'intellectual nomad' came to me from Spengler's *Decline of the West*, read by me as a student in Glasgow. It excited my mind much more than words like 'writer', 'author', 'poet'. In Spengler, the intellectual nomad is a furtive kind of character, lurking about city streets, either nihilism personified, or bearer of a vague kind of spirituality – like, say, Hesse's Steppenwolf, carrying a rucksack full of Buddhist texts in Christianized translations. I did an awful lot of *steppenwolfing* in my own (supernihilistic) way in Glasgow, reading in the ruins and wandering in the macadam desert.

But there were other, related terms. In fact the first term I found really useful was Nietzsche's term *Hyperborean*: 'We are Hyperboreans, we are well aware in what remoteness we live. Beyond the ice of the North lies our happiness. We have found our way out of millennia of labyrinth.' One of the texts I wrote at this time was entitled 'Open Letter to all Hyperboreans' (it was later published in the Dutch, post-Provo magazine *Raster*).

Then there was the 'Western pilgrim', the 'Western navigator' evoked by Toynbee at the end of his *Study of History*, also read, voraciously, in cold rooms in Glasgow, 'piloting his vessel through perilous straits in the hope of making his way into more open waters beyond'. It's these possible 'open waters' that Toynbee calls 'the postmodern', a term that was going to be picked up and used indiscriminately, devoid of any basic historico-cultural reference, by trendy writers and myopic intellectuals, to label masses of ungrounded, uninspired, ineffectual texts. I worked with the basic references and tried to follow them out – beyond the Franciscan kind of spirituality (the sort of thing that was to blossom and wilt in San Francisco, USA) in which Toynbee's mind seemed to find harbour. Which is why, maybe, years later in Paris a critic was to write in a review that the work I was doing was 'the first *coherent* expression of postmodernity' (my emphasis).

Among other terms and references that applied to the field I felt myself moving and working in, there was, for example, the figure evoked in Hegel's *Aesthetics* (Hegel also much read in Glasgow), who 'had separated himself from the contemporary modes of manifestation, acquiring stability and a force of resistance'. Years later, in France, in a book on biology that appeared in 1974, *L'Unité de l'homme, invariants biologiques et universaux culturels* ('The unity of man: biological invariants and cultural universals'), Edgar Morin and Massimo Piatteli-Palmarino, writing the introduction, say this: 'The unity that interests us lies in a *no man's land* to be explored.'

That was my situation, my activity, and my perspectives.

*

When my first books appeared from London, they were received, critically, as being pretty extravagant productions. One critic was more precise, saying they lay 'outside the muddy eddy of contemporary literature', portending the opening of new space.

I was well aware myself how far away I was from 'contemporary literature'.

Looking at it from high up, without getting lost in particulars, post-War Britain seemed to me to have decided that, since ideas could lead to disaster, it was better to have no ideas at all. There was no intellectual energy in the air. As to literature, the novel consisted in a drab social realism, with a little perverse psychology thrown in for spice. Poetry was what I thought of as 'lawnmower poetry' – it hummed along, competently enough, but in a very circumscribed context, and with all the poets sounding as if they'd gone through a 'creative writing' class and got 6 out of 10. One of these English poets asked how one could dare now be 'anything but numb', another was out just to 'keep the good old habit alive'. A lot of the poems sounded like intelligent, but not too intelligent, conversations in a university staffroom 'Was Freud entirely right?' Thom Gunn's motorbike and Ted Hughes' punky crow were more energetic but didn't go very far. The same for the Liverpool scene, pabulum for the babes of Albion, or Concrete Poetry, little more than a parlour game.

I was aware, in the background, representing a range of larger concerns, of Yeats, MacDiarmid, Eliot and Pound. Yeats in Ireland had attempted to impart a much-needed larger dimension to poetry via mythology, till he gave it all up to 'walk naked', asking himself what there was to say about a bit of bone found on the beach – I considered myself as walking farther along that coast. What Yeats had tried to do with mythology, MacDiarmid in Scotland tried to do with information – reams of it. I was interested, excited even, but I felt the need for more coherence, and if I liked MacDiarmid's outlooks on to 'stony limits' and 'raised beaches', I couldn't swallow his nationalist communism. As to Eliot, I was interested in his cultural analysis of the Wasteland, not in his solution, the orthodox bulwark he raised against its ruins. The line of his I retained most was the one in his poem on Cape Ann where he says 'the palaver is over' and that it is time to give the land 'back to the gulls'. Then there was Pound, provincially aesthetic to start with, then ploughing his way through hell, knowing you don't get through it in a hurry, especially if you have no Virgilian guide or Aquinas map – Pound, a worker in the labyrinth, increasingly incoherent, but sensing there was a coherence somewhere and that the aim of fundamental poetic work, of fundamental culture-work, was to *make cosmos* (the Greek *kosmos*: a beautiful whole in harmonious movement).

I'd published three books in London (two books of poems and a prose narrative) when I presented my London publisher with a fourth. If my other books were wild, this one was strange. My man said he was no fool (and he wasn't), he could see where I was going. But I was more 'continental' than 'British'. I just didn't fit into the categories. 'Well', I said, 'invent a new category.' He raised his hands and his eyes to the heavens.

I went with my strange, uncategorisable manuscript to another London publisher. This man was more blunt. He said I should put that weird thing in the fridge for ten years and in the meantime, to really establish my reputation, write a big, fat, seamy Glasgow family novel, full of beery sex, blind violence and general bloodiness (you know the kind of thing). I said I didn't want that kind of reputation, and that what he described and prescribed wasn't my idea of literature. He said that he really wasn't in literature at all any more, he was in the entertainment industry. The fast-food sub-literary industry had definitely arrived in Britain straight from New

York, bringing with it cartloads of gilt-edged platitude, shelves of
lurid nonentity.

After hearing my first publisher's remarks on the new
manuscript, I'd said: 'No problem, I'll get it published in France.'
'Ah', he said, 'but France is a *literary* country.'

*

I'd already spent four years in Paris. That's where my very first
two books were published (*Wild Coal, En toute candeur*), even
before London. After those four Parisian years, I'd come back. Now
I was leaving again, for an indefinite period.

Paris isn't the same thing as an American in Paris (even if he's
Benjamin Franklin). I have the same critical distance to France as the
French writers and intellectuals I feel close to.

That said, I agree with Nietzsche, writing in *The Genealogy of
Morals* (1887): 'Even yet, it's in France one finds the finest and most
intelligent European culture.' Certainly, Nietzsche goes on to say,
you have to look for it, you have to know where to find it, because
there's a fair amount of vulgarity too in France. But the fineness is
there, going along with a grounded strength. That's the fine grain of
France. I say it 'even yet' – roughly a hundred years after Nietzsche
said so. Even now that France is also being invaded by the kind of
slush that hit Britain thirty years ago.

It has been suggested here and there in articles (based both on
inadequate information and intellectual myopia) that I found a
comfortable niche in France. Nothing could be further from the
truth. What I found was a field: a field of forces, certainly more
propitious to the work I wanted to do than what I could have found
in Britain, but with nothing like intellectual comfort.

There are two main cultural traditions in France. One is the
Versailles courtier tradition, the other is the Parisian-Jacobinist
political tradition. The French-based minds I feel closest to stand
outside both these traditions, either because they lived and worked
'on their lands' (like Montaigne or Montesquieu), or because they
moved to and fro (Rousseau, Nerval, Rimbaud, Artaud, Segalen), or
because they holed up in city nests (Diderot, Breton).

The French writers I feel the strongest affinity with have also
written in some sense outside 'literature': the literature that Rémy de
Gourmont called 'a crowded omnibus' and that Raymond Schwab

described as 'a deluge without a dove'. This distinction between two categories of literature, or, more sharply expressed, between 'literature' and 'something more than literature' was maintained, whereas in the Anglo-Saxon countries it tended to get blurred.

Let me just rapidly trace this high line, this 'outsider' context.

In Verlaine's *Art poétique*, he calls, outside all the rest that is 'literature', for a 'winged thing' (*la chose envolée*) and 'adventure redolent with mint and thyme' (*la bonne aventure... fleurant la menthe et le thym*). Verlaine's work is on a minor key, but by extrapolating and projecting a bit you can arrive at the idea of a moving about the earth experiencing freshness at every step and a sense of exaltation. The movement is both more evident and energetic in Rimbaud, first on the roads of Northern France, then all over Europe, finally in the desert of Abyssinia. As to the Surrealists, if they entitled their first review *Littérature*, it was out of irony. One of its numbers had a couple of pages entitled 'Erutarettil', which is '*littérature*' in reverse. What the Surrealists wanted to put in place of literature, in all its dreary psychology, trivial intrigue and commonplace event, was 'magnetic fields'.

That was the context I worked in.

I also descended at times into the literary, cultural and political arena. At one point, I did a whole series of articles on literature in a fortnightly magazine. At the end of it, the editor said the next time I came up to Paris (by then I was living down in Pau, in the Pyrenees), I should come in an armoured car, because 'they' were after my blood. 'They' were certain writers and certain intellectuals I'd rubbed the wrong way. In fact I'd never rubbed them directly at all, I'd never even mentioned them, what I talked about was types of writing.

Anyway mostly I just got on with the work.

The book I'd shown my London publisher was an early version of *Incandescent Limbo*, which I continued to work at in Paris when I returned there for a while after the May revolt of 1968.

Incandescent Limbo, 'the book of seven rooms' is the story – no, there's no story (though there's plenty of incident) – it's the itinerary of an intellectual nomad moving between Montparnasse and Meudon, Pantin and the Porte des Lilas. It's a magnetic field, with flashes of energy coming in from North, South, East and West. It's shot through with references to, *relations* to, taoism, zen and tantric buddhism, quantum physics, complex mathematics and the shaman's journey of ecstasy. 'They still take me for a Scot', you can read at one part. 'But I've become an Eskimo, by naturalisation. In fact, even that's just for my passport – I'm really a Hyperborean. Nobody knows a thing about the Hyperboreans. The Hyperborean is a man engaged on an erratic path to a far-out thing. What people see are the erratics (the stones he leaves on his path), what he sees are flashes of the far-out thing. Nobody can define anything in that area. It's nine hundred miles beyond literature, nine thousand miles beyond civilisation.' And just next to that (this is in the chapter: 'A Short Introduction to Eskimo Studies'), you have the Netsilik Eskimo legend of Atungai: 'Atungai was a great shaman who was seized with a desire to travel around the world. But he didn't want to be *all* alone, he needed a woman with him – a strong woman, with a wild life-desire and no time to waste on family and children. So he set out first on a loving search for such a woman, till he found her. Then he set off. At length he came to a high, steep cliff. When he'd got to the top of the high, steep cliff, he started travelling round the world. But remember, he was a shaman, he kept to the other edges. When he had met up with all the different people of the earth, he came back home. But he came back home by a different road from the one he'd taken on the way out. I tell you, Atungai was a really great shaman.'

Incandescent Limbo was a pivotal kind of book. After it, my prose-books tended to be of two types: waybooks and staybooks.

*

The waybooks: *Travels in the Drifting Dawn, The Blue Road, The Face of the East Wind, The Wild Swans...* aren't novels (even if you think of them, as somebody did, as 'novels without strings'), nor are they travelogues, because they've got more energy and urgency in them, more extravagance and another dimension than what is found in most travel-writing. They roam, physically and mentally, over fairly wide and varied landscapes, through city scapes too, but always end up at some limit, some edge – looking out to Open World.

As to the staybooks, well, while I was engaged in my multifarious historico-cultural research, I came across a study by a late-nineteenth century French sociologist, Henri de Tourville (*Nomenclature des faits sociaux*, 1886), in which he says this: 'What we need now, in the midst of our present world, are hermits able to bear the isolation that new ideas entail, able to work out also a life for themselves.' That was strange talk for a sociologist. But it was the kind of 'strange talk' I was looking for, in all domains. And I always loved it when I saw paradoxical ideas coming from unexpected quarters.

What is certain is that there is a double tendency in my nature, innate or strategical, maybe both innate and strategical. In my life and work there's always been a to-and-fro, a dialectic, between errancy and residence, the traveller and the hermit.

The first of my hermitages was an old farm in the Ardèche. The second was an apartment, with large windows, facing the Pyrenees. The third has been and still is a house on the north coast of Brittany.

Down there in the Ardèche, I was studying Provençal culture, taoism and buddhism, granite, schist and calcite. The book that came out of it all was *Letters from Gourgounel* (Gourgounel – gurgling source). In the Pyrenees, I went deeper into geology and geomorphology, studying primary sediments, magmatic intrusions and moraine complexes (groundings – like the growths of a mind) – that led to a series of *Pyrenean Meditations*. My third hermitage, on the Armorican promontory, is situated in an area known in geology as a centred complex. Out of that 'centred complex' (I'm translating that now into mental terms) emerged the book *House of Tides*.

At the end of that book there's the account of a return trip to Scotland which summed up many such trips (over the years I was often in Scotland, incognito as it were), and symbolic of a general (literary, intellectual, cultural) return to my original ground.

*

When, in the late 80s, from within a whole new set of circumstances as well as a new field of impulses, I was moved to renewing contact with English-language publishing, I decided to do so from Scotland.

Why?

Well, in the first instance, there was, in my genealogy, a whole band of Camerons, MacGregors, Dewars, McNies and McKenzies clamouring at the back of my mind, calling to me that it was time to come back, that there was work to be done.

Secondly, I have always had a deep feeling for this country, an uninterrupted affiliation with it, an awareness of its potential scope, keeping it as my primary reference. In addition, after my long years of intellectual nomadism and the opening of the field of geopoetics, I had a project, a programme. What's a country, after all? It's a physical space, a social context, and an intellectual horizon. Owing to a series of politico-historical-economic-industrial events and to a thickening of circumstance, an obfuscation of opportunity and perspective, Scotland had lost its sense of physical space and intellectual horizon, reduced only to a social context. I felt it was time to remedy that, I felt that there were a lot of people in Scotland wanting to remedy that. I wanted to get at what Heidegger calls somewhere 'the free extent of the country'.

The other reason for my deciding to start again from Scotland was that by now there are publishing houses in Scotland with some kind of distributive capacity, which was hardly the case when I started out.

This return, while it has met with tremendous reception, has not of course gone on without a certain amount of opposition – in some quarters, there has been some grinding of teeth, and of axes. Some would even like to pretend I'm not there at all: ostrich tactics with a vengeance.

It has been suggested, for example, that I am somehow 'exotic' to the country, because I have lived and worked for so long out of it – and in France (not England or America). But throughout Scottish history, some of the brightest, most dynamic and most far-seeing Scottish minds have lived and worked outside Scotland. Think, as I often do, with delectation, because it's a high Scottish line, of the travelling monks of the Western isles, founding monasteries, libraries, schools, spreading literature, language and ideas all over Europe. Think of the *Scotus vagans* of the Middle Ages. Think of Duns Scot, working in France and Germany. Think of Michael Scot, one of the leading minds in Western Europe of the thirteenth century, an *'internationalgebildeter Mann'* ('an internationally, educated man'), as Saxl calls him, evoked in a section of the long poem I wrote just before leaving Scotland in 1967, *Walking the*

Coast. Think of George Buchanan, working in Paris, Bordeaux and Lisbon, writing his books and teaching (among others, one of the finest writers of French and world literature, Michel de Montaigne). Think of David Hume, just as much at home in Paris as in Edinburgh. Think of Robert Louis Stevenson, moving from Scotland to France, and from France to Polynesia. And so on. Were these Scots less Scottish because they wandered over the world? No, they were more Scottish, and it was they who represented Scotland in the eyes of the world. As to France in particular, as David Irving says in his book *The Lives of the Scottish Poets* (1810), it has always been 'a favourite place for Scottish wanderers'. When I left the British context, definitely Anglo-British, which had spread like a thick (pale pink or tartan) quilt over Scotland, I was following a road much older and much livelier than the Johnsonian 'highway to England'. To categorize myself, and *a posteriori* all this line, as 'exotic', is to have a very reduced conception of Scotland and Scottishness.

It is also said, I hear, that I am elitist. That is no doubt because I consider, and make no secret of the fact, that Scottish literature can mean more than kilometres of the chronicles of Kilcuddie or their, shall we say, late-modern equivalent, the death throes of dead-end city. In writing and thought, I look, beyond a literature that is content to reflect a state of things, usually a rundown state of things, to minds that raise intelligence and vision to new levels and open worlds. The early Celto-Christian monasteries did that, working with Greek, Latin, Hebrew, Gaelic, and open to influences from the East. Throughout Scottish cultural history there has been work of this nature, with this kind of field of energy. The last big public moment was the Scottish Enlightenment, with men like Hutton in geology, Robertson in history, Hume in philosophy, Adam Smith in economics, open to ideas coming in from the continent like flotsam and jetsam on Scotland's intellectual shore, and able to produce such massive works as Johnston's *Atlas* or Audubon's *Birds of America*. It's maybe at something like that we could work today. Is that elitist? In politics, I'm a democrat – but a demanding democrat. In other words, I protest when democracy runs down into populist demagogy. In education, I'm a partisan of what George Davie calls 'the democratic intellect', that is, the provision of a high general education for all that want it. I think a people deserves more than the pabulum some institutions and administrations think is the only thing fit for it. If what I try to do is too much for certain writers and certain institutional bodies, it is not too much for Scotland.

About the policies and perspectives of some institutions, here are some amusing and I think illuminating anecdotes.

When, owing to my participation in the May '68 revolt, I had lost my University post, and was down and out in France, Hugh MacDiarmid here in Scotland proposed to get me a writer's bursary. To this end, he applied to the Scottish Arts Council. The SAC of the time told him that since Kenneth White did not live in Scotland, he was not eligible, and application should be made to the British Arts Council. MacDiarmid did this, and was told by the British Arts Council that, since Kenneth White was a Scot, applications should be made to the Scottish Arts Council. MacDiarmid finally got £1000 out of them, telling me in a letter, with rueful apologies, that they were pouring out barrowfuls of money to work that in his estimation had little significance, and mostly no significance at all.

Another example.

A few years ago, in 1996, an exhibition on my itinerary and work was set up by the National Library of Scotland. When the French version was ready to begin circulating in France, the organizers, not only because it seemed an obvious partner, but as a matter of courtesy, turned to the British Council in Paris. The answer came back that the British Council could do nothing for Kenneth White, because he was 'to all intents and purposes a French writer' and that its mission was to promote literature that 'reflected the contemporary state of British society'. No comment on 'the contemporary state of British society', but there again you have that rundown, merely sociological conception of literature-as-reflection, not as breaking new ground, expressing an original relationship to the universe, opening worlds. As to national epithets, call me a Euro-Scottish-universal writer, as Duns Scot was a Euro-Scottish-universal writer (on this score, we've come down a long platitudinous way since the thirteenth century) and let's try and get somewhere, beyond 'contemporary states', whatever they are.

We're badly in need of institutions with revised cultural policies, we're badly in need of renewed cultural perspectives, with people in office able to distinguish between what is secondary and what is primal and necessary. We need a re-mapping of the whole cultural field, something equivalent to Han China's constitution of the classics.

But what we need most is radical work.

*

What do I mean exactly by radical work?

It means a lot more than social agitation, though it can also include that, on occasion.

What vocabulary we have in the domain of intellectual-poetic work stems from a literary criticism largely outdated or, in recent times, brought over, massively, from psychology and sociology. Little of it gets anywhere near the real thing, the thing in movement.

What distinguishes in the first place radical work is the conflict engendered between it and the established context.

Every real artist (poet) is an insurgent against the world 'as it is'. That doesn't mean creating, via idealist symbolism, another world - at least not in my conception of things. What it means is going back to the ground and gathering elements for a world of greater intensity. That kind of 'worlding' can have an effect on society, unless that society be absolutely totalitarian, or crassly mediocratic. It can *always* have an effect on individuals.

An orthodoxy of whatever type (social, religious, cultural, localist) loathes any real, creative movement. The attitude of orthodoxy towards any really creative mind is always one of suspicion and hostility, at times downright repression.

Why?

Because what the builders of city and empire construct (*bona fide* people with good political intentions engage in this area, but what can they do?) is a mass ruled over by codes and symbols: religious symbols, regal symbols, demagogical-republican symbols. Underneath the codes and symbols, there will be an emotional mush, and underneath that, the contortions of the Freudian *id*. Nothing like a creative idea. Ideas don't grow in this kind of context. Ideas, as Gogol says in his *Diary of a Madman*, come in from somewhere across the Caspian Sea.

When I was still a young student in Glasgow, I read a lot of Russian literature. Among the authors and thinkers was Berdyaev. I didn't share his theology, but he did seem to get at something, particularly in his essay 'The meaning of the creative act'. What he says there is that 'the creative act reveals the priority of the "self", the subject, over the "non-self", the object.' About this 'self-action', there is nothing egocentric. It is in fact the opposite of egocentricity. The 'white heat', if I may say so, of creation, implies self-transcendence. It isn't narcissistically in-looking, it is outreaching, transfigurative, liberating. Not just a reflected image of society, not just 'amusing'. It liberates the mind, it creates a freedom, it presents an open conception of world. Berdyaev defends freedom as 'an untraceable, undetermined and unpredictable movement from within outwards'. It comes out of 'nothing' (nothing definable in current vocabulary). Berdyaev talks of 'self' and object. I myself have long thought that the real thing happens beyond subject and object, and that the cosmos contains more than any self. But to come back to Berdyaev's 'nothing'. I don't probe into that 'nothing', I don't symbolize it, I don't mythologize it, I don't theologize it, I don't mystagoguize it. I follow it in its outward movement, I follow its path. Doing so I try to go further than minds that preceded me and dropped on the way.

Outside the confused flurry and the muddy flux of history, outside all the 'contemporary contexts', a dialogue goes on perpetually among creative minds across space and time. The 'selves' in question are those whom Kant described as capable of 'transcendental apperception', and that Hegel considered as being part of 'universal mind'. They live beyond themselves. They do not care to be turned into mere icons or idols. If they be brought into relief, it should always be to see, with more and more insight, into what is implied in their work: a whole landscape-mindscape. In such landscape-mindscapes there are ideas and energies, both manifest and latent, that can, potentially, bring in a live society, an intelligent republic, an open world. What I feel the need to say also is that, however complex the background, minds can catch on to the manifestation intuitively and immediately.

That's what I mean by radical work.

One last remark on this score.

Whatever be the relative merits of representative anthologies and other similar panoramic compendia, whatever be the habits, categories and curriculum of any contemporary context, it is the single, singular work, in its own time and space, that alone corresponds to the full scope and scape of the potentiality.

*

It's to a work of this kind, *opus fundamentale*, that, in my own way, I've devoted the past forty years. Its logic (a combination of *eros, logos* and *cosmos*) is perhaps not yet fully apparent, its topography (wide reaches and abruptitudes), its imagistic and semantic structure (wild coal and diamond country, candour and incandescence, Alba and white world), its *architectonics* (firmly grounded and yet open), but a lot has been done, and a lot more will be done, and I want to thank again all the participants in this St Andrews symposium for their readings and interpretations.

Goethe has a nice phrase about how a work can operate. He says (I'm adapting slightly) that its truth needn't be totally incorporated for it to have effect – it can hover in the air, as a spiritual force, provoking new unity.

It's maybe on that serene image we can close these proceedings, ready to move further into the space they open.

KENNETH WHITE: BIOGRAPHY

1936   Born in Glasgow, south side of the river, in the Gorbals. Father, railway signalman, socially-minded, avid reader of books. Grandfather, musician, dancer, foundryman.

1939-54   Raised on the west coast of Scotland; sea, woods, hills and moor. Physical movement in this territory. Schooling at Fairlie, Largs, Ardrossan. Work on farms and on the shore (shellfish-gathering for Billingsgate), also as postman and purser on the Clyde steamers. Studies local geology and archaeology (first public text on the archaeology of Ayrshire). Reads Thoreau, Whitman, Melville.

1954-56   Student at the University of Glasgow: French and German, with Latin and philosophy. Does a lot of reading in the University library: all sections, from metaphysics to mineralogy. Particular affinities with Ovid, Rimbaud, Hölderlin.

1956-57   In Munich, lodged in a wooden shack on the banks of the Isar. Reading Nietzsche and Heidegger. Tough winter, beautiful Spring.

1957-59   Back in Glasgow. Double First in French and German. Named first student in the Faculty of Arts. With a post-graduate scholarship, leaves for Paris.

1959-63   Marriage with Marie-Claude Charlut. Lodged in 7th-floor rooms in Paris. Exploring Surrealism (Breton, Artaud) and connected fields (Daumal, Michaux). After two years, settles out in Meudon. Begins the manuscript that will become *Incandescent Limbo*. Gives private lessons in English.

1961   Buys Gourgounel, an old farm in the mountains of the Ardèche, with several acres of moor, wood and rock. Hermit kingdom! Spends there summers and autumns, handling mattock and scythe, studying Eastern literature and thought (Taoism, Ch'an Buddhism). Works at the manuscript that will become *Letters from Gourgounel*.

1962-63   Teaching at the Sorbonne. The students of English publish his first book of poems: *Wild Coal*.

1963   Back to Scotland, sense of unfinished business in Glasgow. Much stravaiging in the streets. Assistant lecturer then lecturer at the University: teaching twentieth-century poetry and the Encyclopedists. Founds a para-university group, *The Jargon Group*, for lectures, debates, poetry readings. Talks in terms of 'cultural revolution' (worked out the concept for himself – no reference to Mao).

1964   *En toute candeur*, early poems plus three biographical sketches, appears at the Mercure de France in Paris. The only living author in that collection ('Domaine anglais').

1966   Two books, one prose, one poetry, come out simultaneously from Jonathan Cape, London: *Letters from Gourgounel* and *The Cold Wind of Dawn*. Considered as being outside the norms of contemporary British literature: sort of erratic boulders.

1966-67   Living in Edinburgh, thinking of Stevenson, De Quincey and other physical-mental travellers. Working at a long poem, *A Walk along the Shore*, which sums up his *itinerarium mentis* up to that point. Meets MacDiarmid: affinities and differences.

1967-68   Back to France, living at Pau, in the Atlantic Pyrenees, teaching at the University of Bordeaux in Pau. Founds a group and a review: *Feuillage*. Involved in the May '68 movement. Expelled from the University. The students protest. He goes for a long walk in the Basque country.

1968-69   Out of (socio-economic) work in Pau. Studies and writes a lot, facing the Pyrenees, mountains he comes to know better and better. A book of poems, *The Most Difficult Area*, appears from Cape Goliard, London. As from this date, in Britain, his name is surrounded with silence. Does nothing to change this state of affairs, too engrossed in his own workfield.

1969-73   Still in Pau, but lecturing at the University of Paris VII. Founds another group, another review: *The Feathered Egg*.

1973-75   Senior Associate at the University of Paris VII. Founds a research seminar 'East-West', which will be known familiarly as 'The Cold Mountain Seminar' or 'The Old Pond Seminar'. Moving around Europe, from Dublin to Marseilles, Amsterdam to Barcelona. These trans-Europe trips are the basis of *Travels in the Drifting Dawn*.

1975   White's post as Senior Associate terminating, after a new governmental decision, at the end of two years, he finds himself reduced to the position of 'foreign assistant', while continuing the same work and directing research.

1975-76   Travelling in South-East Asia (Hong Kong, Macao, Taiwan, Thailand...). Working at a manuscript: *The Face of the East Wind*.

1976   As from this date, the manuscripts accumulated during the Pyrenean period begin to appear in Paris at a rapid rate.

1979   Defends a State doctorate thesis on the theme of 'intellectual nomadism': it is recognized by the jury as opening up a new field of studies and several of its concepts (geopoetics etc.) are now being used by geographers and psychologists, not to speak of writers. Leaves on a trip along the north bank of the St Lawrence into Labrador, which will turn into the book *The Blue Road*.

1983   Leaving the Pyrenees, settles on the north coast of Brittany. Appointed to a newly founded chair of Twentieth-Century Poetics at the Sorbonne. The Labrador book, *La Route bleue*, published by Grasset, is awarded the Prix Médicis Étranger.

1984   Trip to Japan, where he follows Bashō's trail from Tokyo north and continues on into the Hokkaido, a trip which will result in *The Wild Swans*.

1985   Awarded the French Academy's Grand Prix du Rayonnement Français for the totality of his work. Archives on his work are established at the municipal library of Bordeaux.

1987   Awarded the Prix Alfred de Vigny for *Atlantica*.

1988   Trip to the Isles of America (Martinique).

1989   After a long exile, renews contact with English language publishing. Publishes *The Bird Path, Collected Longer Poems*, and *Travels in the Drifting Dawn*. Second trip to the Isles of America (Guadeloupe, Saintes, Martinique). Founds the International Institute of Geopoetics.

1990   Publishes *Handbook for the Diamond Country, Collected Shorter Poems*, and *The Blue Road*. Brings out also the first number of the geopoetics review, *Cahiers de Géopoétique*.

1991   Receives an Honorary D.Litt. from the University of Glasgow. Third trip to the Isles of America (Dominica, St Vincent, Grenada).

1992   More progress is made in getting his work available in English with *Pilgrim of the Void*, which brings together two books recounting his Asian travels published separately in Paris: *The Face of the East Wind* (Hong Kong, South China Sea, Taiwan, Thailand) and *The Wild Swans* (Japan). Fourth trip to the Isles of America (the northern section of the Antillian Arc).

1993   Promoted in Paris from Chevalier des Arts et des Lettres to Officier des Arts et des Lettres. Fifth trip to the Isles of America (the Virgins).

1994   Is awarded the prize of the Société de Géographie in Paris for *Frontières d'Asie*. Sixth trip to the Isles of America (the Virgins).

1995   Trip to Corsica. Seventh trip to the Isles of America (the Virgins).

1996   The National Library of Scotland stages an exhibition on his work: *White World, the itinerary of Kenneth White*, which is later shown in other cities and towns. Publishes a collection of interviews, *Coast to Coast*. Travels in Italy, Sweden, Norway, Canada. In Italy, receives the Aleramo Prize for his work in poetry. Eighth trip to the Isles of America (the Virgins). Withdraws from the Chair of Twentieth-Century Poetics at the Sorbonne.

1997   Travels and lectures in Serbia, Montenegro, Sweden, Germany, Scotland, Spain. At Malaga, is awarded the Insignia of the Generación del 27. Ninth trip to the Isles of America (the Virgins). Publishes in Paris *The Shores of Silence*, the result of nine years' work in the poetic field.

1998   Travels and lectures in Poland, Sweden, Scotland and Morocco. Awarded a D. Litt. *honoris causa* by Heriot-Watt University, Edinburgh. Tenth trip to the Isles of America (the Virgins). Publishes in France the book *Strategy of Paradox*, which sums up his socio-political itinerary. Commences the publication of his essays in English with *On Scottish Ground*. In France, is awarded the Prix Roger Caillois for his work as a whole. The French version, adapted and augmented, of the National Library of Scotland exhibition, retitled *Open World, the itinerary of Kenneth White*, begins to circulate in France. Le Vaudreuil, March; Trouville, April-May; Rouen, June-July.

1999   Travels and lectures in Sweden and in Scotland. Trip to Spain and Portugal. First trip to the Indian Ocean: Reunion, Mauritius. Eleventh trip to the Isles of America (the Virgins). Elected to a three-year fellowship at Edinburgh College of Art. The exhibition *Open World* is presented at Rennes in January.

2000   Publishes a new book of poetry in Paris, *Limits and Margins*. Second trip to the Indian Ocean (the Seychelles archipelago). An exhibition of his artist-books (close on a hundred) is held at the Librairie Nicaise in Paris. The exhibition *Open World* is shown at Evreux in March, at Le Lavandou in June, at Pau in November.

2001   Publishes *House of Tides* at Edinburgh. Elected honorary member of the Royal Scottish Academy. Member of the executive council of the World Academy of Poetry (Verona, Italy). Founding member of the Atlantic Academy (France). Delivers the Consignia lecture at the International Book Festival in Edinburgh: 'The Re-mapping of Scotland'. Third trip to the Indian Ocean (the Seychelles archipelago). *Open World*: at Besançon in January, at Châteauroux in February-March, at Mende in April, at Fontainebleau in December.

2002   Is awarded the ARDUA prize (Bordeaux) for his work as a whole.
Prepares the edition of his *Collected Poems*. Fourth trip to the Indian
Ocean (the Seychelles archipelago). *Open World*: at Nancy in April-
May, at Dunkirk in November.

2003   A symposium 'Horizons of Kenneth White – literature, thought,
geopoetics' is held at Bordeaux (February) and another 'Forty Years
of the White World' in St Andrews (October). Trip to Polynesia: a
lecture on Gauguin at Tahiti in the context of a conference organized
by the University of French Polynesia, followed by a journey from
island to island. In May, back to the Indian Ocean. In June: lecture
on a French cruise boat down the Caledonian Canal and up the
Hebrides. Publishes *Open World: Collected Poems 1960–2000* and
Geopoetics: place, culture, world. *Open World* at Brussels in
January.

2004   Takes part in an international poetry symposium in Italy at Stresa-
Orta organised by the literary review *Atelier* (February). March: An
international colloquium on geopoetics is held at Geneva, organized
by the University of Geneva. Delivers a lecture on Rimbaud, at the
poet's birth-place, Charleville-Mézières. September: delivers another
lecture on Saint-John Perse at Paris in an international colloquium on
that poet organized by the Sorbonne. Publishes two new books in
Britain: *The Wanderer and his Charts* and *Across the Territories*.
Receives the Édouard Glissant prize attributed by the University of
Paris 8 for his 'openness to the cultures of the world'. *Open World* at
Charleville-Mézières, March-April.

KENNETH WHITE: ENGLISH BIBLIOGRAPHY

Wild Coal, poems (Paris: Club des Etudiants d'Anglais 1963).

The Cold Wind of Dawn, poems (London: Jonathan Cape, 1966).

Letters from Gourgounel, narrative (London: Jonathan Cape, 1966).

The Most Difficult Area, poems (London: Jonathan Cape, 1968).

Selected Poems of André Breton, translation (London: Cape Editions, 1969).

Ode to Charles Fourier by André Breton, translation, with an essay on utopian socialism (London: Cape Editions, 1969).

The Tribal Dharma, essay on Gary Snyder (Carmarthen: Unicorn Bookshop, 1975).

The Coast opposite Humanity, essay on Robinson Jeffers (Carmarthen: Unicorn Bookshop, 1976).

The Life-technique of John Cowper Powys, essay (Swansea, Galloping Dog Press, 1978).

The Bird Path, Collected Longer Poems (Edinburgh and London: Mainstream Publishing, 1989). [Also in Penguin paperback edition, 1989.]

Travels in the Drifting Dawn, narrative (Edinburgh and London: Mainstream Publishing, 1989). [Also in Penguin paperback edition, 1989.]

Handbook for the Diamond Country, Collected Shorter Poems, 1960-1990 (Edinburgh and London: Mainstream Publishing, 1990).

The Blue Road, narrative (Edinburgh and London: Mainstream Publishing, 1990).

Pilgrim of the Void, narrative (Edinburgh and London: Mainstream Publishing, 1992).

Van Gogh and Kenneth White, an encounter (Paris: Flohic Éditions, 1994).

Coast to Coast, interviews (Glasgow: Open World in association with Mythic Horse Press, 1996).

On Scottish Ground, selected essays (Edinburgh: Polygon, 1998).

House of Tides, narrative (Edinburgh: Polygon, 2000).

The Remapping of Scotland, essay (Edinburgh: edbookfesteditions, 2001)

Open World, Collected Poems 1960-2000 (Edinburgh: Polygon, 2003).

Geopoetics: place, culture, world (Glasgow: Alba Editions, 2003)

The Wanderer and his Charts, essays (Edinburgh: Polygon, 2004).

Across the Territories, narrative (Edinburgh: Polygon, 2004).

Into the White World, two cassettes of poem readings, 1992. Available from: Scotsoun, 13 Ashton Road, Glasgow, G12 8SP.

The paradox of White's situation is that his work, written in English, with the exception of the essays mostly written in French, has appeared in French, and substantially in other languages before it has appeared in English. With the ongoing publication of White's work in English, the paradox is diminishing, but it is still there.

KENNETH WHITE: FRENCH BIBLIOGRAPHY

Narrative

Les Limbes incandescents, trans. Patrick Mayoux (Paris: Denoël,
  Les Lettres Nouvelles, 1976). [New edition: Paris: Denoël, 1990.]
Dérives, several translators (Paris: Laffont,
  Lettres Nouvelles/Maurice Nadeau, 1978).
Lettres de Gourgounel, trans. Gil and Marie Jouanard (Paris: Presses
  d'aujourd'hui, 1979). [New edition: Paris: Grasset, Les Cahiers rouges,
  1986.]
L'Écosse avec Kenneth White (Paris: Flammarion, 1980).
  [New edition: Arthaud, 1988.]
Le Visage du vent d'Est, trans. Marie-Claude White
  (Paris: Les Presses d'aujourd'hui, 1980).
La Route bleue, trans. Marie-Claude White (Paris: Grasset, 1983). [Prix Médicis
  étranger, Livre de poche n° 5988.]
Les Cygnes sauvages, trans. Marie-Claude White (Paris: Grasset, 1990).
Corsica, l'itinéraire des rives et des monts, trans. Marie-Claude White
  (Ajaccio: La Marge, 1999).

Poetry

En toute candeur, bilingual edition, trans. Pierre Leyris
  (Paris: Mercure de France, 1964).
Mahamudra, le grand geste, bilingual edition, trans. Marie-Claude White
  (Paris: Mercure de France, 1979).
Le Grand Rivage, bilingual edition, trans. Patrick Guyon et Marie-Claude White
  (Paris: Le Nouveau Commerce, 1980).
Scènes d'un monde flottant, bilingual edition ('revue et augmentée'),
  trans. Marie-Claude White (Paris: Grasset, 1983).
Terre de diamant, bilingual edition ('revue et augmentée'), trans. Philippe
  Jaworski, Marie-Claude White (Paris: Grasset, 1983). [New edition: Paris:
  Grasset, Les Cahiers rouges, 2003.]
Atlantica, bilingual edition, trans. Marie-Claude White (Paris: Grasset, 1986).
  [Prix Alfred de Vigny.]
Les Rives du silence, bilingual edition, trans. Marie-Claude White
  (Paris: Mercure de France, 1997).
Limites et Marges, bilingual edition, trans. Marie-Claude White
  (Paris: Mercure de France, 2000).
Le Passage extérieur, bilingual edition, trans. Marie-Claude White
  (Paris: Mercure de France, 2005).

Essays

Victor Segalen: théorie et pratique du voyage (Lausanne: Alfred Eibel, 1979).
La Figure du dehors (Paris: Grasset, 1982). [Livre de poche, Biblio essais 4105.]
Une apocalypse tranquille (Paris: Grasset, 1985).
Le Poète cosmographe, interviews (Presses Universitaires de Bordeaux, 1987).
L'Esprit nomade (Paris: Grasset, 1987).
Le Monde d'Antonin Artaud (Brussels and Paris: Éditions Complexe, 1989).
Hokusaï ou l'horizon sensible (Paris: Terrain Vague, 1990).
Le Plateau de l'Albatros, introduction à la géopoétique (Paris: Grasset, 1994).
Le Lieu et la Parole, interviews, 1987-1997 (Cléguer, Éditions du Scorff, 1997).
Les Finisterres de l'esprit, essays (Cléguer, Éditions du Scorff, 1998).
Une stratégie paradoxale, Essais de résistance culturelle
      (Bordeaux: Presses Universitaires de Bordeaux, 1998).
Le Chemin des crêtes, avec Stevenson dans les Cévennes
      (Esparon: Études et Communications, 1999).
Le Champ du grand travail (Brussels: Didier Devillez Éditeur, 2002).

On Kenneth White

MICHÈLE DUCLOS (ed.), *Le Monde ouvert de Kenneth White*
      (Bordeaux: Presses Universitaires de Bordeaux, 1995).
JEAN-JACQUES WUNENBURGER (ed.), *Autour de Kenneth White: espace, pensée,*
      poétique (Dijon: Presses Universitaires de Dijon, 1996).
OLIVIER DELBARD, *Les Lieux de Kenneth White, paysage, pensée, poétique*
      (Paris: L'Harmattan, 1999).
PIERRE JAMET, *Le Local et le Global dans l'œuvre de Kenneth White*
      (Paris: L'Harmattan, 2002).
JEAN-YVES KERGUELEN, *Kenneth White et la Bretagne*
      (Moëlan-sur-Mer, Éditions Blanc Silex, 2002).
LAURENT MARGANTIN (ed.), *Kenneth White et la Géopoétique* (forthcoming).

NOTES ON CONTRIBUTORS

ANNE BINEAU lives in Saint-Malo where she teaches French at the lycée Maupertuis. Publications include various articles in *Filigrane, Area, Poésie 89* and *Cahiers de Géopoétique*. Author of a doctoral thesis, "Kenneth White - Théorie et pratique de la poésie intégrale". She is currently preparing a DVD on *Les Travailleurs de la mer* by Victor Hugo.

NORMAN BISSELL is an Area Officer of the Educational Institute of Scotland, Scotland's largest teaching union, and formerly taught history. As a student in Glasgow he joined the Jargon Group set up by Kenneth White, and has since had many articles, reviews and poems published. He founded the Open World Poetics group, 1989–1999, based on Kenneth White's ideas, and is now director of the Scottish Centre for Geopoetics.

GAVIN BOWD is Lecturer in French at the University of St Andrews. He attended Kenneth White's seminar on 'Poétique du monde' at the Sorbonne 1989-1990. He is the author of an essay, *The Outsiders. Alexander Trocchi and Kenneth White* (Akros, 1998).

OMAR BSAÏTHI is presently teaching English literature at Mohamed I University, Faculty of Letters, Oujda, Morocco. In 2003 he completed a PhD thesis on geopoetics in the Arab context under Kenneth White's supervision. His present field of interest is travel literature, particularly that composed by English travellers to the Orient.

OLIVIER DELBARD wrote his doctorate thesis on *The Poetics of Landscape: Kenneth White's European approach and Gary Snyder's American approach*. His book on White *Les Lieux de Kenneth White* was published at L'Harmattan (Paris) in 1999. He teaches in Paris and is also a translator (Gary Snyder). He lives in Burgundy near Dijon.

MICHÈLE DUCLOS was lecturer till her retirement in Modern British Literature at the Université de Bordeaux 3. She wrote her thesis on Kenneth White, "Les Chemins de la pensée poétique", and created an Archive for research on his work at the Bibliothèque municipale de Bordeaux. For the Presses Universitaires de Bordeaux she has edited two volumes by Kenneth White: *Le Poète cosmographe – Entretiens* (1987); *Une stratégie paradoxale, Essais de résistance culturelle* (1997), and a book of essays on his work and itinerary: *Le Monde ouvert de Kenneth White* (1995). She currently reviews contemporary British poets for the Belgian review *Le journal des Poètes*, and has translated books of poems by Thomas Kinsella, Ruth Fainlight and Alan Sillitoe.

MARCO FAZZINI has a PhD from the University of Venice. After teaching English literature at the University of Macerata, he is now at the University of Venice. He has translated into Italian selections from the poetry of Norman MacCaig, Hugh MacDiarmid, Kenneth White, Douglas Dunn, and Edwin Morgan, among others. His most recent publications include *Crossings: Essays on Contemporary Scottish Poetry* (2000) and *Alba Literaria: A History of Scottish Literature* (2005).

CHARLES FORSDICK is the author of *Autoscopy and Self-Reflection: fiction and pathology from Musset to Segalen* (1995) and *Victor Segalen and the Aesthetics of Diversity: journeys between cultures* (2000). He has recently co-edited, with David Murphy, *Francophone Postcolonial Studies: a Critical Introduction* (2003). He is James Barrow Professor of French at the University of Liverpool.

KHALID HAJJI was born in Oujda, Morocco, where he studied English literature, then settled in Paris after years of peregrination in Europe. In 1994 he obtained his doctorate from the Sorbonne with a thesis on T. E. Lawrence under the supervision of Kenneth White. After a prolonged sojourn in Germany where he taught French, English and Arabic, and learned German, he joined Mohamed I University English Department. With some colleagues he founded 'Science and Culture', a multidisciplinary research group that has organized important international conferences, is a founding member of the "Circle of Wisdom for Thinkers and Researchers" and is the Editor-in-Chief of *Al-Munaataf*, an Arabic quarterly magazine. Among his published works is *Lawrence d'Arabie ou l'Arabie de Lawrence* (Paris: L'Harmattan, 2001).

JOHN HUDSON is an award-winning poet, critic, filmmaker and editor of *Markings* literary magazine. Born in London, he has lived in southwest Scotland since 1987. He regularly works in France and his publications include *Medusa Muse* (Abbey Hill, 1996) and the bilingual *A rose by your heart* (CIAC 2004). He collected and edited *The Collected Poems of William Nicholson* in 1998 and his film *Solway Fire* was released in 2002. He has just completed a long, collaborative poem, *Collateral Damage* with the Solway Festival Poets which has been read around Scotland and in London.

PIERRE JAMET is Lecturer in English at the University of Franche-Comté (France). He has published a book on Kenneth White, *Le local et le global dans l'oeuvre de Kenneth White* (Paris: L'Harmattan, 2002) and was a critical friend of geopoetics until 2004. He writes essays and "prosetry" under various pen names.

STUART KELLY is a critic for *Scotland on Sunday*. His *Book of Lost Books* will be published in August 2005.

JEAN-PAUL LOUBES is an architect and anthropologist. A member of the
International Institute of Geopoetics, he teaches at the School of
Architecture in Bordeaux, directing a research seminar on the
anthropology of space, with field work in China and Central Asia. For
him, in addition to its other aspects, geopoetics provides a basis for new
projects in architecture.

TONY McMANUS was an inspirational teacher, writer and musician who
studied the work of Kenneth White in French and English, and gave
lectures and published many articles on that work and on other subjects.
He was curator of the *White World* exhibition for the National Library of
Scotland in 1996, which has since toured extensively in Scotland and
France; and he founded the Scottish Centre for Geopoetics in January
1995, becoming its first director and securing its future before his untimely
death in April 2002.

PADMAKARA is a member of the Western Buddhist Order. He has lived
monastically in the Spanish mountains, taught at various UK Buddhist
Centres, helped establish a Vegan Café in Manchester, and recently
published a book *Verses of Inspiration*. He is currently a creative
photographer living with his partner in Lancashire.

ANNE SCOTT is a lecturer in the Department of Adult and Continuing
Education at the University of Glasgow where she works mainly on Irish
and American Literature. She has been a member of Scottish Geopoetics
through all its developments since 1989 and has run day and longer
courses on the writings of Kenneth White.

MICHAEL TUCKER D.Litt is Professor of Poetics at the University of Brighton.
He has published widely in the field of contemporary art, music and poetry
and has worked with, and written about, Kenneth White several times. He
organised the symposium on the life and work of Kenneth White which
accompanied the showing of the exhibition *White World* at the University
of Brighton in May 1998.